BEATING THE ADOPTION GAME

by
CYNTHIA D. MARTIN

OAK TREE PUBLICATIONS, INC.
PUBLISHERS, LA JOLLA, CALIFORNIA

To my very special family

. . . David for his strength to be himself and his love
and understanding which allows me to be myself.

. . . Scott, Dru, Nohl, and Shaine, our natural children
both adopted and non-adopted, for enriching our
lives.

Beating the Adoption Game text copyright © 1980 by
Cynthia Martin

First Edition
Manufactured in the United States of America
For information write to Oak Tree Publications, Inc.,
P.O. Box 1012, La Jolla, CA 92038

Library of Congress Cataloging in Publication Data

Martin, Cynthia.
  Beating the Adoption Game.

  Includes index.   1. Adoption—United States.   I. Title.
HV875.M369   362.7'34   80-16883
ISBN 0-916392-60-0

1 2 3 4 5 6 7 8 9   84 83 82 81 80

CONTENTS

1. ADOPTION OPTIONS 9
   Adoption: A Personal Issue 11
   Purpose of This Book 12
   A Time for Needed Change 13
   About the Book 14
   Summary 16

2. WHERE HAVE ALL THE BABIES GONE? 17
   Why Fewer Babies? 17
   Unplanned Pregnancies: A Source of Babies 19
   Contraceptive Alternatives 20
   The Pill 20
   Diaphragm 21
   Intrauterine Device 22
   Abortion 22
   Sterilization 23
   Condoms (Rubbers) 23
   Rhythm 24
   Foam 25
   New Contraceptives 25
   Unconscious Desire to be Pregnant 26
   Dilemma of Unwanted Pregnancies 29
   Summary 32

3. FACING INFERTILITY 35
   Causes of Infertility 38
   Infertility in the Male 38
   Infertility in the Female 40
   Consequences of Infertility 42
   Infertility Help 46
   Finding a Physician 46
   Learning About Infertility 47
   Options to Infertility 49
   Experimental Methods of Reproduction 49
   Adoption 50
   Foster Parenting 50
   Substitute Parenting 52
   Childlessness 53
   Summary 55

4. MAKING BABIES WITH A LITTLE HELP 57
   Artificial Insemination 59
   Test-Tube Babies 64
   Embryo Substitutions 66

Surrogate Mothers 66
Reproduction to Specification 68
Summary 73

5. THE ADOPTION AGENCY GAME 75
The Agency Process 76
Criteria for Selecting Adoptive Parents 82
Financial Status 82
Age 83
Educational Background 84
Medical History 85
Race and Nationality 86
Religion 87
Marital Relationship 87
Employment of the Mother 88
Involvement with the Adoption Agency 89
Flexibility 90
Personality Factors 90
Parenting Skills 91
Fighting the Adoption Agency's Rejection 93
Creative Flexibility Needed Within the Agencies 95
Power of the Adoption Agencies 98
Summary 100

6. YOUR OWN GAME 103
Private Adoptions 104
How Private Adoptions Work 106
Making Contacts 106
Hiring a Lawyer 107
Determining the Amount of Contact 109
Paying Pregnancy Costs 110
Securing Medical Consent Forms 112
Working with the State Agency 112
Signing Relinquishment Papers 113
Going to Court 116
The Risks of Private Adoption 117
The Advantages of Private Adoption 118
Family Adoptions 120
Black Market Adoptions 120
Why Not Sell Babies? 121
The Risks in Black Market Adoptions 124
Summary 126

7. LOOKING ELSEWHERE AND EVERYWHERE 129
Potential for Finding a Child 130
Beginning Your Baby Search 133
Limits for Your Search 133
Establishing Priorities 138

Presenting Yourself   138
Contacting Everybody   139
Physicians   140
Lawyers   140
Groups of Adoptive Parents   141
Infertility Groups   142
Free Clinics   142
High Schools   144
Colleges   147
School-Age People   147
Friends, Neighbors, Acquaintances and Everyone   148
Advertising   150
Summary   152

8. **FARAWAY BABIES   153**
   International Adoption: A Changing Scene   154
   A Different Way for Different People   155
   International Adoption Through Adoption Agencies   157
   Procedures for International Agency Adoptions   157
   Criteria for Parenting International Children   159
   The Costs of International Adoptions   160
   One International Agency Adoption   160
   Private International Adoptions   162
   State Regulations   163
   Understanding Private International Adoptions   163
   Making International Contacts   164
   Risks of Private International Adoptions   166
   One Private International Adoption   167
   Health of the Child Adopted Internationally   171
   Summary   171

9. **THE SPECIAL KIDS   173**
   Handicapped Children as Adoptees   176
   Physically Handicapped Children   176
   Mentally Handicapped Children   179
   Emotionally Handicapped Children   181
   Older Children as Adoptees   184
   Siblings as Adoptees   187
   Racially Mixed Children as Adoptees   189
   Summary   192

10. **THE SPECIAL MOMS AND DADS   193**
    Single Parents as Adopters   194
    Physically Handicapped Adopters   198
    Older Parents as Adopters   200
    Parents with Medical Problems as Adopters   202
    Parents of Large Families as Adopters   203
    Foster Parents as Adopters   205

Homosexuals as Adopters 209
Summary 211

11. DEEP DARK SECRETS 213
Current Laws on Adoptees's Birth Record 214
Definition of Terms 215
Sealed Birth Record 215
Adoption Record 215
Good Cause 215
Searchers 215
Reunions 215
Changes in Adoption 216
Clamor for More Change 216
The Emotional Issue of Opening the Birth Record 217
A Suggested Approach 219
Different Views on Opening the Sealed Record 221
The Adoptee and the Sealed Record 221
The Adoptive Parents and the Sealed Record 225
The Birthparent and the Sealed Record 227
The Adoption Agencies and the Sealed Record 230
Preparing for Opening the Birth Record 232
Summary 234

12. LETTING IN SOME LIGHT 237
Individual Honesty in Adoption 237
Honesty and Openness in the Adoption System 243
Adoption Agencies and Birthparents 243
Adoption Agencies and Adoptive Parents 246
Adoption Agencies and Foster Parents 247
Open Adoption 249
Different Kinds of Open Adoption 249
Minimal Contact in Open Adoption 249
Moderate Contact in Open Adoption 251
Maximum Contact in Open Adoption 252
Adoption Agencies and Open Adoption 254
Open Adoption Historically 255
Risks in Open Adoption 256
Summary 256

13. CLEANING UP THE GAME 259
Adoption Agency Recommendations 260
Legal Recommendations 267
Recommendations for Adoptive Parents 271
And Finally 275

FOOTNOTES 277
BIBLIOGRAPHY 285
INDEX 300

ACKNOWLEDGMENTS

Acknowledgments in books always seem so ritualistic. Yet the thanks and appreciation I wish to express to the people who have helped write this book are sincerely and deeply felt.

My deepest appreciation to my husband who helped me learn about adoption and then helped me write about it. His suggestions, confidence, and hard work were essential ingredients in completing this project.

I owe thanks to the many adoption agencies throughout the United States who supplied information for this book. Their cooperation and encouragement greatly aided this project.

I am indebted also to the many people who have come to me about adoption. These people who asked for help in finding a baby or told me of their success comprise many of the case studies that are presented. Adoptees who have talked with me about their searches have significantly altered my feelings about adoption birth records. These people and those in adoption classes I have taught continue to impress me that adoption statistics tell little about the human needs of the individuals so involved in the adoption game.

Several people read the manuscript and made helpful suggestions. Leona Heth's positive view and warm hugs greatly encouraged me. Dr. Warren Baller, a dear friend, added significantly to the book.

Other people, too, helped in special ways. Allwyn O'Mara spent hours with me researching books for children related to adoption. My daughter, Dru, has become my special critic by reading every children's book I could find on adoption. My friends, Cindy and Charles Tillinghast, who suggested I write the book and who published it gave me this exciting opportunity.

Books are not written by individuals but by groups. The group that helped me on this one has been absolutely wonderful.

THE PROPHET

And a woman who held a babe against her bosom said, Speak to us of Children.
And he said:
Your children are not your children.
They are the sons and daughters of Life's longing for itself.
They come through you but not from you,
And though they are with you yet they belong not to you.
You may give them your love but not your thoughts.
For they have their own thoughts.
You may house their bodies but not their souls,
For their souls dwell in the house of tomorrow, which you cannot visit, not even in your dreams.
You may strive to be like them, but seek not to make them like you.
For life goes not backward nor tarries with yesterday.
You are the bows from which your children as living arrows are set forth.
The archer sees the mark upon the path of the infinite, and He bends you with His might that His arrows may go swift and far.
Let your bending in the archer's hand be for gladness;
For even as he loves the arrow that flies, so He loves also the bow that is stable.

KAHLIL GIBRAN

1
ADOPTION OPTIONS

You can get a baby. You can get a baby even if you cannot get pregnant and even if you are turned down by the adoption agencies. You don't need a lot of money or a fancy house. You can get a baby if you are overweight, old, handicapped, or even if you are single. There is a baby somewhere for you if you are willing to try some new ways.

Babies are available. Actually it is quite a simple matter. The people who want babies and cannot make them need to meet either those people who are good at making babies or those medical people who are good at fixing reproductive problems. These are the only options. The means to get to them are varied.

If you want a baby, you must look at the choices and then look at yourself. There is no right or wrong choice or direction, but there is a right way for you.

You need to explore which ways of seeking a baby are comfortable for you. At first glance, some of the methods may seem inappropriate for you, but think about them. You may need to try familiar approaches first; later, if you have had no luck with the familiar ways, it is possible that you may become more comfortable with some of the newer or riskier ways.

Part of making your choice of alternatives is to understand your limits and whether you can stretch those limits.

For some people, the traditional modes of obtaining a baby are the only ones with which they would be comfortable. These are the only ways they have ever considered. Go through the routine medical tests for infertility. If a medical problem is discovered that cannot be corrected, you seek some level of acceptance of your infertility and then you contact the adoption agency to ask for a baby. Assuming you are accepted by the adoption agency, you follow the set process until the exciting day you are called about your baby or child. You raise your family just like any other normal family and soon no one knows you are different at all. This procedure has been followed by thousands of people. However, for many people this method will not lead to a baby.

This traditional approach is in sharp contrast to the risk taken by a couple who had the same goal, a baby. After the initial medical exams, John and Debbie learned she could not get pregnant. In attempting to deal thoroughly and openly with their feelings about Debbie's infertility, they discovered that it was important for them to have a child, at least partly, from their genes. They decided to hire a surrogate mother to carry John's child. They placed an ad in a national magazine. Risky? Of course. However, sixteen months later they got their baby. They took the risks and got the payoff.

For others, the need to be more exhaustive about all the medical possibilities in order to have a child of their "own" is a critical factor. England's baby Louise, the so-called "test-tube baby," was one couple's way. Hundreds of other couples wait to try the same methods or other methods considered far more radical.

Adoption may be considered by these couples, but only after trying every reasonable medical remedy for their infertility. Some would say these people are disturbed or poor risks for adoption because they have been unable to resolve their feelings about their infertility. Others would admire their perseverance. For this group of people, their willingness to pursue advances, which seemed improbable a short time ago, will get them a baby.

The desperation of some couples drives them to utilize procedures that are currently considered illegal . . . the black market. People are willing to pay $20,000 or more to get a baby. Most people are shocked that a couple would elect to *buy* a baby. However, if you really want a baby and have been thwarted in every way until someone tells you that for $20,000 you can have a baby about to be born, what would you do? Patty and Jim, a couple in their late thirties who had been turned down by the adoption agencies, had that chance and they took it. They know they got a bargain!

The people willing to seek babies in non-traditional ways are a different group than have ever before been searching for babies. They are creative in their approach. They look at every means to reach their goal. They are willing to take great risks to get what they want . . . a baby.

Are they different from "normal" couples who get pregnant or who adopt by traditional means? Yes, definitely. They are desperate. They want a baby and cannot get one the regular way. Their choice is to be creative, be risky, or be childless; they take the risks.

Some people will find it hard to identify with these people and their search. Others will tell them to fill their lives in other meaningful ways like taking in foster children, raising some nice pets, or becoming teachers. While these substitutes may be enough for some people, they do not provide a baby to love and be loved by. There is no substitute for your own baby.

I strongly support and encourage these people . . . you, if you are searching for a baby. I know there are children available. Open up to the ways to find a baby. Create new ways to find one that have never before been tried. Think, explore, search, try . . . you *can* find a baby!

Adoption: A Personal Issue

Rules and procedures are set up in adoption to accommodate groups. Adoption studies talk about the trends of *most* people. Statistics deal with large numbers of people who do one thing or another in adoption. Yet adoption is an individual, personal issue. The intent of this book is to present the many options which are available in adoption to many people . . . not because these options are appropriate for everyone, but rather so that individuals can make an individual decision.

Personal issues must be pursued personally. Others don't have quite the circumstances in their life that you do. Your accumulated life experience puts you where no one else has been. No one can tell you about the best way for you to pursue obtaining a child. This book is meant to be a guide to options . . . options in the methods of finding a child to adopt . . . options to beat the adoption game.

Adoption is personal for me also. The options available to the individual pursuing adoption have increased over the years. Choices I believed were open to me at one time in my life have changed and others have appeared.

Consistently I have known that being a mother is very important to me. It is a role I wanted to have and I always thought it would be easy to achieve. I grew up, got married, but the next step . . . children, did not happen. Being a product of my time, I labored over the pangs of infertility that confronted my husband and me. At times, I could minimize where a child would fit in my life; at other times, my insides would not allow these pretenses.

We adopted three children in the next eleven years. The first two we adopted through adoption agencies, the third child we adopted independently. When our third child was four, for some reason, I got pregnant. Our jokes over the years about how I would get pregnant when I was forty weren't too far off. Our last child was born the week before I turned thirty-eight.

Our first two children were easy to get. Our third child we adopted at the time children were becoming hard to find, so we were fortunate to find her. Our fourth child, our surprise, was truly unplanned, but after the initial shock and disbelief, she was, and is, a most welcome addition.

Adoption for our family is something very special. It is not important for us to have the children look like us. Our blonde, blue-eyed daughter is a sharp contrast to our dark-haired, brown-eyed daughter. Each one looks and acts differently from the others. Adoption is not the same as having children biologically. It is neither more nor less satisfying, but it is different . . . it is special.

My views on adoption are very different from when we first adopted, but then so are my views on life. One thing remains the same . . . I know, no matter how hard it might be to adopt a child, I would find one to adopt. Having children remains important to me. I *know* I would find a child.

Purpose of This Book

An issue as important as adopting a child should never be turned over completely to someone else to handle and to solve. While many people can and will help you in adopting, you are the one who needs to learn thoroughly about adoption . . . you need to understand the adoption process and the different options open to you in adoption. If you want to beat the adoption game, you need to understand the rules. The players who have control and who understand the game thoroughly are the ones most likely to win . . . to get the child they want. That is what this book is all about . . . getting the child you want.

A passive approach to adoption may work. Maybe someone will find you and give you a baby. Maybe an adoption agency will be the one to open the door for you to form your family. No question about it, this is the easiest way to adopt a baby. For some people this will work.

For others, this approach will fail. They will not be able to get a child from an adoption agency. Perhaps it will be their looks, a simple statement they make, their income, their rigidity, their age, or their view of life. They may never know why they were rejected. Not being sure of what the adoption agency wants, they do or say something wrong and they fail the adoption agency entrance examination. Without admittance to the system, they cannot get a child from the adoption agency.

For others, the adoption agency will be rejected by them. The couples who cannot tolerate the adoption agency system must seek children some other way or remain childless. Those people who are likely to reject the adoption agency system would be likely to be rejected by the system even if they continued.

This book is written for the potential rejects from the adoption agency who want to know what the game is before they start in order to increase their chances of becoming a winner. This book is written for the rejects who want a child and were turned down by the adoption agency to help them see other options in adoption. This book is written for the people who are rejecting the system and who want to know other ways to find a child to adopt. This book is written for the adoption agency worker, the decision maker for people in adoption, who needs to look at adoption in a more creative and flexible way. This book is also written for me, because I believe it is time to change what is happening in adoption and I want to be a part of that change. I want adoption to be possible for many kinds of people because *adoption is special and it shouldn't be a game.*

A Time for Needed Change

We are living in a time of rapid change in the world in which we live . . . environmental changes, technological changes and attitudinal changes. In order for people to be able to emotionally cope with the changing world, they too must change. The next level of change then that must be made is in the institutions which serve the people.

When we find that institutions serving people are not working, we are seeing institutions that are in need of revitalization . . . institutions in need of change. Adoption is one of these institutions.

The institution of adoption is theoretically designed to help all of the people involved in adoption. Yet cries of dissatisfaction are heard from each of the adoption participants.

Potential adoptive parents are being turned away by adoption agencies for inconsequential, unproven reasons, denying them the child they want. The emphasis in screening of potential applicants seems to be on how people can be eliminated rather than how they can be helped. The reasons for rejection are seldom given to the applicants and there is no recourse within the system for these potential adoptive parents. Anyone "different" who seeks to adopt a child has little chance of getting through the system unless they find a child on their own to adopt.

Parents who have already adopted children from agencies are beginning to wonder if they were told as much about their children as the adoption agency knew. The secretiveness surrounding adoption brings the fear that there is unknown negative material which for some reason must not be revealed. The secret side of adoption creates stress and suspicion in the adoptive home.

Birthparents complain of agency pressure to relinquish their child and the harshness of the procedure. They deplore the lack of financial help from the adoption agencies that say they want to help them in this stressful time. Birthparents wishing to have a more flexible approach to this difficult procedure have a tough time trying to get the adoption agency to bend its approach on how adoption should be. The suddenness and finality of adoption for the birthparents allows little room for their grief.

The adoptees object to the sealed records that prevent them from knowing about their backgrounds. They feel cut off from their past with no recourse. The prize of the game, the adoptee, whom the entire institution of adoption is currently set up to serve, says something is wrong with the system.

Something is drastically wrong when so many people seem unhappy with what is currently taking place in adoption. Institutions should be molded to fit the people who use the institution. Adoption, like any institution, needs to change to fit the people who want to adopt or who want to place children for adoption. People will remain disgruntled if they are forced to fit the agency rather than the agency fitting the people it is supposed to serve.

While the suggestions in this book are designed to help people work within the system, this is in reality a compromise. The best way is for the institution to change and develop new, creative ways to serve their clients. Most people can't wait that long so they need to know how the adoption system works now and what their options are for making a defective system work for them.

About the Book

Adoption is a beautiful way to have a family. It is only beautiful, however, if it works. If you can't adopt, the disappointment can be overwhelming. This book is intended to help you understand the current scarcity of infants and the way the adoption system operates. With a thorough understanding of the system and the options you have, you can try new things which you have never imagined. Hopefully, your new approaches will lead you to the baby you want.

All of the incidents used as examples throughout the book are true. The people cited are real, but their names and identifying data have been changed.

Chapter 2, "Where Have All The Babies Gone," explores what has been happening in our society to create a lack of babies available for adoption. Sometimes the way to get a baby is to understand the right places to search for one. Knowledge of the underlying factors creating the diminished supply of babies will enable you, the baby searchers, to deal realistically with the potential choices that are open to you.

Infertility—its causes, cures and consequences are discussed in Chapters 3 and 4. Pursue having a child biologically as far as you want to . . . this is an essential process for most people. No one profits from fooling themselves about how important having a child is to them. These chapters explore ordinary and extraordinary means of becoming a parent.

Chapter 5, "The Adoption Agency Game," is intended to help anyone who goes to an adoption agency better understand the agency system and how it operates. Since adoption agencies are the place most people begin in adoption, this chapter will help you, before you begin the process, to know what the adoption agency social worker is looking for in order to consider you as potential adoptive parents. It will also help you know what *eliminates* you from the list of potential adoptive parents.

Since many will not survive the adoption agency screening, Chapter 6, "Your Own Game," will help clarify the state of private adoptions in the United States. Many people know very little about private adoptions or how they operate. Knowing ahead of time of the potential problems in private adoption lessens the problems. The distinction between private adoptions and black market adoptions is discussed in this chapter.

Chapter 7, "Looking Elsewhere and Everywhere," tells about the many sources of potential children for adoption. There are children out there if you know where to look and how to look for them.

For many people, the adoption option they will choose is a foreign adoption. Chapter 8, "Faraway Babies," discusses how foreign adoptions operate. Knowing what to anticipate helps simplify this complicated process.

Many people do not fit neatly into "normal" categories of people wanting to adopt or children needing to be adopted. These "specials" are discussed in Chapters 9 and 10, "The Special Kids" and "The Special Moms and Dads." Knowing how to present yourself, even if you are what might be called a "special" mom or dad, increases your chances of finding a child to adopt. Opportunities are also increasing for people who consider adopting "special" kids. One method of increasing your options in adoption is to look at children with "special needs" that you may not have previously considered.

Chapter 11, "Deep Dark Secrets," discusses the opening of the sealed birth record of the adoptee who wants information on his or her birthparents. The controversy surrounding this issue is critically important to the entire institution of adoption. Anyone entering the process of adoption today, or anyone who has adopted before, needs to understand the implications of opening the sealed birth record of adult adoptees. The potentially positive changes in adoption that this opening might precipitate will do more than any other single factor to take the secrecy out of adoption. But, as with any change of this magnitude, the personal implications far outweigh the implications for the institution of adoption.

The issue of honesty in adoption is dealt with in Chapter 12, "Letting in Some Light." Individual honesty in adoption is one way you influence the direction of adoption. Ways that the adoption system can encourage more openness and honesty in adoption are discussed. With the many kinds of people in our society who wish to adopt, we need many ways for them to adopt. Some of the more open and honest ways to have adoptions are explored in this chapter.

Chapter 13, "Cleaning Up the Game," discusses the specific areas of change needed in the adoption system to make it healthier and more vital. Recommendations for change in adoption agency procedures and for legal change are made. Suggestions for the general framework of a search for a child are also recommended.

Summary
Babies are available. Most people simply need the information and the courage to find them. This book is designed to provide that information and to encourage that search. While adoption needs change, don't wait. If you want a baby go out and find one. *Be creative, be flexible,* and *be assertive.* Be open to new ways to find a child. This is a time for openness. There are many avenues you may never before have considered. The many options that are open to you can help you beat the adoption game!

2
WHERE HAVE ALL THE BABIES GONE?

Babies used to be a natural product of marriage. Now through our scientific advances, we have learned to maneuver our way around nature by techniques that prevent or interrupt conception. Babies in our society are sometimes not an asset; they are all too often a liability.

As a result, the birth rate has dramatically declined in recent years. The goal of environmentalists concerned with population control is zero population growth (two children per couple). This goal is now closer to being achieved than ever before.

Fifteen years ago, a couple who wanted to adopt a child was welcomed with open arms by the adoption agencies. The agencies had more babies than adoptive parents. Then times began to change and change rapidly. To understand where all the babies have gone, we need to look at the multiple causes of our declining birthrate.

Why Fewer Babies?
Society has undergone radical changes in the last generation. People are questioning how to get the most out of life. Survival is no longer the issue; quality of life is the goal.

The assumed goals of the past are being carefully scrutinized. People no longer use Disney movies as the model for the good life. Perhaps we can afford to question the old goals because of the material abundance we now enjoy in our lives. Perhaps our view of life has been forever altered by television; the world seems smaller now and traditions are often relics of the past. We now question where we are going because we have choices that were never before available.

One of the choices being considered by couples is whether or not to have children. For the first time in history, people are questioning whether children are a high priority in their lives. A recent survey of priorities of young married people found them rating a car over a child as an ingredient in what makes a good life.[1] People are looking at children to determine why they should have them. Will they add enough to their lives to warrant the inconvenience of having them?

At a minimum, a couple has the contraceptive capabilities to determine when, as well as if, they will have children. As a result, more and more women are postponing having children. Having children later means having fewer children and sometimes later becomes never. Instead of asking what do you want to do when the children are gone, they ask, "Why not do what you want with life before having children?"

The search, first to see what life holds, and later to experience children, exemplifies the strivings of the young person. "We'll try living together first, marriage later, maybe." "We'll have kids after we get what we want first, maybe." "Let's travel now and see about children later, maybe." "I want to try everything . . . I'll see later where and if children fit."

The theme is clear, "Me first; then we'll see." Many older people view what is happening as selfish. Perhaps it seems selfish, but maybe it is our envy at not having had the same choices.

The decline in birthrate has been significantly affected by women choosing to work outside of the home. World War II put more women in the labor force than ever before. Society has never since been the same.[2] More women work outside the home than those who choose to be housewives only. This one single factor, working women, has altered the structure of the family as nothing else in recent years. Working women have a choice they never before enjoyed. The choice is when and if these women will have children. The financial liability of a child becomes a big deterrent to a woman whose income is an integral part of the family income. The choice is sometimes between a lower standard of living or not having a baby.

Choosing sterilization has also decreased the birthrate. Population control issues have brought sterilization to the forefront. For many years, the United States has advocated sterilization as a method of population control for other countries in the world, especially the poor countries. We have also gently suggested sterilization for the poor or the mentally handicapped in our own country. The recent shift in our attitudes about sterilization for "regular" people is now demonstrated by the push for vasectomies and tubal ligations for people of all ages, with or without children. The healthy, bright person without children who was considering sterilization was discouraged a few years ago. Today, few questions are asked.

Divorce, as well as changing marriage statistics, has also decreased the birth rate. Divorce is the end result for nearly half of all marriages. [3,4] Because of the large numbers of divorced people who will be unmarried for some period of time, the birthrate has decreased. If you take three years off between a first and second marriage, you have also taken three years out of your normal reproductive life. With marriage being viewed with less permanence, people who fear divorce may choose not to have children at all.

With the high divorce rate, singleness has found greater acceptability. The world of the single person is no longer the dismal world of spinsters and undesirable bachelors. The changing divorce rate has created a need for social patterns to change in order to accommodate the sometimes or temporarily single person. Singleness does not have the disadvantages that were present in the past. In fact, it may be such a desirable state for some people that it discourages marriages and, of course, babies.

The continuing changes in our sexual attitudes have also altered the birthrate. Under contraceptive protection, women seek the same freedom as men. To be totally free and have children is difficult. Consequently, children are postponed or eliminated while freedom is retained.

Contraception is the basic reason for fewer babies. Never before have so many contraceptive choices been available. The age of the condom (rubber) gave men freedom from venereal disease and, as a by-product, freedom from fatherhood. The tide has turned and women now have the freedom to choose "motherhood at their convenience."

Yet, despite all of these factors, some women get pregnant when they don't want to. These pregnant women need to know why they got pregnant and what alternatives are open to them.

Unplanned Pregnancies: A Source of Babies

Despite all of the reasons for the birthrate decrease, there are still women who get pregnant who don't want to be. Why? Why would a woman who says she doesn't want to be pregnant, get pregnant? Why would a woman not take the necessary precautions to prevent an unwanted pregnancy?

Some women will get pregnant because of contraceptive failures. Other women believe the risks or the disadvantages of taking the necessary contraceptive precautions are too great and they would rather take a chance on an unwanted pregnancy. Some of these women will also fit into another group of women who experience unplanned pregnancies . . . women who at some deeper level, desire to be pregnant.

Women who experience unplanned pregnancies are obviously a potential source of babies for people hoping to adopt. Therefore, people seeking a child need to thoroughly understand the reasons women get pregnant when they say they don't want to be pregnant.

Contraceptive Alternatives

The current state of our knowledge about contraception is far more sophisticated than before. Just about every one, no matter what his or her age or socioeconomic status, knows about contraception. Most large cities have free contraception available upon request.

Fear of pregnancy in the past prevented women from being sexually active. Most women need not have that fear any longer if they choose to use contraceptives or have their partner use contraceptives.

Even with our knowledge of how to prevent a pregnancy, the availability of this knowledge to most people, and the advantages derived from this ability to control unwanted conceptions, women still get pregnant. Several explanations account for these pregnancies:

1. Contraceptive failures account for some of these unplanned pregnancies.

2. Some of the contraceptive techniques are not easily used, which discourages their faithful or effective use.

3. Contraceptive availability does not offset a woman's deliberate, although unconscious, exposure to an unwanted pregnancy.

4. Some women don't care if they get pregnant because they view abortion as an easy way out.

Contraceptive availability sounds like an easy preventative to unplanned pregnancies. It would be, if only people weren't so complex. Contraception is not a simple answer. In order to fully appreciate the causes of unplanned pregnancies, contraceptive techniques and people's emotional responses to them must be understood.

The Pill When we think of contraception, the first technique that comes to most people's minds is the pill. While many women like the convenience, the ease and the effectiveness (98-99 percent) of the pill, there are growing numbers of women not using the pill because of the side effects. Studies linking the pill to gall-bladder, liver and heart disease, stroke, blood clots, anemia and cancer cause many women to say no to the pill.[5] This increasing anxiety about the safety of the pill has caused a significant decrease in the number of women who elect the pill as their chosen contraceptive technique. While the results of some studies involving the risk of the pill are open to debate, two groups of women appear to be unquestionably high health risks if they take the pill . . . older women and women who smoke. Physicians frequently refuse to prescribe the pill for women over forty or for women who are smokers.

If you were to select a random sample of women and ask them to cite reasons for not taking the pill, high on the list of reasons would be weight gain. Physical attraction is of prime importance to people in our society and the fear of possible weight gain will deter many women from using the pill. The fact that the pill may not be the cause of this weight gain does not matter; if women believe the pill will cause them to gain weight, it will prevent many of them from choosing the pill as their contraceptive.

The younger woman is the best candidate to use the pill because she risks fewer health problems. Unfortunately, the younger the woman, the less likely she is to use the pill regularly. Adolescent pill users who believe nothing will "happen" to them, frequently do not take the care needed to be effective pill users. They forget and they get pregnant.

The woman who does elect to use the pill must assume the responsibility for her reproductive life. She must take the pill religiously, for the woman who "usually" takes the pill will usually get pregnant.

Although the negative publicity about the pill has caused many women to reject it, the same publicity seldom emphasizes that the woman who gives birth to a child or who has an abortion is at a higher risk than the woman on the pill. Nevertheless, the woman who fears the pill will generally not use it.

Women, fearful of using the pill, may or may not experience unplanned pregnancies. They may seek other contraceptive means.

Diaphragm Currently, a resurgence of faith in the diaphragm as a means of contraception is taking place. When the pill came into prominence, the diaphragm lost out as one of the major contraceptive techniques. The pill was originally reported to be far more effective than the diaphragm. Recent studies on the effectiveness of the diaphragm indicate that if used regularly and correctly, and not left in the drawer, it is as effective as the pill.

The younger generation is questioning chemical means we commonly use to change our bodies . . . food additives, sugar, caffeine and the pill. Pills change our body chemistry. The diaphragm does not. As a consequence, use of the diaphragm has increased 140 percent in the last three years.[5]

In order to use the diaphragm, the woman must plan ahead for intercourse. This has serious drawbacks, especially for the woman who wants sex to be spontaneous. The effectiveness of the diaphragm is directly related to the motivation of the user. As with all contraceptive techniques, the younger woman is frequently less motivated to use them.

Intrauterine Device The intrauterine device (IUD) is another contraceptive technique that has come under considerable criticism in recent years. The IUD is a device which, when inserted into the uterus, prevents a pregnancy from being continued. It is not clear if the pregnancy is interrupted or if the pregnancy never starts. The technique has been used by millions of women in the last twenty years.

The primary objection of potential users to the IUD is that the woman has a foreign object in her body at all times. Fears of infections, increased menstrual cramping and the possibility of the IUD being "lost," with a resulting pregnancy, are some reasons many women choose not to use an IUD. Women who have not previously had children usually experience slightly more cramping than women who have had children.

The positive side of using an IUD is that the woman does not have to plan ahead for intercourse . . . her spontaneity can be retained. Neither does she have to remember to take a pill each day. Her only regular task is to make sure that the IUD remains in place.

Therefore, the IUD is an effective contraceptive means for women who have difficulty remembering to use contraception. Since the IUD must be inserted by a physician and with some degree of discomfort, it has never been as popular as the easier contraceptives. Again, the IUD is an effective means of contraception if the woman really does not want to be pregnant.

Abortion One of the reasons that people may have gotten more casual and even fussy about using contraceptives is the legal availability of abortions. Abortions are considered by some people to be a method of contraception. I do not believe abortions are a form of contraception. Abortion is a solution to poor contraception.

As a preventive measure against babies being born, abortion has become popular. In the United States it is estimated that currently three out of ten pregnancies end in abortion.⁶ This popularity exists in spite of the fact that it is a costly technique in terms of money, psychological aftereffects and physical trauma. The long-term physical and psychological consequences of abortion are not known but are being studied. Even in countries where abortions have been legal for many years, the long-term effects are still unclear.

Historically, abortion has been a means of preventing births for millions of women. Its recent legalization in this country has caused abortion to be used by women who previously might have used contraceptive techniques more effectively, by women who previously would have married because they were pregnant, or by women who might have placed their unplanned child for adoption.

Sterilization Another method of preventing conception which has grown in acceptance, is sterilization. Government figures indicate that nearly one third of America's married couples of childbearing age have been surgically sterilized. Men openly discuss their vasectomies. Women view their tubal ligations as guarantees against unplanned pregnancies.

Of all the methods most likely to prevent conception, sterilization is the most sure. However, there are cases of unexpected pregnancies for women who thought they or their partners were sterile. Fortunately, the chances of this happening are quite rare.

The obvious drawback to sterilization is the permanence of the procedure. Cases of reversal of the technique are not common. It is critical that the person be certain about what he or she is doing when considering sterilization. When young people consider this type of decision, there is always the possibility that they might later change their minds. It is too early to see the long-term consequences for the many people currently using sterilization as their contraceptive choice.

The second major drawback to sterilization is that it too must be done by a physician. For women it is a major surgical procedure which usually necessitates hospitalization. For both men and women, the procedures cause discomfort and sometimes pain. The motivation to use this contraceptive technique must obviously be strong.

Condoms (Rubbers) Condoms are the only effective means of male contraception other than sterilization or abstinence. Condoms are actually quite effective (90 percent) in preventing pregnancy.⁷ They are easy to acquire without any medical intervention; if the man is properly motivated, they are relatively simple to use. The only ways pregnancy can occur is if there is a tear or hole in the condom, or if it comes off during intercourse.

The interruption of sexual activity in order for the man to put on the condom is a significant deterrent to its large-scale use. Some men will reject it on that basis alone. Many men feel that the use of the condom decreases the pleasurable sensations of sexual activity.

Men's reliance on women for contraception also decreases the potential usage of condoms. At present, the condom is the only method that gives contraceptive control to the male. Other devices are under experimentation, but because of potential dangers, they are not yet available.

The lack of men's involvement in contraception is clearly demonstrated in the way birth control clinics are aimed toward women. The San Francisco Department of Public Health recently took a pioneering step in its opening of a birth control clinic for men. This innovative approach, while only a small step, will undoubtedly help foster a feeling of shared responsibility toward preventing unplanned pregnancies.

The vulnerability of males in the contraceptive arena is apparent. He is legally responsible for the financial support of any child he fathers. At the same time, he is usually dependent on his partner to be responsible for preventing conception. In long-term relationships, this reliance may be justified; in short-term relationships, the man takes some significant risks.

Rhythm Rhythm is a method of contraception that is occasionally suggested because of its acceptance by the Roman Catholic Church. There is no question that rhythm decreases the number of pregnancies. Unfortunately, many babies are conceived by couples using rhythm. In order to be really good at using this technique, the woman needs to be regular in her menstrual cycle and she must be able to keep track of where she is in her cycle.

I remember asking a woman attending an anti-abortion lecture in the Roman Catholic Church what contraceptive alternatives she thought young people who were sexually active should use. She was adamant in her response that rhythm had worked well for her and it would be the only method she would discuss with her children. She had five children.

Actually there are two ways to use rhythm as a technique of contraception. The first way is a general rhythm technique. We know that a woman who has a twenty-eight day cycle is likely to ovulate about the fourteenth day after her period begins. In general then, intercourse should be avoided for about two or three days immediately preceding and following ovulation. Unfortunately, the pattern of ovulation can be easily upset by circumstances in a person's life. Woman's emotional well-being, or lack of it, changes her physiologically.

The second type of rhythm technique is more precise; it takes into account the individuality of the woman's cycle. In order for it to be accurate, the woman needs to take her oral temperature each morning just before getting out of bed. When she ovulates, her temperature will go up slightly but noticeably . . . especially if she uses a basal thermometer, which emphasizes these slight changes. The other indication of her ovulation and subsequently increased fertility is a cervical discharge. These two occurrences together—temperature and discharge—have been found to be an effective indicator of maximum fertility. Most people, unless they are trying to get pregnant, will not go to all this hassle to find out when they are most likely to get pregnant.

Rhythm is a rough gauge of pregnancy susceptibility. One of its primary values is that it is a natural means of contraception. Rhythm might also be called timely abstinence. Some people will not feel that the number of "safe" days for sexual activity warrants use of this method.

Foam Foam is a popular contraceptive technique. It is simple to use but takes some advanced preparation. The foam contains a substance which kills the sperm on contact and thus prevents pregnancy.

The advantages of foam are that it requires no prescription and it has no known long-term effect on the body. Unlike the pill it does not remain in the woman's system.

The disadvantages are that foam requires last-minute preparation. Like the condom, it interrupts sexual activity prior to intercourse. As a contraceptive method it is less effective than many of the others.

New Contraceptives New techniques of contraception are constantly being studied by scientists throughout the world. Many pharmaceutical firms are actively searching for a better means of contraception.

Vaginal sponges are expected to be on the market soon.[8] These sponges are filled with a substance which destroys the sperm on contact. This technique does not require fitting and it can be left in place for several days. The sponges are not likely to be any more effective than foam or spermicidal creams.

Testing is being done on a condom designed to dissolve during intercourse.[8] The condom would then release a spermicide which would prevent pregnancy. The primary advantage of this technique over a regular condom would be the lack of disposal problems.

Another technique being explored to replace the pill is a vaginal ring that gradually releases hormones.[9] These hormones are the same ones released by birth control pills but in smaller doses. The advantage would be that a daily pill would not be necessary. The ring is designed for use for about three weeks at a time. Another advantage is that the drug is absorbed through the vaginal wall and, as a consequence, bypasses the digestive system.

Research is being conducted throughout the world on numerous other experimental contraceptive techniques.[9] Ultrasound to suppress sperm formation, injections to eliminate the sperm production, cervical caps, reversible sterilization, and bracelets that release hormones through the skin are among some of the methods being studied. Researchers are trying to make contraceptives more effective and easier to use in order to increase their use and to eliminate unplanned pregnancies.

Whether rhythm, abstinence, condoms, IUD's, pills, withdrawal, diaphragms, or a technique of the future is best, it doesn't matter. All are likely to decrease the number of children conceived. Each is best used by properly motivated people.

Some day contraceptives may be in the water supply or administered in some way by the state. Perhaps we will have to be licensed to become pregnant after we have proven our fitness to parent. For now, however, parenting takes little forethought or aptitude for those who can readily get pregnant. For now, no matter how good contraceptive techniques are, they are only effective if the woman does not want to be pregnant.

Unconscious Desire to be Pregnant
The second reason that unplanned pregnancies occur is that many women at some unconscious level, desire to be pregnant.[10] The fact that contraception is available but not being used substantiates the possible existence of this unconscious desire. If you *really* don't want to get pregnant, you do something to prevent it. The woman who cannot find any method of contraception that is acceptable to her may be saying she doesn't want to find any method to prevent a pregnancy. The woman who is a sometime contraceptive user is one who sometimes may want to be pregnant.

Women who have had abortions as a means of resolving an unwanted pregnancy at times find themselves deliberately exposing themselves again to the same predicament. The woman's stated desire not to be pregnant must seriously be questioned if she keeps putting herself in a position to get pregnant.

These women, who may have some strong underlying reasons for wanting to be pregnant, are a source of babies who might be available for adoption. For that reason, we have to look closely at the factors which cause a woman to expose herself to a pregnancy when she says she doesn't want to be pregnant.

Pregnancy means a lot of different things to different women. For some women, especially the adolescent woman, pregnancy is a means of establishing her identity as an adult woman. The adolescent's primary psychological task is her search for a firm sense of who she is, her identity. The adolescent girl struggles to find her identity as a woman, not as a girl; as an adult, not as a child; and as an individual, not as an extension of her parents. Seeking to find her unique identity, she may use her developing sexual behavior as a form of saying, "Look, I am an adult, too!"

For some adolescent girls, having sexual feelings and the recognition of their developing bodies adds enough to their sense of identity. For other girls, further proof of their adulthood is needed and is achieved through active sexual behavior. Still others, unsure of who they are, need a pregnancy to prove to themselves that they are women. However, bearing the child or mothering the baby may not be essential in developing their female identities. Some of these young women with a need to be pregnant would be good candidates for allowing their pregnancies to go full term and placing their babies for adoption.

Another reason a woman might expose herself to an unwanted pregnancy is to maintain a relationship with a man. Perhaps the relationship is deteriorating and she seeks pregnancy as a way to maintain it. But babies make poor cement. In fact, in most cases, accidental pregnancies cause the breakup of a non-marital relationship. Historically, this tactic may have prompted many marriages, but this is no longer as frequent. Her reason for exposing herself to an unwanted pregnancy may have left her, however, her pregnancy does not leave that easily. Again, women in these circumstances might be a good source of adoptable children.

People help others who are in trouble. At times this well-intentioned help might in itself lead to a pregnancy as it did with Sharon. She was a lonely nineteen year old who had few friends. She had difficulty talking to people. In fact, she said that sometimes, it was easier to go to bed with a guy than to try to talk to him. Not surprisingly she got pregnant. Agencies opened their doors to her. Volunteer counselors spent time with her whenever she needed them. People, new "friends," helped her get to and from the agencies. Sharon said it was the best time of her life. Then she had her abortion and was back where she was before her pregnancy. The "friends" were no longer there. Her next pregnancy was not much of an accident. She needed help and the second pregnancy gave her that opportunity even though it was short-term abortion counseling.

Sharon needed professional counseling to avoid unwanted pregnancies and to help her solve her personal problems. If she had considered carrying her pregnancy to full term and placing the baby for adoption, at least she would have received longer-term counseling.

At times a pregnancy may result from an attempt to rectify a previous abortion. The woman, feeling the unresolved loss of the previous pregnancy, is likely to get pregnant again. She may inadvertently expose herself to an "accidental" pregnancy to "undo" her abortion. For this woman, carrying the child to term in the first instance may be a better choice. She may feel better about herself if she allows herself to complete the pregnancy and she would provide another child for adoption.

Fears of sterility can motivate women toward an unwanted pregnancy. A doctor told Evelyn, who was adopted as an infant, that she was unlikely ever to get pregnant. To prove her womanliness to herself she soon became pregnant. Evelyn typifies the woman who gives birth to satisfy her fears of infertility. She may also have to reject abortion since she owes her existence to her natural mother's choice not to abort when pregnant with Evelyn.

Some women deliberately keep their lives in a constant negative state. Jennifer was one. She had a late abortion which made it a difficult, labor-like procedure to abort the fetus. She was in labor for over fourteen hours and left the hospital angry with the staff and with the father of the child. Her primary way of relating to people was through the negative things that were "happening to her." She saw herself as a victim. The new man in her life did not treat her as she deserved. She was angry that he did not pay for her birth control pills, so in spite she quit taking them. Unable to take responsibility for her own actions, it was clear that Jennifer was a victim of her own making, paying for her anger with another pregnancy. She was a victim in her own unhappy way. At one of these pregnancy crisis points in her life she might consider placing the baby for adoption as an alternative to abortion.

In order for people seeking babies to succeed, it is essential they understand the motivation for unwanted pregnancies. The aforementioned are only some of the unconscious reasons a woman gets pregnant. Counseling services seldom find out why the woman gets pregnant. They get her an abortion, the cheaper, the better. Some of these women being given quick abortions are good prospects to give up their babies for adoption. Many of these women may never have considered adoption as an alternative.

Dilemma of Unwanted Pregnancies

No matter what the reasons for an accidental pregnancy, contraceptive failure or unconscious desire to be pregnant, once the woman is pregnant she faces a new dilemma. She is no longer involved in risk taking . . . she is on her way to having a baby. Whether she is single or married, she has only three choices open to her:

1. She can have the baby and raise it.
2. She can have the baby and place it for adoption.
3. She can terminate the pregnancy with an abortion.

If she doesn't want a baby, all of the choices are bad and she chooses the least offensive.

She is now ready to be bombarded by all of the people who would like to have input into her decision-making process. She begins with her own view which involves her feelings about herself and her relationship to others—the father of the child, parents, siblings and friends. Her personal view of what to do is influenced by her religious and moral feelings. Her view of herself as a woman and as a "maybe" mother enter into the decision. She is usually filled with ambivalence and confusion.

There is in each woman a view of herself as a potential mother. The ambivalence between the feelings of singleness and motherhood is viewed with alarm by the woman who is not sure that she wants to be pregnant. She resents the child's intrusion on her life, while at the same time fantasizing about her new life with a baby. She immediately begins to form a view of herself as a "mother," no matter what decision she makes about the baby she carries.

In this moment of great uncertainty, many others have their say in her pregnancy decision. The father of the child has his say, even though it is legally quite limited. He has no legal right to prevent or to force termination of the pregnancy. Jeff, aged fifteen, found this out the hard way. He had convinced Sue, aged sixteen, that they should "get rid of the baby" the first time she was pregnant. A friend told her if she took a lot of birth control pills she would miscarry—she did. (Probably not because of the pills.) The second pregnancy in the same year found her more reluctant. He convinced her to get an abortion. She delayed as long as possible then finally aborted twins. Jeff insisted to no avail that she use the pill or something. She never remembered. Her third pregnancy at seventeen, which she decided to complete, surprised him. He tried to convince her to abort the pregnancy, but she refused. He was responsible financially for the baby boy she later delivered. He is only seventeen now, but if she chooses, he will be forced to support his son for quite some time.

The father has no legal right to prevent the pregnant woman from placing the child for adoption; however, he does have a legal right to be considered as the appropriate home for the child in such cases. Amy was faced with a problem because of this new legal right for fathers. Amy was an active student in high school when she became pregnant with Kevin's baby. Her parents, mindful of their community involvement and social standing, were appalled. They made plans for her to visit relatives in another state until she delivered and could quietly place the child for adoption. Everything was so clear until Kevin's parents said they wanted him to keep the baby and they would raise it. His parents were willing to go to court to get the baby if Amy relinquished it. Amy was unwilling to deal with this so she kept the child she had wanted to place for adoption.

The influence of the father greatly depends on the relationship he and the mother have. While his rights are limited, they are increasing.

No one else has legal rights in the mother's decision making about the fate of her unborn child. The impact of others is likely to be felt but cannot be sustained in a court of law.

Everyone *knows* what she should do. Everyone tells her what she should do. Parents, siblings, friends—all give her their opinions on the subject. And all she gets is more confused. It's a relatively easy decision for a thirty-five-year-old woman with three children who, through contraceptive failure, becomes pregnant. She doesn't want the child and decides to get an abortion. It's an equally easy decision if you have been married for a year and wanted to wait a bit longer to have a baby. You accidentally got pregnant, so you merely change your time plans a bit. The decision isn't difficult if all the indicators point the direction for you. It's hardest when the pressures go in all different directions.

At this point the woman, confused and hurried by time pressures, needs to look objectively at all available alternatives. There are advocates, not necessarily equally represented, for each of the alternatives. Unfortunately, it is difficult to find someone who advocates exploring all of the alternatives.

In recent years, the pro-abortion counseling groups have become the loudest. Abortion as a legal choice is fairly recent in the realm of options. Over one million abortions per year are being done in the United States alone. Today, most young women finding themselves pregnant consider only abortion or keeping the baby. That is what their friends did and those are likely to be the only choices they consider.

The choice to raise the baby, if the mother is not married, has only recently been viewed as an option by other than special minority groups. At one point, the single mother was viewed with alarm. Now with single mothers merging with the serially married mother, society barely takes a second glance. Celebrities who have elected to remain single while carrying a child also glamorize this choice as an alternative to unplanned pregnancies. The romanticism and independence of having a baby and handling it on your own also encourages single parenting. From time to time even adoption agencies put their seal of approval on single parenting by placing children with singles. Like abortion, single parenting has an advocacy group.

Adoption has no effective advocates. The adoption agencies' workers are not a visible group. Out-reach programs and searching for potential biological parents to place children for adoption is unheard of. We do not recruit babies! I don't know why not. With advocates for two of the three alternatives available to the unhappily pregnant woman, the need for greater publicity of the adoption alternative is clear. "Pregnancy counseling" as it is popularly offered is a deception. All of the alternatives to a pregnancy are not presented in an unbiased manner. Each group that does "pregnancy counseling" has something to advocate—to sell. Most groups are selling a philosophy: zero population growth, abortion is murder or, women's liberation. Other groups are selling a product: adoptable babies or abortions. The concept of advocacy by any group might be acceptable if each group were equally represented. This, however, is not the case. If you open your newspaper, you are likely to find classified ads for "pregnancy counseling" under the personal heading. The young woman who turns to these "counselors" for help is trying to make a good decision about her unborn child. Unfortunately, she seldom has a chance to explore equally all of the alternatives open to her.

A few years ago I called a number of agencies in one area and told them about my "fifteen-year-old friend" who was pregnant and did not know what to do. The responses were astounding.

One agency, with the little information I had given, told me to get her in tomorrow and she could have an abortion and be out by noon. I asked where they did the abortion. . . . Did they do it in the office, or where? The worker-counselor told me they were working on that, but for now they went to a nearby hospital. She said they didn't have women doctors, but they hoped to soon because sometimes the male doctors "treat you like a hunk of meat." I told her that my friend thought she might get married or place the baby for adoption. The worker said, "Oh, she is too young to get married and the adoption agencies are a bunch of crooks." My fifteen-year-old friend might have had difficulty exploring alternatives with this group.

The bias of this agency was blatant, but not singular. I called another agency about the same friend. The volunteer indicated the agency had "trained counselors" who would help her through her abortion. Again, I told her my friend was uncertain whether she would be better off keeping the baby or even getting married. The woman said they would talk to her about her choices. I asked about adoption. The worker said they had a number for her to call if that is what she wanted. I asked her whose telephone number it was and she did not even know whose number she was distributing.

The woman who might consider placing her child for adoption would have great difficulty getting through this "counseling" system. The bias against adoption is as strong in these agencies as the bias against abortion is in anti-abortion groups. Because many volunteer counselors know little about adoption, or view it as being too difficult, they seldom bring it up as a choice for the woman to consider. Yet this is the time for the woman to consider *all* of the alternatives.

The fact that the major source of revenue for many volunteer pregnancy counseling agencies is "kickbacks" given by hospitals which perform referral abortions cannot help but influence the counseling they provide. Some agencies are on quota systems, which means they guarantee referring a certain number of women per month to a specific hospital for an abortion. While these innovative approaches have significantly lowered abortion costs, they have been at the expense of women who deserve to know *all* of the alternatives to her pregnancy. The sad part is that the unsuspecting woman, usually young, does not even realize she has not explored all the alternatives. She believes she had pregnancy counseling in order to make the best decision. Women who truly explored all of the alternatives might consider adoption. Women who have not even considered adoption represent a virtually untapped source of babies for people seeking a child to adopt.

Summary

Adoption for many women who are unhappily pregnant might not be considered by the woman because she does not understand the current scarcity of babies available for adoption. She simply doesn't know how many people would like to have the child she is carrying. Even today, the pregnant woman is likely to view her child as unwanted. The need to change this misconception is evident. In reality, the woman carries within her a valuable person desperately wanted by thousands of people. Perhaps the fact that her unborn child is in great demand could help effect a decision that offers the best solution for herself, the child and some potential parents. She needs to feel she could do something beneficial with the baby.

With fewer and fewer babies available today than ever before, adoption is a viable, healthy alternative to unwanted pregnancy and needs to be promoted. It is time to try new, open and different approaches to adoption. It is time to advocate adoption as an alternative to an unwanted pregnancy. It is time to make adoption a desirable, known alternative the pregnant woman might consider.

3
FACING
INFERTILITY

To want a child and not be able to have one is one of life's ironies. People throughout the world desperately seek the means to prevent unwanted births while others with equal desperation seek to conceive. Millions of dollars are spent to find the "new" method of contraception while few but the infertile would equally value the research being done on helping couples conceive. Overpopulation alarms the world as it overtaxes our resources, while you want only to add one more to the number but can't. Abuse of a child shocks the community and cries for a solution, while you would be so willing to take and love this abused child and solve the problem. One woman panics as her period is late, while you are again filled with anxiety that yours will come. Infertility is not an easy cross to bear in a society which seems to be going in absolutely the opposite direction.

In this age of people increasingly choosing not to have children, it is hard for many to understand the plight of the infertile. The instinctual side of motherhood causes heated debate on both sides. Whether there is an instinctual side of motherhood or not, there is little question about the intensity of the desire to have a child by those women who want to but cannot have one. Fertility is not an issue for most people *except* if they are infertile.

Medical advances in solving the problems of infertility could provide solutions for about half of the people who would otherwise be unable to have a child.[1] Advances in our knowledge about conception, in corrective reproductive surgery, and in the correction of hormone deficiency have significantly decreased the number of couples who would otherwise have been unable to produce a child. Some of these advances have been a direct result of the increased interest in infertility due to the lack of children available for adoption.

New reproductive techniques continue to make headlines. People marvel and cringe at the burgeoning power of medical science. The infertile watch with hope each new experimental success. Infertility is not just a medical problem, it is also an emotional problem. In the past, the emotional side was frequently blamed for infertility. Evidence does not support this belief. All the friendly advice about "relax" or "forget about it and you will get pregnant," while well meaning, does not usually help you get pregnant. Instead, the physiological problems causing infertility can cause serious emotional problems.

Many hints are available to help a couple conceive. Simply following some of the advice given by fertility specialists will solve the problem with no further medical intervention. The following types of suggestions are frequently given to couples who are having difficulty getting pregnant:

1. Just because you haven't gotten pregnant doesn't mean you are sterile. It simply means you have not yet become pregnant. About 80 percent of couples get pregnant within the first year they try to have a baby. The odds are that you will also. Unless you are sure there is some reason you have a fertility problem, give nature a chance.

2. Regular sexual intercourse is necessary to get pregnant. Regular means every two or three days. To have sexual relations more frequently may, in fact, decrease your chances of getting pregnant because it decreases the quantity of sperm available to fertilize the egg.

3. Be mindful of keeping yourself in good shape. This will increase your chances of getting pregnant and of being healthy while you are pregnant. Maintain a balanced diet, exercise regularly and get the right amount of rest for you.

4. No specific coital position is necessary to achieve a pregnancy. As long as there is full penile penetration and the man ejaculates

inside the woman's vagina, he is doing everything just the way he should.

5. Both of you, but especially the man, should avoid excessive use of alcohol, tobacco, caffeine and other drugs. Research shows that the number of sperm and their consequent ability to travel effectively are significantly altered with the use of drugs, chemicals and tobacco.

6. The man should also be aware of his local environment so he isn't exposed to excessive or prolonged heat. Heat—as in hot baths, hot tubs or saunas—just before intercourse decreases sperm production and interferes with the correct environment to store the sperm. This decrease lessens the likelihood of pregnancy. Loose-fitting underwear is generally a good idea, since the male body will keep the sperm at the right temperature if clothing does not interfere.

7. Learn about the female's menstrual cycle so you know when you are most likely to achieve a pregnancy. For the woman to become pregnant, she must have intercourse shortly before or after the time she ovulates. This is usually between 10-17 days after she starts her period. In order to know about your individual cycle, you need to learn when you ovulate. Thinner vaginal mucous discharge generally indicates you have ovulated and are most fertile. You can also get a basal thermometer which measures small changes in your oral temperature. Just before you ovulate, a slight drop in your temperature will occur. Knowing the right time to try to achieve a pregnancy significantly increases your chances.

8. If you have an obvious problem that might be interfering with your ability to conceive a child, correct it. If you are overweight, try to reduce. If you are under considerable stress at work, see if you can change that situation. If you have been sick a great deal, try to discover what is creating your susceptibility. Make any necessary corrections you can to increase your chances of getting pregnant.

For most couples, these hints will solve their infertility problem. They really didn't have a problem with infertility at all; they merely were waiting the normal period of time to get pregnant. They really didn't belong to the 10 or 15 percent of the population that is infertile. [2,3] If you have tried all of these suggestions and they didn't work, then it is time for you to look thoroughly at infertility and what it means to you. You need to understand the causes, the cures and the consequences of infertility to see where you fit in the picture.

Causes of Infertility

Generally men and women are equally afflicted with infertility problems. Women account for about 45 percent of the medical problems preventing conception; males account for about 40 percent of the medical problems. The cause of infertility in the remaining 15 percent of the couples is unknown.[1]

In order to understand the causes of infertility, you need to understand the reproductive process. The male produces a large number of sperm which he ejaculates into the woman's vagina during intercourse. If one of the sperm meets and penetrates the egg released from the woman's ovary each month, at the right time, the egg will be fertilized and conception occurs. Therefore, assuming nothing stops sperm production, that the sperm and egg are healthy and not incompatible and this occurs at the correct time to fertilize the egg, a baby will begin. That is a lot of assuming. For the couple experiencing infertility, one of these conditions does not occur. Let's look at the specific causes of sterility in both men and women.

Infertility in the Male Infertility in males always has something to do with the sperm. The problem involves at least one of three areas: (1) sperm production, (2) sperm storage, or (3) sperm transportation.

First the sperm must be manufactured. If anything interferes with this process, there may be too few sperm or they may be defective in some way and incapable of fertilizing the female egg. In a normal ejaculation, which amounts to about a teaspoonful of fluid, there are between 150-600 million sperm. Despite the gigantic number of sperm, most of the liquid in each ejaculation is not sperm but semen. In order for a woman to get pregnant, 100-150 million sperm are needed even though only one sperm actually penetrates and fertilizes the egg.[2] Checking the number of sperm the man produces is one of the easiest medical fertility tests and should usually be performed in the beginning phase of any fertility study.

One cause of a lowered sperm count is frequent ejaculation. The man who has intercourse one or more times per day for several consecutive days will temporarily lower his sperm count. Couples trying to get pregnant may sabotage their efforts by having intercourse too frequently.

Infectious diseases that involve the testes (where the sperm are manufactured) may decrease sperm production or cause sterility. The most common infectious disease associated with sterility is mumps; the adolescent boy having mumps is vulnerable to becoming sterile. Infections of the prostrate gland are also a cause of infertility.

Physiological and anatomical disorders can cause low sperm counts. Diabetes and thyroid dysfunction as well as abnormal hormone levels are associated with decreased sperm production. Varicose veins in the scrotum reduce the blood supply to the testes and also can cause decreased sperm production.

Occupational hazards contribute to male sterility. Thirty years ago, men who worked in shoe stores and used fluoroscopes in shoe fittings at times found themselves sterile from the prolonged and repeated exposure to radiation. Radiation is known to decrease sperm production. People today who work closely with radiation—X-ray clinicians, physicians, dentists, nuclear plant workers—are likely to increase their chances of becoming infertile unless they take the necessary and recommended precautions. Certain chemicals also present hazards that inhibit sperm production. Some drugs used to treat cancer decrease sperm production.

Temperature is a crucial factor in the production and storage of sperm. The testes must remain at the correct temperature or the sperm production will be lowered. The sperm are stored in an elongated tube inside the scrotum called the epididymis. Nature has planned well to keep the storage of sperm at just the right temperature. The wearing of clothes which keep the scrotum too close to the body and at too high a temperature, may cause infertility in the male. Taking a hot bath or sauna before intercourse may also destroy sperm in storage.

The sperm being stored in the epididymis in the scrotum must then travel up a small tube called the vas deferens (this is what is cut in a vasectomy) past the seminal vesicles and the prostate, where fluid is added to produce semen. Semen is the fluid that is ejaculated from the penis during intercourse. If the travel of the sperm in the semen is blocked anywhere by scar tissue, conception can be prevented. Common causes of this scar tissue are infections, especially gonorrhea. Sometimes hernia operations result in scarring also. Exposure to radiation may also scar the route the sperm must travel in its attempt to unite with the female egg.

Many of the causes of male sterility are correctable. Some tubal blockages, if they are not too advanced, can be corrected by surgery. Varicose veins of the testes may also be corrected by surgery. Hormone deficiencies can be corrected at times by supplemental injections. Even low sperm counts can be overcome by having a doctor store the male's sperm until a sufficient amount has been accumulated to impregnate the woman by artificial insemination. Drug therapy is also being used to increase sperm production in males.

The male experiencing a problem with infertility has some problem related to the production, the storage, or the journey of the sperm. Frequently these problems are correctable. For any couple who is having problems getting pregnant, a semen analysis should be one of the first diagnostic tests. If no problem is identified with the male sperm, then the female needs to be thoroughly examined.

Infertility in the Female Slightly more women than men have infertility problems. The greater difficulty for women is that the problems are usually more complex to diagnose and to treat. In order to understand infertility problems in the female we have to see what happens in the reproductive system of the female before and after male sperm enters.

The journey of the sperm from production through storage, and its travel through the male's reproductive system has been briefly described. When the male's sperm enters the female's vagina, it encounters new obstacles on its journey toward the egg.

The most common obstacle the sperm first experiences on its journey to the egg is at the cervix. The cervix, which is the entrance from the vagina to the uterus, normally has a thick cervical mucus. However, during the time of the month when the ovary releases an egg, a hormone causes the mucus to become thinner and therefore, allow easy passage of the sperm through the cervix and into the uterus. If the mucus does not get thinner, the sperm cannot pass.

Sometimes a woman's immunity system becomes activated against her husband's sperm. She is actually somewhat allergic to her partner. She may send out antibodies that destroy the sperm.

An inadvertent cause of sterility may be the use of feminine hygiene products. Commercial douches or vaginal deodorants may inhibit the journey of the sperm or completely destroy it. This is probably related to the changed pH of the vaginal environment. If the vaginal secretions are strongly acidic, the sperm are destroyed quickly or, at a minimum, the movement of the sperm is considerably slowed.

At the other end of the reproductive tract, in the ovaries, a different set of circumstances which might prevent pregnancy can occur. Ovaries are like the counterpart of the male testes . . . this is where the female sex cell originates. Unlike the male, the female starts life with all of the eggs already in her body. She does not produce new eggs each month, she simply releases one egg a month (usually) after the egg has spent two weeks maturing. Several problems can go wrong at this particular stage of reproduction.

One of the major causes of female sterility occurs when an egg is not released because of some hormonal problem. Deficiencies of thyroid, adrenal, or pituitary hormones may interfere with the woman's ability to ovulate, or to release an egg. Malnutrition, vitamin deficiency, anemia, or stress may also interfere with ovulation. If the woman fails to release an egg, there is no possibility that conception will occur.

When the egg is released from the ovary it is swept into the Fallopian tube. The ovary is not connected to the Fallopian tube, but the egg mysteriously finds its way to the Fallopian tube. Under normal circumstances it takes about three days to travel down the three- to five-inch tube. It has no means of propelling itself as does the sperm, but it is carried by a current of small hairs lining the tube and by the muscle contractions in the walls of the tubes. At some time during this part of the journey, the sperm meets the egg and fertilization occurs.

The critical role of the Fallopian tubes makes it another source of infertility problems. If the tubes are obstructed by scar tissue, the egg's or sperm's journey can be prevented. Over one million American women have obstructed or damaged Fallopian tubes; half of these women would like to have this problem corrected. Tubes may be blocked because of previous infections or surgery. Tests using a gas (Rubin's Test) or an oily dye (hysterosal pengogram) injected through the cervix into the Fallopian tubes determine if tubes are blocked. These tests can be helpful in clearing the tubes also. Usually the dye test is used because it is more effective and is less painful.

Infections other than Fallopian tube infections also cause female sterility. Infections of the uterus, vagina, cervix or ovaries may cause infertility by inhibiting or preventing passage of the egg or of the sperm on their journey toward each other.

Given the number of times a couple may have intercourse, the probability of fertilization occurring at any one time is extremely low. In animals, intercourse occurs at the time when fertilization is likely to occur . . . the animal is "in heat." With humans, intercourse is not restricted to the woman's fertile time. Without this condition, the correct time of the month, the egg will not be fertilized. Of the several hundred million sperm that the male ejaculates at the right time of the month, only about 2,000 reach the Fallopian tube down which the egg is traveling and then only one sperm (usually) gets the chance to do fertilization.[2] The male has enough sperm to produce millions of babies at each ejaculation and it takes those huge odds to produce one sperm that has the chance of meeting, at just the right time, the one egg that the female sends out.

Many women experiencing infertility can be successfully treated. Drugs are now available to treat women unable to ovulate because of hormone deficiencies. Current advances in the use of varying amounts of hormones appropriate for the individual woman are decreasing the multiple births frequently associated with the use of "fertility" drugs.

Delicate microsurgery, which is surgery using tiny instruments, is being used to open Fallopian tubes that are blocked or damaged.[4] The 70 percent success rate with this surgery is wonderful and is preferable to the procedures used in the well-publicized "test-tube baby" which was developed to solve the same problems (See Chapter 4).

Fertility problems in women, like those in men, are frequently correctable. The infertility problems women usually experience are related to blocked tubes, unreleased eggs, or incompatible environments for the sperm. Procedures are available to correct about half of the problems in sterile women.

For both men and women experiencing infertility, it is difficult to decide how far to go in order to try to medically correct a problem. Statistics indicate that if a specifically identified cause of infertility exists, the person has a 50-60 percent chance of correcting the problem.[4] If a person is infertile and the cause of the infertility cannot be determined, the rate of success drops to about three percent.

Each person needs to identify for himself or herself, how far to go in terms of medically correcting a fertility problem. In recent years more couples are seeking "cures" for their infertility and the increased interest is directly related to the lack of available infants for adoption.

Kinds of infertility problems and their common cures are what have been discussed in this chapter. More experimental and riskier techniques of having babies are discussed in the following chapter. Most people will find the answers to their problems of infertility in the more usual and common medical remedies currently available.

Consequences of Infertility

In some ways, not having a child "proves" to the world an individual's deficiency. If we are poor, financial inadequacy may or may not show to the world. If we are insecure, the world may not necessarily know. But if we are childless, our sexual deficiency is there, exhibited for all the world to view. To understand the emotional consequences of infertility is to understand the plight of feeling inadequate.

Sexuality still remains so blurred and confusing to most people that fertility is one of our primary means of demonstrating our sexuality. Our society headlines the older male who fathers a child. In Southern California, an old lion at one of the animal parks was eulogized for fathering so many lion cubs late in his life. Shirts with his picture on them were printed in admiration.

Young people, too, brag about sexual conquests to bolster their feelings about sexuality. Roger is a good example of confused feelings about sexuality. Roger was sixteen and had few friends. He felt very unsure of himself in most situations. He told his school counselor and a few acquaintances about getting a girl pregnant at church camp. Everyone started to listen to him a bit more, so he related that the girl gave birth to their daughter. Then he told how his girlfriend's parents made them get married. Now a lot of people knew about Roger. He told his counselor he had gotten her pregnant a second time and wasn't sure what he should do. The counselor suggested he seek legal help, but Roger did nothing. The counselor then learned, from Roger, that the girl had stepped out in front of a car and had been killed and her parents had brought his baby over for him to raise. Everyone knew about Roger's story by now. His story had been told at school for over a year. He had added prestige with his peers and he felt more confident about dealing with people who knew of him. He spoke positively about his daughter to the counselor who was impressed with his strong commitment to the child. The counselor spent long hours with him helping him to learn how best to raise a baby since Roger's parents were not helping him with the child. Then one day, someone from the school office contacted his home and found out from Roger's mother that Roger didn't have a baby. Roger hadn't caused anyone to become pregnant. Roger didn't even have a girl friend. In fact, Roger had never been sexually active at all. Roger had made up the entire story. He needed to have the same kinds of stories, or better ones, to tell the guys in the gym. He needed to have people see him as a sexual creature who knew what he was doing sexually just like he thought others knew what they were doing. Roger couldn't feel comfortable doing the same things others did to establish their sexual identities so he made them up. Our sexual identities are frequently very fragile.

Early sexuality and late sexuality "prove" adequacy for some uncertain reason. Lots of sex is another way of proving sexuality. Frequently, men seek to improve their sense of sexuality by the number of times they can reach a climax or the number of women they have had sex with . . . sexuality proven by the frequency of intercourse. Number of children is another way of proving sexuality. Contraceptive clinics in low-income areas have frequently failed because too often the identity of low-income groups is based on how many children they have. They may be poor, but they are "good" parents because they have lots of children.

With so much emphasis on demonstrated sexuality, the infertile couple is obviously in some trouble. They are forced into feelings of inadequacy. In order to survive emotionally as complete persons, they have to learn how to handle feelings of deficiency since they are unable to establish their sexual identity by producing a child as others do.

The couple experiencing infertility must first come to grips with how this factor affects each of them individually. Each individual must grope for new ways to establish a firm sexual identity through means other than getting someone pregnant. The person who is sure of his or her sexuality will be less effected than the person who is less sure. If you are sure of your sexuality, demonstrating it to yourself or your friends or the world becomes less important. Generally, the woman who is doing other things in her life places less emphasis on her fertility as her only means of viewing herself as a woman. The man who is successful in other areas of his life is less concerned about his lack of success in impregnating his wife. Basically, the more together the person, the easier time he or she will have accepting his or her infertility . . . easier, but still not too easy.

The couple experiencing infertility must also face the strains it puts on their relationship. All major problem areas—a new job, a new home, the woman beginning to work outside the home, someone being fired, a relative coming to live with them, the death of a relative, an injury to one of the partners—cause shifts and changes in the marital relationship. Sometimes the changes are for the better and sometimes for the worse. How the relationship comes back determines where the couple goes from there; these are vulnerable periods in marital relationships. Experiencing infertility may be one of the most significant experiences a couple will ever have.

Couples, at this time above all, need to communicate openly. To harbor feelings of blame toward your sterile spouse can cause long-term, irreparable damage to the relationship. Scheduled sexual relations and the stress of medical tests put severe strains on any relationship. If this is coupled with hidden hostility and unspoken blame, the couple will have difficulty overcoming the strains of infertility. They may end up not only without a child, but also without a partner.

The problem of relatives and friends is another consequence of infertility to be overcome. Relationships with others are filled with references to the couple's infertility. The potential grandmother has her advice to give. The potential aunts and uncles, going through their own period of child rearing, are quick to offer tips and reminders of your childlessness. Baby showers where people say, "You're next" become ordeals and alter your relationships with your friends.

Society, with no knowledge of your pain, views you with confusion and skepticism. You are likely to be pictured as selfish in not wanting children—which is ever so far from the truth. Even if you are viewed as childless not by choice, society is likely to offer little sympathy because people with children have difficulty identifying with your infertility plight. People openly sympathize with mourning couples whose child has been lost through death; people fail to comprehend the mourning of the couple whose child is lost through infertility.

At times, outsiders will view you in your childlessness as neurotic or immature. Articles you read will relate your childlessness to your frigidity and sexual immaturity. In this time of overpopulation, your problems will be viewed as insignificant and lacking in substance.

As the desire for pregnancy supersedes most things in your life, you need to find adequate and acceptable ways to handle your feelings about infertility. The primary way to deal with feelings about your infertility is to talk with people . . . especially your partner. Express your feelings to sympathetic listeners, if you have feelings of guilt or deficiency. Talking with others helps to eliminate the irrational feelings you have about your infertility problem. If you continue to have difficulty finding someone to talk with, seek professional help from a psychologist or psychiatrist.

A second means of coping with your feelings is to redirect your energies. For months you may have been engrossed with fertility tests, temperature charting, medical appointments and scheduled sexual activities. Infertility has dominated your existence. At some point you have to accept the fact that there is no solution to your infertility that will produce a pregnancy. So now what are you going to do? You need to change directions. One new direction may be trying to find a child to adopt. It may be toward a different kind of creative approach to life. A change in your direction, however, is critical.

Don't expect the feelings you have to go away immediately. You need to be prepared for a period of mourning. This might be called mourning for the child you couldn't have. Expect the period of mourning to last at least six months. You will find your feelings of depression, anger and anxiety decreasing with time, with redirection of your energies and by talking openly about your problem.

The medical cures for infertility may sound difficult to surmount. So, too, are the emotional consequences, but they *are* surmountable. The individual dealing openly, honestly and thoroughly with his or her feelings of inadequacy and anger is much more likely to overcome these emotions than the person who pretends everything is fine when in fact it isn't. The lack of babies available for adoption makes it even more critical that the individual's feelings about infertility are resolved and not simply denied. Your options, now that you are certain of your infertility, take strength to pursue. If you remain handicapped from the discovery of your infertility, you will be less likely to be able to pursue effectively the options you still have to get a baby.

Infertility Help

As you become aware that a baby is not going to "happen" to you, get ready to find help. This is a difficult step for many people because it, more than any other thing to this point, admits openly that you have a problem. This is the point at which you are forced to confront the reality of sterility. Infertile is harsh enough but *sterile* sounds so much worse. Yet someone in your relationship is sterile at this time; you need to figure out what you are going to do about it.

Finding a Physician As the tears increase with each new menstrual period, it becomes more apparent that other steps need to be taken. The first step you are likely to take is to talk with the physician you know the best. From this departure point, you are on your way.

Your physician is likely to recommend another who knows more about infertility. When your physician makes a referral, find out on what grounds he is suggesting this new person. This is also a good time to consult other people because it is important to find a physician who offers an expertise about infertility and additionally is the kind of person with whom you want to work.

This is a time to shop around and to ask questions. Call your local infertility association or write to the American Fertility Society, 1608 13th Avenue South, Birmingham, Alabama 35205, for general information on doctors working on infertility in your area. Go to the nearest university medical school and get their suggestions. You may be involved with this physician for the next year or more; find the right one for you. Even though the initial stages of an infertility study are relatively simple, find someone with whom you can work well because your infertility work may be more involved; you may be spending a lot of time and money with him or her over the months ahead.

After you have gathered names of the people you have heard are the best, contact them. By this time you will have formed some opinions on what kind of person you are seeking. Interview your potential doctor to make certain this is the person you want. Find out the background he or she has in infertility work. Ask questions about his opinion on the kind of problems you have and what the possibilities are for you. Know enough about what is happening so that you can try to assess his state of knowledge in infertility. Not all physicians, in fact not even all infertility specialists, know equal amounts. By talking with him about his background and your problem, you should be able to determine who he is and what his working knowledge is about infertility.

Pam and Sean found out about their physician the hard way. After Pam and Sean had tried for over a year to get pregnant, they decided to consult a physician. They asked their friends and one woman suggested Dr. Hall, a gynecologist. Pam began fertility studies. She went through test after test, appointment after appointment. She did everything he told her— she took her temperature regularly, had intercourse at the prescribed times, went through the tests he suggested (even the painful ones) and looked at the X-rays he showed her. After all, he was the expert. After six months she was still not pregnant. He suggested major surgery "to straighten out the Fallopian tubes." This was his diagnosis of the reason for her infertility. At this point Pam and Sean sat down to survey what had happened and what was being suggested to them. They somewhat apologetically approached Dr. Hall and asked if he felt it might be worthwhile to have Sean examined before performing major surgery on Pam. The doctor agreed. Sean's examination revealed a sperm count so low that it would have been highly unlikely he could impregnate Pam. Pam and Sean felt very foolish for the passive role they had played in their infertility studies. Since the doctor hadn't suggested that Sean be examined, they felt they should have known enough to suggest it far earlier in the process. They were right . . . they should have. They had the most to lose and the most to gain. They needed to know more about their infertility and they needed to know more about their doctor.

If you find one physician isn't all you hoped for, consult another one. There are some outstanding physicians in this field and they are the kind you want. Take the time to find the right one.

.If a physician suggests major surgery for your infertility problem (or for any other problem as well), consult another physician for a second opinion. Most times it will verify the recommendation. The time to make certain of your decision is before surgery.

In the past, physicians have held a position of unquestioned authority with most people. Don't be intimidated by your physician; you are trying to find someone to hire to do a service for you. More and more we are learning that physicians can help most if we, the patients, are actively involved in the treatment plan. *No one knows more about you than you!*

Learning About Infertility How can you, a lay person, ask intelligent questions of a physician, the expert, if you don't know much about the subject? You can't. This is why it is important to learn about infertility. You will end up learning about infertility somewhere along the way whether you want to or not. You may as well find out about the subject right at the beginning and have your information work for you.

Many sources of information are available on infertility. Some of these may be too technical in the beginning stages especially, but others are aimed at people without medical backgrounds. The more you find out about the subject, the more difficult and technical information you will understand.

One of the best sources of information on infertility is the local infertility society. If you don't know about the one closest to you, check with the American Fertility Society, 1608 13th Avenue South, Birmingham, Alabama 35205, to see where your local chapter is located. These groups frequently have meetings with people who are experiencing infertility problems. They discuss the general procedures used with infertility studies, innovative techniques in reproductive medicine, the psychological consequences of infertility and other areas of concern to people who are having difficulties getting pregnant. They frequently have guest lecturers who are experts in this field. The informal knowledge passed from individual to individual is priceless. You will learn about the best physicians to go to and the newest techniques that are being tried. You will also have found a support system that is exceedingly valuable in many ways.

Another source of information is obtainable through reading. Information on this subject is published in many different forms. Become familiar with all of them.

Books are available on infertility. [5,6,7,8] Some are written for physicians but some are also written in less technical language. Read current books because this is a rapidly changing field. Your library or a college library will have some appropriate books for you on this subject.

Articles in popular magazines regularly discuss infertility. Some of these are excellent sources of material since they are frequently more timely than books can be. If nothing else, they will help you understand enough about the subject of infertility to talk with and to ask questions of your physician.

As you become more knowledgeable about the subject you may wish to go to the medical libraries and read current articles on infertility that are written for physicians. These are not as difficult to read as you might think, especially after you begin to acquire a greater background in this field.

Newspapers also have articles on recent advances in reproductive medicine. They may not give a lot of detail, but it may be enough to at least talk with your physician. They may also give you another source to contact.

In all of your sources of information, don't hesitate to write to the people who are the "experts" about whom you are reading. They can answer questions and be a valuable source of additional information to you.

You can understand why it is so important to have a cooperative working relationship with your physician as you begin this process. If he can't answer your questions or doesn't like you "meddling" in the treatment, you will be restricted in how much you can be involved. You may also find out some ideas that will help him in your treatment. No one is so much an expert that he doesn't have more to learn. Patients are a primary source of learning for physicians.

The issue of infertility is one of the most important issues you are likely to face in your life. Face it intelligently, openly, frankly and thoroughly. Seek the help of experts but trust yourself to be involved in this important life experience.

Options to Infertility

If you have not become pregnant and have consulted a physician or physicians who specialize in infertility problems, he or she will have done the ordinary tests and the regular corrective procedures to try to remedy the apparent problems. But what if you still are not pregnant? What choices are now open to you?

Many ways exist to meet your need for a child. Some are direct means of getting a child and others emphasize a redirection from parenting. People will choose different options. As in many areas we are discussing, there is not a right or wrong way; there is a way with which you are likely to feel most comfortable. You may pursue several options before you find the one that best suits you. You may eliminate an option now that later on might suit you better. Meet your needs in your own way.

Experimental Methods of Reproduction Some people will try to go further than others would to correct their infertility problems. More extraordinary help is available in the area of fertility studies than ever before in history. Yet there are some problems with pursuing this option.

You have already spent over a year, maybe more, on trying to become pregnant. Your life has been thoroughly absorbed in this primary goal. It is likely that the strain of the pursuit is showing in your relationships with spouse, family and friends. It is important that you evaluate this option in terms of the costs to you if you continue still further on this same path.

Find out from your physician what your chance of success is before you decide how far to go with extraordinary medical procedures. Only in this way can you evaluate how worthwhile it might be to continue. As in many areas of life, you are playing the odds; you want to calculate the costs versus the possibilities of the payoff.

On the other hand, as long as you have hope and this is indeed your desire, go after it. Hopefully you strive for this objective with the full support of your partner. If you have been communicating regularly and openly you will know if this is the case.

In order to continue on this path it is important for you to keep current of every new development in the field of infertility. You are very likely to become quite an expert on this subject. It may take your appropriate questions about a certain technique to jog your physician into finding out about it. It may take trips across the country to consult with an expert in the development of a new technique. It may take trips to the medical library, many more medical tests, a great deal of patience and a hopeful outlook. The kinds of experimental or more unusual techniques of reproduction are discussed in greater detail in Chapter 4. So, if being pregnant is what you want and nothing else will do, go as far as you can.

Adoption For some who choose not to pursue the more elaborate or experimental techniques of reproduction or for others who have pursued them unsuccessfully, adoption may be the option they choose to attain parenthood. The many avenues to finding children are discussed in this book. Find the one that best meets your needs.

Both private and agency adoptions should be considered when you are thinking of adopting a child. They each have advantages and disadvantages which will be discussed in detail later in this book.

In order to seek a child via adoption you should first know that reasonable medical corrections of your infertility problem have been attempted. If these are tried and you have allowed yourself some time to digest the fact of your infertility, adoption can be almost or just as meaningful as producing a child biologically.

Foster Parenting A different kind of parenting possibility exists through becoming a foster parent. This can be a rewarding opportunity to participate in the raising of a child.

At times people confuse foster parents with adoptive parents. There are very few similarities. Foster parents are usually temporary parents. Foster parents do not have legal custody of the child. The child can be taken from the foster home at any time. Foster parents are paid for the care of the child. Adoptive parents on the contrary, provide permanent homes where the parents have legal custody of the child. In adoptive homes the parents are legally responsible for the upbringing of the child and receive no pay for this responsibility.

The foster care system of this country has come under considerable attack in recent years. Agencies running foster care programs are often adoption agencies. Not all, but many of these agencies, have been accused of deliberately keeping potentially adoptable children in foster care because the state pays the agencies for each child it keeps in the foster care system. If these children are placed in adoptive homes, the agency no longer receives funds from the state. Critics of the system say the agencies are being supported by state funds and therefore have no incentive to place these children in adoptive homes. The state cost of raising a foster child from early childhood to age eighteen can be several hundreds of thousands of dollars. This tremendously expensive parenting system is not only a burden on the taxpayers, but is also offers little stability for the child raised in these "temporary" facilities. It is estimated that as many as 500,000 children are currently in foster care.[9] The average stay will be between four to six years. It has been estimated by representatives of the Health, Education and Welfare Department that between 50 to 85 percent of the children in foster care will remain there through the age of eighteen. This type of permanent "temporary" home situation causes tremendous confusion to the child who belongs nowhere.[10,11]

None of these criticisms negates the great good being done by foster parents who willingly offer temporary homes to children in need. The ideal foster parent is one with an ability to love without having to feel the relationship will go on forever. This is not an easy kind of love for many people to offer. As a consequence, there is often a lack of good foster parents.

With this scarcity of foster homes, little screening of potential foster parents may actually occur. As a consequence, large numbers of foster parents are not truly involved with their foster children. At times, the primary reason people become foster parents is to have the income from caring for the foster children. Some homes have large numbers of foster children as a means of having a significant income.

Children in the foster care system come from one of three groups. The first group are children who are waiting to be placed in adoptive homes. These are usually the most temporary children in foster homes. Older children waiting to be adopted are frequently kept in foster homes for a long period of time to make certain the correct type of home is found. The second group are children whose parents are temporarily unable to care for them but who do not want to place them for adoption. This is a temporary situation that allows the parent to maintain contact with the child while the parent stabilizes his or her life. Some of these children are voluntarily placed by their parents and at other times the court system has intervened because the parent has not adequately cared for the child. The third group of children are the ones whose parents have little contact with them. These children are likely to remain in foster care through their eighteenth birthday. The Child Welfare League of America maintains that children whose parents do not take the child back within a year and a half probably never will. As with the previous group, these children are placed in foster care both voluntarily and by the courts.

Cases have recently been publicized of foster parents being allowed to adopt their foster children. In the past this was strictly forbidden by the adoption agencies. While more cases are occurring, it is usually with great effort that foster parents are accepted as the adoptive applicants for their foster child. This is not a very sure way to find a child to adopt. Adoption agencies, I believe, should begin with the foster parents if a specific foster child they are raising does become adoptable. The home the child knows should be the first one to be considered permanent. This is not usually the case.

Substitute Parenting Some people will choose to remain childless but will find themselves intricately involved in parenting vicariously. There are many means of being a substitute parent.

One of the ways to be a substitute parent is with children of your relatives. Some aunts or uncles are extremely involved with their nieces and nephews. They take them places, spend time with them, travel with them, baby-sit them. They are involved in their holidays and in their other joyous events. They are able to participate in these children's growing years.

Other childless people, wanting to participate in child rearing, seek out close relationships with children in the neighborhood or do extensive baby-sitting. Other people become Big Brothers or Big Sisters for children who do not have an adult of that sex in their life. They find that part-time parenting meets some of their needs for contact with children.

Another way people become substitute parents is by teaching children. Becoming a teacher or helping in a nursery school will sometimes substitute for not having children. The teacher spends four to six hours a day with lots of children. That may be far more hours of parenting than many actual parents spend.

The people who choose substitute parenting are saying it is important to them to have children in their lives. They are not actually remaining childless. They simply have children who are slightly more "borrowed children" than those who adopt or who have foster children. All our children, the ones we produce, the ones we adopt and the ones we merely nurture for awhile are borrowed; no one *owns* a child.

Childlessness One of the options to infertility is to remain childless. This is an option that is chosen far more frequently than is generally believed. Figures on how many childless people actually tried to get pregnant and failed are impossible to find. It is difficult to determine how many people are childless and how many people are childless but not by choice.

Childlessness has only recently been studied. It is known that greater numbers of couples have not had children during certain periods of our history such as during the Depression. The reasons for the decreased fertility rates are purely speculative.

A resurgence of childlessness has been seen in the seventies and is likely to continue into the eighties. Organizations advocating childlessness, like the National Alliance for Optional Parenthood (2010 Massachusetts Street, Washington, D.C. 20036), are widely publicized. Their push toward childlessness has undoubtedly increased the acceptability of non-parenting as a viable alternative open to couples. They offer support groups in local areas for childless couples. They generally have speakers who are available to publicize their cause. It is worthwhile to contact them if you wish to know more about childlessness.

Studies are only recently being undertaken to assess why people are childless and how this affects their lives. One recent study dealing with life satisfaction of older people compared childless couples and those with children.[12] The interesting result was that childless couples were found to be just as satisfied with their lives as those who had children. The common assumption has been that the childless couple will be lonely in later life and that life will have held no meaning for them if they have not had children. This assumption appears invalid.

Another group of studies published in the fifties focused on the failed marriages of childless couples. The results were presented to the childless as a further reason to have children. If you don't have a baby, the marriage is more likely to fail. In recent years, these same studies have been shown to be faulty. Early divorces are frequently childless by nature of the length of these marriages. To try to assess the effect of having children on the failure of the marriage becomes impossible.

So where does this leave people who remain childless not by choice? Is there a negative effect on their marriages or on their lives in general as a result of their childlessness? What can people do to minimize any negative effects remaining childless might have on them?

Marriages are not held together by babies for long. The quality of a marriage is most directly related to the commitment and work of the two people involved. Open communication can help any couple surmount a specific difficulty encountered. Marriages neither succeed, nor fail because of children.

The *primary* means of making sure your life is fulfilling is not necessarily having children. Children may or may not add to your feelings of satisfaction with life. If you decide to remain childless, it is important to have other means to feel good about yourself. Satisfying jobs are one means. Doing worthwhile things in your life are another. If you feel good about yourself, you won't need any specific things like a child to prove your worth. Validation from others or from society in general based upon your parenting or non-parenting become less important to you. You know you are worthwhile . . . you feel it . . . no one needs to tell you that you are okay.

Basically these are the options to infertility. You may elect to try some of the options simultaneously. You may try new experimental ways to get pregnant, at the same time you are trying to find a child to adopt. You may elect to go from one option to another. You may try being very active with children as a substitute parent and decide later that it isn't what you want. Then you might decide to pursue medical remedies further or to pursue adoption.

Nancy and Warren are a good example of a couple trying many options to their infertility. Nancy and Warren went through infertility studies and found that Warren had a low sperm count that probably was the cause of their infertility. They decided it was "no big deal" and went ahead to adopt two children. Everything was going along fine until they began to have marital problems. As they came closer and closer to a divorce, they realized the unexplored and undiscussed areas of Warren's sterility were a significant factor in the hostility Nancy was feeling. As this came more to the foreground, they saw that many areas of concern revolving around their infertility had been ignored or denied. With the discussion came improvement in the marriage. What had started out to be a dissolving of the relationship ended up with their deciding to resume their fertility work to see if they had gone as far as they needed to in trying to produce a child. After some additional tests, they decided to try artificial insemination; it didn't work. As a result, they discovered that Nancy, too, was part of the infertility problem. They decided to adopt another child while continuing their medical possibilities. Nancy and

Warren exemplify the multiple attempts and changes a couple can try while they seek an acceptable alternative to their infertility.

Try what sounds best to you. Don't hesitate to say after a time that the option you chose is the wrong one and you want to try another one. Life changes and so can you.

Summary

Your infertility journey is not an easy one. It will take a lot of strength and stamina. As with all areas of your life, the more knowledge you begin with, the easier will be the way on this difficult road. Know the easy things that may correct your early symptoms of infertility . . . these are what you do to get pregnant if there really isn't a problem with infertility. Know the kinds of problems that exist when there actually is a fertility problem . . . pursue your problem intelligently and openly and it will be easier. Consider your option to infertility . . . having choices after you know you are infertile makes accepting the problem easier.

Many people and sources are out there to help you to solve and to accept the problems you are experiencing. This very emotional issue is difficult to handle alone. Seek out the support you need. Seeking help from loved ones or from professionals is not a sign of weakness . . . it's a sign of intelligence.

Sterility hurts. It makes people cry, it makes them angry, it makes them feel incomplete. It's hard to determine and it's hard to accept. It's clinical and it's emotional. It can dominate your life and yet it is painful to know when to let it go. Only the strong should suffer sterility.

4
MAKING BABIES WITH A LITTLE HELP

Years ago, books predicting the time that babies would be artificially produced outside the mother were looked at with disbelief and alarm. This could never happen! Today the scientific capacity exists to produce a child and to maintain it through the time of "birth" outside the mother.

When this real possibility is discussed, most people are alarmed. Yet all of the techniques necessary are being successfully tried. These techniques are being utilized by people like the parents of baby Louise (the first test-tube baby), by parents who conceive via artificial insemination, and for premature babies. Most people can readily accept the lifesaving means used for a child born prematurely; few would put limits on how far we should go as we attempt to sustain the life of a fetus outside the mother. The majority of people have voiced support for the miraculous birth of baby Louise, who was conceived outside of her mother's body and then implanted within her to await birth. It probably took the normal, beautiful face of Louise after her birth to win support for this awesome technique. Fewer people would support the concept of artificial insemination with an unknown father's sperm; the lack of publicity of this technique of reproduction in many ways accounts for its limited acceptance with the public.

Our scientific capacities today amaze us and make us fearful, but we are confused on as basic an issue as at what point in the birth process does life begin to exist. Questions of this magnitude—debated scientifically, religiously, morally and publicly—create confusion for all of us on an issue that just a generation ago was so simple.

The whole issue of abortion has significantly altered our thoughts on life. At what point in an abortion is a life being taken? Then after the debate begins to subside an aborted fetus survives, and the debate is fueled once again.

Our medical capabilities to sustain life have changed our beliefs on what life is. We have panels to determine if a person is dead or alive. Relatives wrestle with the responsibility of how long they should maintain their loved ones on life-support systems that prolong their "life."

The revelations following World War II on the efforts of Hitler to produce a master race and his horrendous attempts to eliminate a given race of people, have caused the world to shudder. Yet the very issue of genetic screening and selective breeding to eliminate "defects" looms closer today than existed then. Legally we can eliminate a child that does not meet the criteria we have set for it in certain areas . . . as long as we do it early enough.

The opportunities to fertilize the infertile and to manipulate the process of conception have now been altered. Nature, in its most basic form, reproduction of life, has been found to need help. Our scientific advances have been able to help animals and humans to breed more effectively. Many people ask, have we gone too far?

Throughout the controversy on life and selective life, the infertile wait. The reproductive advances that shock us hold hope for the infertile. The medical advances being made may give the infertile couple the child they so desperately want, yet many people are critical of these same scientific advances. People say we are tampering with Mother Nature. Others say we are interfering with God's design, but the major critics are not those who are infertile. The fears of society about the impact of science on our lives and the hope of an infertile couple for a baby are on a direct collision course.

Ultimately, scientific advances that alter the direction of life are determined by personal decisions. You cannot debate the long-term effects on society in having your baby conceived in a laboratory . . . you really debate your chances of getting the baby you want so much. The effect on society of having someone else's embryo implanted in you after your partner has fertilized the embryo cannot be determined . . . the only determination to be made is how this will affect you, your partner and your hoped for child. Reproduction decisions are not society decisions . . . they are personal decisions.

Experimental ways of having a child are never first choices for the people who try them. In fact, they are generally third or fourth choices. Ask the couple attempting to have a child by artificial insemination why they are doing this. You are likely to hear that first they tried to get pregnant and failed, so they sought the usual medical remedies for their infertility. When these failed, they tried to adopt a child and failed and now they are at this point. You get to this point only by a process of elimination . . . you have no other choices left or this choice seems better to you than the remaining ones.

What then are these newer ways to make babies? What hope is open to the couple who does not respond to the usual medical remedies to infertility?

Artificial Insemination

Of all the more *unusual* methods of conceiving a child, artificial insemination is probably the oldest, the most secretive, the least studied and the most used. It is estimated that in this country alone between 10,000 and 20,000 children per year are produced by this method.[1] Yet we keep few records on the outcome of artificial insemination, we know little about the psychological consequences for the people involved, and we offer little help and support to those considering this procedure.

Artificial insemination takes many forms. Basically, when we speak of artificial insemination it means fertilization of the egg by artificial, or not regular, means. This technique is used when a husband has a low sperm count that would prevent his sperm from impregnating his wife (under 100–150 million). Some people would say that the artificial part of artificial insemination means using some other man's sperm . . . it's not from the *real* father. Other people would say the artificiality is when sperm is put into the woman's vagina by means other than intercourse.

Historically, couples experiencing infertility were helped by having another man get the woman pregnant if the husband could not. Friends or relatives were usually willing to help the couple in distress. Little thought was given to the long-term consequences because society was less complex. This type of infertility remedy was simply a part of society.

For some people today, this attitude still remains. Joyce and Leon wanted a child. Leon and Joyce were both carriers of Tay-Sachs disease— a common metabolic disease, found in Jewish families, which causes blindness, muscle tone deterioration, and death of the child at an early age. As a consequence, Joyce and Leon were unwilling to take the 25 percent chance that their child would have Tay-Sachs disease. They debated at length about what they could do, given their specific problem. They very much wanted to have a child which at least came partially from their genes. They also knew how difficult it was to adopt a child. After a long period of discussions, they decided to approach Leon's sister and her husband, David, about the possibility of David fathering a child for them. David was also Jewish, but he did not carry this negative genetic defect. If only one parent, Joyce, was a carrier, the child would not be affected. David and his wife indicated they were willing. They went ahead with this course of action and Joyce got pregnant. The only ones who knew about this artificial parent swapping were the four of them. Joyce and Leon's baby is now two years old. They say their son will never be told. They all seem comfortable with what they have done. If there are long-term consequences waiting for them, they have not as yet surfaced. Having a healthy son was more important to them than the possibility of running into problems some time in the future.

Another type of artificial insemination occurs when a husband has a low sperm count. One technique mentioned in the previous chapter is the accumulation of the father's sperm. Once a sufficient number of sperm are acquired, the physician identifies the most ideal time of the woman's cycle to insert the accumulated and concentrated dosage of her husband's sperm. This form of artificial insemination sometimes produces the desired child.

Some women seek artificial insemination because they are single and wish to become mothers. Approximately 10 percent of artificial insemination is done on single women.[1] Undoubtedly, most single women who wish to have a child would simply go out and get pregnant. Others would have moral objections to having sexual relations and not being married, so they would seek the help of a physician. Holly found herself in a situation similar to this. Holly was thirty-five, unmarried, very religious and she wanted to be a mother. She knew that if she wanted to pursue this objective, she had better hurry because of her age. The adoption agencies said she had no possibility of getting the infant she wanted from them. In fact, one of the adoption agencies said, in her circumstances, she would only be considered for an older, mentally disturbed child. Since she was a social worker by occupation, who worked all day with mentally disturbed people, she felt she wanted something different for her home life. Her only choice then, was to find an infant to adopt elsewhere or to get pregnant. A very close, married man told her he would be willing to father her child. She felt this man would be an excellent father, but she could not bring herself to be involved in a sexual relationship with him . . . it was against her moral code. Artificial insemination using the sperm of her male friend was her answer. She had the strength to withstand the social disapproval of her unmarried pregnancy, but she could not go against her moral standards.

The most common form of artificial insemination that is currently practiced by physicians is artificial insemination by donor (AID). The woman who is fertile, and whose partner is sterile, is artificially inseminated by a physician who uses sperm from a donor. The donor is generally unknown to the couple.

Men who donate sperm to be used in artificial insemination are usually paid a small sum for the sperm they provide. The donors are frequently university or medical school students, so they are generally above average in intelligence. In one recent study on artificial insemination, the researchers found that little screening existed for genetic disorders among donors. The main concern seems to be for the current medical health of the donor. The donors who are sought are those who would blend in with the characteristics of the father-to-be. Since the techniques used are fairly crude, no elaborate matching is done. Matching means having the child look not too different from the father. A donor with hazel eyes will fit most fathers' characteristics; a donor of between 5'8" and 6'2" will produce a child most men could accept as not looking like someone else's child. This screening is rudimentary at best.

At times, sperm of several donors are mixed so that it is impossible to know which donor's sperm impregnated the egg. This is an additional safeguard to protect the donor's anonymity. Sometimes the sperm of the father, even if it is quite low in numbers, is mixed with a donor's sperm so that there is a possibility that the sperm of the father may have actually been the sperm that impregnated the wife's egg. Many times this mixing of the father's sperm with the donor's sperm makes this technique acceptable to the couple where otherwise it would not have been.

A modification of artificial insemination by donors is a new type of selective sperm bank called the Repository for Germinal Choice.[2] This unique sperm bank is the dream of a Nobel Prize-winning geneticist who was concerned about the declining genetic qualities of mankind. A sperm bank made up of donations from brilliant men, such as men who were Nobel Prize winners, is now in operation based upon this man's dream. It is currently run by Robert Graham in Escondido, California. This year the first women to become pregnant by the sperm of men selected for their intelligence are due to bear these children. Women who are selected for insemination must be young, bright, married women, preferably with a husband who is sterile. Once the woman is selected, the only cost involved is in transporting the sperm she has selected. The woman is given information sheets the special donors have filled out; the forms include the specific donor's weight, height, age, IQ, color of eyes, skin and hair, and number of normal children. The woman can choose the man who seems to be the best choice for her, but she also agrees to keep Dr. Graham of the Repository of Germinal Choice informed of the progress and IQ level of the child as he or she grows. Graham admits his concept of greater genetic control may not yet be popular but at least it has a foothold. He maintains we have ignored the potential for genetic improvement in our society even though it has been clearly demonstrated that it is possible to improve the quality. Graham has also suggested that other forms of sperm banks could be established, like an Olympic-athlete bank. This specialized sperm bank, and others like it, demonstrate the most selective human breeding mankind has ever attempted.

In the more usual type of artificial insemination currently being done, records are seldom kept on whose sperm is used to inseminate which woman. While this assures anonymity for the donor, it also presents some additional problems. The sperm of a single donor may be used to impregnate many women in a given geographical area. The possibility of the resulting children meeting and marrying at a later time obviously exists. This possibility is far greater in artificial insemination than it is with adopted children who might ultimately marry siblings unknown to them as brothers or sisters.

Another problem comes from the lack of medical history available to the child who is the product of artificial insemination. The valid cry from adoptees who seek their medical history can also exist for the child produced by artificial insemination. Half of their parental medical history is lost to them forever.

The anonymity for the donor, on the other hand, is critical. If the identity of the donor is known, he could potentially be sued for the support of his child. Few men would be willing to donate sperm if there existed potential for being identified.

The donor's response to fathering multiple children has never been studied. A team of researchers at Vista Del Mar is attempting to do research on this subject and other factors related to artificial insemination by donors. Barren, Panor, and Sorosky (AID Research, P.O. Box 49809, Los Angeles, California 90049) are seeking donors, parents through artificial insemination, and children from artificial insemination to measure and understand the consequences of using this method to produce a child.[3]

Certain legal consequences exist for the people involved in artificial insemination by donors. Not only can there be risks of legal problems for an identified donor, but in divorce cases, a father by artificial insemination might try to deny support for the child who was produced by this procedure. One father supported his wife while she became pregnant through artificial insemination, but later changed his mind. The reality of his wife carrying another man's child proved overwhelming. As this procedure is used more frequently, partially due to the lack of children for adoption, the potential for problems also increases. Some states have ruled that artificial insemination is illegal.

Religious implications also exist for couples using artificial insemination. Some churches object to artificial insemination. As in other areas where people ignore the doctrine of their church, the potential problems they can experience is increased because of their religious guilt.

The secrecy surrounding artificial insemination is designed to protect everyone involved. Yet it is known that secrecy can compound psychological problems. How does one lead a healthy life when secrecy is such a critical underlying ingredient in the relationship. Couples electing this process must develop a healthy communication between themselves to offset the effects of this lifetime secret they share. People trying to hide adoption from the adopted child seldom succeed in their attempt. Their failure is usually because others know and tell the adoptee. At times they fail because they get angry and use the secret as a weapon to hurt their spouse or their child. The secret of the child conceived through artificial insemination is usually considered far more important to guard than the adoption secrets.

While there are some significant drawbacks to this procedure, it is important to remember that this is not usually anyone's first choice as a way to get a baby. If a couple had a choice they would simply get pregnant, but remember . . . they can't. So while there are lots of problems to having a child through artificial insemination, this may be the best chance a couple has to get a baby. If the choice is a child through artificial insemination or not having a child, which would you choose? It's your choice, no one else can make that choice for you.

Many unexpected problems can result from having any child ... the child can be disturbed or handicapped ... the child could be seriously injured in his or her early years ... your marriage could potentially break up and you might have to raise your child as a single parent. All of these and many other circumstances would seriously and forever alter your life. In deciding to have a child from artificial insemination you are saying the child is worth the risks. You are saying:

> I want a child ... I want a child even if there are some big problems in how I get the child. It is more important for me to have a baby to love and be loved by than to let the potential problems deny me this chance. I want to enjoy watching my child grow, even though I know my methods of producing this child are not ideal. I can offset the lack of ideal conception by my love, my warmth and my support. I want to try even though there are some obvious problems. I want a baby.

Test-Tube Babies

Of all the new ways of producing a child that an infertile couple could try, the "test-tube" baby method has been given the most recent publicity. The concept of a child being conceived outside of the mother is at once exciting, futuristic, awesome, interesting and frightening. With all of these emotional responses, the world heralded the arrival of baby Louise, the first "test-tube" baby.

Baby Louise was born in England in 1978 amidst publicity that rivaled the birth of the Dionne Quintuplets two generations before. Her birth brought hope for thousands of infertile couples, and fear of the tremendous power of science. Her family was paid handsomely for her story, which was sought for broadcast throughout the world. The mother of Louise had blocked tubes that prevented her from conceiving a child. Her physicians, after several attempts, successfully removed one of the mother's eggs, fertilized it in the laboratory with the father's sperm, and then implanted that fertilized egg and two others, which did not stay implanted, into the mother's womb. Louise was the result.

Another similarly produced child was delivered by the same doctors. The attending physicians, Dr. Patrick Steptoe and Dr. Robert Edwards, recently discussed a number of failures that have also resulted from this same procedure. They had one hundred fifty-six failures before attaining success. They also have discussed two fetuses that were grossly distorted and that aborted spontaneously, one after ten weeks and one after twenty weeks.

The work of Dr. Steptoe and Dr. Edwards has met with mixed response. The majority of Americans (93 percent) knew of the birth of baby Louise soon after the story hit the newspapers. Of those who knew of her birth, the response was two to one in favor of the use of this new technique of conception.[4] Prior to the birth of Louise, the public outcry in the United States against research on this technique temporarily halted the work being done.

Now, partly because of Louise and how *normal* she seems, and partly because of pressure from infertile couples seeking a child, a new clinic is being opened in Norfolk, Virginia as part of the Eastern Medical School. Already over 3,000 women have applied from throughout the world to be part of the program. Unfortunately, only about ten to twenty women per month can be treated. A second clinic will be opened in Cambridge, England. Both of these new clinics will be associated with Doctors Steptoe and Edwards and their now famous technique. The estimated cost is several thousand dollars for the procedure.

Although this technique has enjoyed tremendous publicity since the birth of baby Louise, it is not the best technique to correct sterility in women whose tubes are blocked through scarring. The technique of microsurgery, discussed in Chapter 3, has been found to be far more effective for the majority of women with this problem.[5]

Some of the unfavorable response to this new conception technique is centered around the research that has been done to develop the procedure. Right to Life groups have been critical of the procedure based upon the number of fetuses that have been destroyed while trying to perfect this method.[6]

Other criticisms of this method of conception question the impact science is having on the family. No longer is a child the result of a shared, loving moment between a husband and a wife. No doubt this is true. Neither, however, are conceptions that result from rape or forced sexual contact, or from scheduled sexual contact for infertile couples, or from artificial insemination that is clinically performed in the stirrups of the gynecologist's treatment table. This is simply another technique that opens the way for a couple to get a child. Couples merely learn to make the best of a situation that is not their ideal, but a reasonable substitute.

Embryo Substitutions

Another new way to make a baby involves the use of a surrogate (substitute) mother's embryo being fertilized (inseminated) outside the surrogate mother and then implanted into the new mother to develop until birth. This technique falls slightly more into the questionable area for some people because it uses another woman and not just the mother and father. Embryo substitutions are similar to artificial insemination but instead use the embryo of a donor rather than the sperm of a donor.

Embryo implantation has occurred in the cattle industry for years. Embryos of cows have been frozen until needed. Then they are artificially inseminated and implanted in the mother-to-be cow. The increase in the number of calves the individual cow can produce has been dramatic and the cattle industry and consumer have profited.

Using animal research as a basis for their experimentation, physicians in India experimented on infertile women in a similar manner. As a result, in 1978, a baby was born that was fertilized using a frozen embryo from a surrogate mother. The physicians responsible for the birth of this child had over one hundred failures before they achieved success. Predictably, the response from people was mixed. The government of India became embroiled in this experimental event that was both lauded and condemned simultaneously.

Researchers experimenting with this technique look toward the near future when they envision embryo banks available for infertile couples. Infertile couples will be able to purchase the frozen embryos, catalogued by type. The chosen embryo will then be fertilized by the sperm of the father and implanted in the uterus of the mother-to-be.

The same difficulties discussed under artificial insemination by donors exist in this procedure. While details are lacking because these facilities are not currently in existence, it is likely that the same privacy concerns for the donor will exist. At some point in the future, it will be necessary to do research to learn how women feel about having their children born and raised by someone else just like we need to understand how this affects sperm donors.

This type of conception is too new to tell what the long-term effects will be on those involved. Much of its acceptance will depend on the publicity agents who sell it to the public. Much of its acceptance will also depend on time ... time creates familiarity which in turn creates acceptance.

Surrogate Mothers

Surrogate mothers are not new. They probably have existed long before adoption became a legally formalized process. Basically, an infertile couple, because of the wife's sterility, has the father impregnate another woman either directly or through artificial insemination. The surrogate mother agrees to carry the child to term and give it to the couple to adopt after it is born.

Legally this is permissible. Most states will allow this to occur as long as the woman receives no money for her services. The reason that the woman cannot be paid is that no laws relate directly to surrogate parenting; instead, the surrogate mother comes under the adoption laws which forbid paying for a child. Medical and pregnancy-related expenses can be paid, but nothing can be paid for her time or effort to produce this child.

A judge in Michigan ruled that it was illegal for a couple to pay a woman $5,000 for bearing and relinquishing to them a child conceived through artificial insemination by the father's sperm. The judge ruled that it would violate Michigan's adoption laws. The prosecutor maintained that to allow them to pay the woman would lead to a commercial market for babies and would affect a woman's decision on placing a child for adoption. The attorney for the infertile couple said the suit would do just the opposite, since it would clearly establish a legal precedent for couples seeking surrogate mothers.

Another woman in Maryland, where payment is also forbidden, decided to proceed as a surrogate mother for a couple in which the wife was sterile, even though she could not be paid for her services. The surrogate mother came under considerable criticism from friends and relatives because of her decision.

I spoke with one woman, Kris, who responded to a couple's ad for a surrogate mother. I asked her why she would be willing to do this? Kris said she was twenty-eight and unmarried, with no prospects of getting married soon. She was involved in the health care services of a hospital and knew a great deal about the ideal time to be a biological mother. She said she wanted to have this experience before she was too old. She felt she would be able to do something "significant for society" by having a child for this infertile couple. She was sure she could produce a healthy child now, but was not willing to be a single mother at this time. She wanted to experience a pregnancy while she was still at the healthiest time of her life to be pregnant. She seemed to know very well what she was doing. She produced a healthy baby girl that the couple hiring her adopted. The child is three and Kris and the child's parents remain in contact.

Finding a woman to do this does not seem to be very difficult. A couple in Kentucky placed an advertisement seeking a woman to bear them a child in a "pregnancy for pay" heading. Five women responded within a month.

People get concerned about the possibility of paying a mother to carry their child. Perhaps paying the woman would be an advantage to everyone. Some women are good at making babies and others are not. Why not let the ones who are good at it produce children for the ones who are not good at it? The law of supply and demand would decrease the cost and couples seeking a child could afford to get one.

Far out? Yes, but it only seems so if you have a baby the easy way. If you don't have one and you want one, it sounds so much more reasonable.

Reproduction to Specification

With the current capabilities of science, it is now possible to know very specific things about a given child before the child is born. With this capacity, it is also possible to "throw away" the developing fetus that doesn't meet our stated criteria. We have the capability to create children to specification.

Amniocentesis is the primary medical development which has allowed us to monitor fetal development. This medical procedure, developed in the late sixties, is a fantastic improvement in detecting possible genetic defects of a fetus before birth. The test is done by a physician using only local anesthesia. A long, thin needle is inserted through the lower abdominal wall into the uterus of a woman who is about sixteen weeks pregnant. A small amount of amniotic fluid which surrounds the fetus is withdrawn. The fetal cells are cultured in a laboratory and then analyzed for chromosomal and metabolic abnormalities for indication of possible genetic defects. It takes approximately three to four weeks to obtain the results after the fluid is taken. From the results of this test, approximately one hundred different kinds of genetic defects can be determined. If any of the problems which are found seem too serious, the woman can then elect to terminate her pregnancy through a legal abortion.

Amniocentesis is being used more frequently. Two primary groups of women are encouraged to use amniocentesis: older women and women who are at high risk for having genetically defective children.

Older women face certain types of increased risks for the children they bear. The reasons for this higher risk are not certain. The fact that a woman is born with all of the eggs she will ever produce, ready to be fertilized, may be the cause; the eggs simply might be too old when the older woman gets pregnant. Women who are over thirty-five run a significantly higher risk of producing a child with Down's syndrome (Mongolism). It is possible for a younger woman to produce a Down's Syndrome child but the risk is considerably greater as age increases.

Age of Mother	Incidence of Down's Syndrome
20	One in 1,923
25	One in 1,205
30	One in 885
35	One in 365
40	One in 109
45	One in 32

The overall risk of having a child with Down's Syndrome is one in seven hundred but you can see how the risks increase with the age of the mother. Amniocentesis can determine if the child will be affected by Down's Syndrome. In the child with Down's Syndrome, there is actually an extra chromosome which is evident when the chromosomes are examined following amniocentesis. The child with Down's Syndrome is severely retarded at birth and usually has heart problems which prevent most of these children from living long lives.

With more women delaying pregnancies until later in life, you can see the importance of utilizing this procedure.[7] Frequently women who have experienced infertility problems will have children later than they had planned; these children might then be in the high-risk categories.

The second group of women who need to use amniocentesis are women who are at high risk for certain genetic disorders. The way you can tell if a woman is at high risk is if she has previously had a child who was born defective, or if there is a family history of a genetically transmissible disease. In all thorough work-ups for amniocentesis, a significant part is the family history of medical problems.

The most well-known diseases that can be detected through amniocentesis in high-risk groups are Tay-Sachs disease, Turner's Syndrome, Klinefelter's Syndrome, spina bifida, cystic fibrosis, and Rh-factor incompatibility between the mother and the child.[8] Sickle-cell anemia and thalassemia, both blood diseases, can be detected by more elaborate forms of amniocentesis which also involve taking fetal blood; this procedure involves significantly greater risks to the unborn child than the usual risks of amniocentesis.

As a result of the development of amniocentesis, many other characteristics about the child are being learned. The sex of the child is one of them. As the chromosome chart of each unborn child is examined, the sex of the child is readily determined. Currently, people who only want to know the child's sex are not considered appropriate candidates for amniocentesis. The procedure costs several hundred dollars if done privately. Foundations that might consider paying for the cost of amniocentesis would not pay for it just to determine the sex of the unborn child. In fact, some physicians refuse to tell couples the sex of the child even when the couples have had amniocentesis for another reason: these physicians believe that couples have chosen to abort a child of the "wrong" sex even though the amniocentesis indicates there are no defects present. As this test becomes less expensive and more utilized, people may wish to know the sex of the child before it is born. Undoubtedly the test will be used for couples trying to produce a child of a specific sex.

Since the sex of the unborn child can be learned through amniocentesis, perhaps the next step is the manipulation of the sex of the child prior to conception. Researchers are filtering sperm to increase the likelihood of producing a child of the desired sex. If the couple wishes to have a girl, the researcher will filter out the sperm carrying the "Y" chromosomes and inseminate the mother with highly concentrated "X" sperm. The chances of the mother producing a desired girl baby will be significantly increased because we have altered the natural probability.

Another use of amniocentesis that is only now being developed is preventing and correcting defects in the unborn child. It is possible, especially as we become more sophisticated through research, that the very problems that are being diagnosed in utero are amenable to correction. Amniocentesis is even more valuable when the correction of defects in utero becomes possible, rather than just the identification of the defects.

A more distant possibility exists in terms of determining the intellectual level of the unborn child. Researchers in Canada have been working on a new method of measuring intelligence. Ordinarily, if you want to know the level of intellectual functioning of a person, a psychologist administers an individual test that shows how smart you are in relation to the rest of the population. The procedure takes approximately one hour. The Canadian scientists are saying that possibly you can measure intelligence by how fast the brain registers a response to a stimulus; therefore, the intellectual functioning can be assessed neurologically in less than a minute. If their results can be validated, the potential exists to measure the intellectual functioning of an unborn child. This is not now being done, but the capabilities may be developed to determine how bright a fetus will be after birth.

At this stage, amniocentesis is used for few pregnant women. A dramatic increase in the use of this procedure is likely to be seen in the very near future.

A strong impetus to the increased utilization of amniocentesis is found in the legal system. A court ruling by the New York State Court of Appeals held that the obstetrician/gynecologist of Dolores Becker, aged thirty-seven, could be held liable for the cost of caring for her child with Down's Syndrome. [9,10] The reason for only the potential liability is that the Beckers must prove by medical testimony that a "competent" doctor in 1974 would have offered amniocentesis to Mrs. Becker. Physicians obviously will be more inclined to use this procedure for women who are at risk as a result of the determination in this case.

With the increased use of amniocentesis will come increased sophistication. More information will be learned about the potential use of amniocentesis. We have just begun to tap the potential of this new technique and the possible uses are being expanded daily. The selective breeding this method encourages is obvious. The message is clear ... eliminate the defectives. This is not an easy message for everyone to accept.

Risks exist in this procedure as in all medical procedures. These risks are especially important to the couple who have had great difficulty getting pregnant in the first place. How much are they then willing to jeopardize this carefully planned and much-sought-after pregnancy once it has finally been achieved?

While certain risks exist with the use of amniocentesis, the risks are quite small. The overall risks are usually between one half to one percent in this country.[10] The greatest of these risks is that the woman will have a miscarriage as a result of the procedure. Risks have been significantly decreased when ultrasound is used in conjunction with amniocentesis. Ultrasound allows the physician to measure the head of the fetus to make certain the mother is far enough along for a sufficient quantity of amniotic fluid to be drawn and to get a sample that will be possible to culture. The other important risk to a woman and the fetus is when multiple insertions are made to draw amniotic fluid. The physician needs to take the fluid at the right time in the woman's pregnancy to get enough fluid and to get the fluid at the point of development when it can be cultured. Obviously, a second amniocentesis doubles the risk.

There are ways to minimize the risks of the procedure. Women should know what the important considerations are before permitting amniocentesis. The following suggestions are intended to provide some guide in the decision of whether or not to have amniocentesis.

1. **Find a facility that performs amniocentesis on a regular basis.** If you don't know where to go to find out about the procedure, write the National Foundation—March of Dimes (Box 2000, White Plains, New York 10602), or the National Genetic Foundation, Inc. (9 West 57th Street, New York, New York 10019) for a referral in your area.

2. Find out how frequently your physician performs amniocentesis; the more often, the better.

3. Find out what information can be derived from the test results. Some places do more test analysis than others.

4. Find out if ultrasound will be used with the procedure.

5. Find out how likely it is that more than one needle insertion will be made during the procedure. Find out the likelihood of more than two insertions being made. The fewer the better. See what the history of your physician is in this area.

6. Find out where the laboratory is in relation to the place the fluid will be drawn. The best situation is to have the laboratory on the premises. The least time taken to begin the culture, the more likely the culture will be successful.

7. Find out what the laboratory's rate of success is in getting cell growth from the cultured amniotic fluid on the first sample. Some laboratories are significantly better than others.

8. Find out if there is a genetic counselor to whom you can speak about the results of the procedure. Someone should be willing to provide answers to your questions, as well as to explain what the test results mean.

9. Find out how long it takes to get the test results.

10. Find out the costs of the procedure. The woman who has a working knowledge of what amniocentesis is and what risks are involved knows better what she is getting into and why. Without this information, she has no way to minimize the risks she is taking.

The psychological implications of amniocentesis are significant. In a routine abortion, a woman may experience psychological effects following the procedure despite the fact that she *doesn't want* to be pregnant and chooses to have an abortion. The woman undergoing amniocentesis is in a completely different set of circumstances. She *wants* the child but is concerned about knowingly bringing a defective child into the world. The psychological implications for the woman who aborts a child she *wants* to have are likely to be greater than for the woman who does not want the child. The additional fact that abortions following amniocentesis are necessarily late abortions magnifies the potential psychological problems the woman may suffer. In many cases, the woman who decides to have an abortion because of the genetic problems that have been discovered by amniocentesis will have already felt fetal movement. Under the best of circumstances, late abortions are more difficult psychologically. As this procedure becomes more commonly used, the possibility is clear that significant numbers of women will suffer over the decision made to abort a wanted child. In no single group is this more likely to occur than with women who have had great difficulty getting pregnant.

Amniocentesis is a technique of great importance to the field of reproductive medicine. Because it is a relatively new procedure, its potential has only just been tapped . . . far greater uses are likely to be found in the future. The implications for developing more perfect babies are both exciting and frightening. Few would turn down the possibility of eliminating unnecessary suffering in the world. At the same time, the long-term implications of our feelings about life are acutely involved in this possibility. Saying unborn, defective children should be eliminated also makes a statement about defectives or unproductives who are living. We are in effect creating minimum criteria you must meet to be allowed to stay alive in our society. The issue deals with control . . . how much control shall we exert over our lives and the lives of the unborn? The knowledge and the techniques are available to have greater quality control over life than has ever before been possible. The moral implications for the living, as well as the unborn, are staggering!

Summary Despite the far out concepts that are being developed, the desired goal is quite simple . . . *a baby*. Genetic manipulations, highly selective donor insemination, and embryo implants are all techniques that have far-reaching implications for society, but the implications for the infertile are rather limited . . . *a baby*. The complexities of infertility pose huge hurdles to the infertile couple who only want what to others is so natural . . . *a baby*.

Choices, again we are involved with choices! What do we do with the knowledge of reproduction we have available to us? Do we ignore it because it sounds too far out? Do we ignore it because it sounds too futuristic? Do we ignore it because it sounds too elite or too cruel? Do we ignore it because this is tampering with nature or with God? Or do we use the information we have to allow people to choose the direction they believe best suits them?

5
THE ADOPTION AGENCY GAME

A new baby is a joyous event. A beautiful night and nine months later the infant wriggles into the world. The pregnancy complete, the baby arrives and a new life begins.

The underscored simplicity of this scene contrasts sharply with the arrival of an adopted child. Medical test after medical test are needed to prove infertility as well as interviews and endless questions to "qualify" for becoming a parent. Clouding the entire process is a veil of secrecy and evasion. The couple necessarily approaches the process of adoption filled with ambivalence. Feelings of inadequacy and fulfillment, fear and joy, anticipation and anxiety, distrust and determination are emotions experienced by the participants in the adoption picture. Adoption is *not* like having a baby.

Fifteen years ago, if you wanted to adopt a baby, you merely gave your name to the agency you liked best, did what they told you to do, and as long as you weren't blatantly inadequate, you got the baby you asked to have. Of course, you had to be able to play the adoption game, but the rules were not hard to follow. The game plan was apparent because there were lots of babies available. The agencies needed you.

Today the picture is markedly changed. Few babies are available. The sought-after blonde, blue-eyed baby girl is seldom available. Agencies are looking for couples who will accept a wide range of children. To be too specific about your desires as a potential adoptive parent may very likely spell your elimination from the agency's waiting list. To tell the agencies you want an infant or a child without any physical disabilities, or a child who is not from a mixed racial background, is cause for your elimination from those being considered appropriate to receive the valuable commodity, "a baby." The emphasis is on how to eliminate applicants, not on how to serve couples wishing to adopt a child.

Waits of two or more years are now common in adoption agencies. Many couples are judged unacceptable for parenthood by the agencies' unstated and unknown criteria. Adoption agencies seek ways to cull down the ever lengthening list of adoptive parent applicants. Consequently, couples have four choices: rely on being accepted, tell the agencies what they want to hear, abandon hope for a child, or look elsewhere. Looking elsewhere includes alternative methods of pregnancy, private adoptions and black market adoptions.

Let me say at the outset, that I believe adoptions through agencies, if done properly, are the most advantageous kind of adoption. I do not mean adoptions as they are currently being done in the agencies, but as they *could be* done. Agencies have the greatest source of babies and children, adoptive parents, trained workers and facilities to get the job done really well. The entire setup for healthy, open adoptions exists within the current adoption agency structure; however, it is not being utilized to the advantage of all the parties concerned.

Even though not all of the agencies are handling adoptions in the best way possible, they are still the largest single source of adoptable babies or children available. Since they have what prospective adoptive parents want, it is critical to understand how they work, what they are looking for and how to work with them.

The Agency Process

Assuming you are going to start with adoption agencies, as most people do, how do you begin? If you understand the process thoroughly, you will significantly increase your chances of being one of the chosen parents.

Most adoption agencies work in similar ways. You call the agency and they tell you of a group meeting which will be coming up for prospective parents. Anyone wishing to consider adoption is encouraged to attend. This means you *must* attend.

The meeting goes into the lack of children available and the general time period couples should expect to wait before a baby might be available for adoption. The social worker discusses the types of children they have available to place. The worker tells the sequence of interviews they have with couples seeking to adopt. The fees of the agency and their general requirements are outlined.

This meeting sounds fairly innocuous. It isn't. Listen carefully, because the worker at this point is telling you exactly what this particular agency is looking for in each couple it examines. At no other point in the adoption process will they provide you with this much information.

If you decide to continue after hearing the general information regarding the agency, they ask you to get an application and set up an appointment with a social worker. Remember, they have not said they will take your application, but you may submit one. At the point they meet with you for this initial individual interview, your entire case is on the line. Many agencies will screen you in or out on the basis of this one interview and your application. Be careful.

Flexibility of attitude is the single most important characteristic that agencies are seeking in prospective parents. At this initial interview session, both parents' flexible attitude is what the worker is seeking. The worker asks you in general what you want in terms of adoption. If you answer you want a Caucasian infant under four months with no physical problems, you are in trouble. The reason is clear. They have approximately fifteen couples for each child. They need to select the couple who would work with just about any of the children they have. So another couple is far more likely to get on the waiting list if they say they want a child under eight, the younger the better, and they are willing to take a child with physical or emotional problems. If you don't even get on the list, you have no chance. You may not even get another interview. Most people don't know this, but if you don't make it through the first interview successfully, that is your last interview and the agency is finished with you, period.

Does this mean you should show no preferences? No, not exactly. It means you should be careful not to show too many preferences.

Does this mean you will get an eight-year-old, mentally retarded child of mixed racial background? No, not necessarily. It means you have kept the door open and have at least gotten far enough so that they will take your application. You still have a lot of other interviews ahead of you.

If you pass this initial interview, they will accept your application and your application fee. All this means is that you are doing all right so far. It doesn't mean they will necessarily give you a child.

After the initial interview, they usually ask for medical histories and doctor's reports dealing with the couple's infertility. Most agencies will no longer place infants with couples who do not have a fertility problem.

Letters of recommendation on how you would be as a parent are usually expected. It is obvious, as in all letters of recommendation, that you get the right people to send them. People who are good references would be verbal people who like you and who can say that clearly. People who meet lots of other people, like ministers, who can make comparative judgments, are usually good references. People who have seen you with children and who can comment on your ability to deal with children are good references. Do not hesitate to tell people what to put in their letters. If you see a couple with children a lot, make certain you tell them to write about your good interaction with their children. Letters of recommendation are important . . . select them carefully.

Some letters of recommendation will not help you even if they should. Usually it is unwise to have your therapist send in a letter. In fact, you probably should not tell them you have had psychotherapy unless you are certain they could accept this information positively. If you do tell them you have been in psychotherapy, first make certain that your therapist will send a letter on your qualifications for parenting.

Another interview is usually scheduled after your application has been accepted. At this point, questions are geared again toward what you will accept in a child, but now the worker is likely to get into your experience with children, your acceptance of the infertility problem, your marital strengths and weaknesses, and your current support systems of friends and relatives. Ideally you will come across as a couple who loves and accepts children, even those who are not yours. Hopefully, you present an image of one who wished you could have a biological child, but who has come to accept the infertility. Your marriage should appear sound but not unrealistically perfect. Your friends and relatives should seem important, but not people upon whom you are unduly dependent for your emotional well-being. In general, you want to appear normal . . . whatever that means. You want to present a picture of someone who is emotionally stable and secure.

The next step is an interview with each member of the couple alone. The intent of these sessions is to make certain both partners are in agreement. The worker is checking to see if the least verbal partner believes the same things as the more vocal partner.   The final interview is usually in the prospective adoptive parents' home. The agency wants to see how you live. The worker will not go into drawers and check for dirt in the corners. The worker will be seeing how the couple lives and what arrangements are planned for the potential child. The house that appears too perfect is just as suspect as the house that appears to be in shambles.

After your final interview, you receive notice that your home study is complete and you now enter the waiting stage. The time varies, but for everyone it seems long. For some it means forever because, even though they have been approved, the "right" child never comes along. Most agencies, after a long wait, will suggest the couple drop off their list, since no child is coming available. One of the reasons this may happen is that many agencies now allow the biological mother a chance to read several histories, or to hear about several families of potential adopting parents, and to choose the one family for her child. It is possible no mother ever chooses you. It is also possible that you just get shuffled around and after a period of time are somewhat forgotten. If you haven't heard from the agency in two or three months, demonstrate your continuing desire to adopt by calling them.

If you are finally selected to receive a specific child, you are called into the agency to see if you like the background of the child the agency has chosen for you. The worker will tell you about the child and the history of the natural parents. If you find anything objectionable in the background information you hear, the worker will want to discuss it at this point. This is your opportunity to discuss anything you have heard about which may prompt questions. Perhaps you are confused about the father, or perhaps you want to know more about the evaluation of the child's physical health. If your questions do not clear up your hesitation at this point, the worker may choose not to go any further in placing this specific child with you. However, if you hear about the child and everything meets with your approval, you will be allowed to see the child. Seldom would the agency let you take the child home at this point. Most frequently they will give you until the next day to allow you time to change your mind or to prepare for your new child, now that you know the age and sex of the child.

If you are selected to receive an older child, more emphasis is placed on your reaction to the child and that of the child to you. Several meetings may occur before an actual placement is made. At times, a temporary placement is made to see how readily everyone is able to adjust to the new situation.

Assuming you are the winner of a child, you still continue to be scrutinized by the worker from the adoption agency. Remember the child is not yours until you go to court to finalize the adoption. This usually takes at least six months from the time a child is placed. During this period you have visits from the worker who sees how you, your spouse and the child are adjusting. Ideally, these visits should be a chance to explore all the difficulties you have encountered, but the specter of the agency still being the guardian of the child is real. The child belongs to the agency, not to you. The Wilsons found this out. The Wilsons were the ideal couple the adoption agency cited in their introductory group interview for prospective adoptive parents. They were both professional people who had ample money and two previously adopted children who seemed very happy and adjusted. Dan, the husband, was exceptionally involved with the children, far more so than most fathers. Ellen presented a beautiful combination of the traditional mother mixed with a moderate approach to working outside of the home. They luckily had a third child placed with them. After five months, their marriage had some problems and they considered divorce. Because they believed what the agency had said about calling them if they ever needed help, they told the agency of their marital difficulties. The worker was understanding and said it was no problem and they would give Dan and Ellen time to work out their problems. One month later, when all of their problems had not been resolved, they were told the agency wanted the child returned. All their pleas notwithstanding, the child was taken back. Dan and Ellen had no recourse because they had no legal rights to the child. Seven months later they had reconciled, but there was lasting trauma over the loss of a child they had loved and nurtured for almost six months. The trauma extended, of course, to the two previously adopted children as these children had to cope with their own fears of their possible return to the agency. The adoption agency is definitely in control until the child is legally adopted.

After the six-month waiting period is completed, you obtain a lawyer and go to court for the finalization of the adoption. This is a step in the process that warrants celebration. The court appearance is not a very elaborate process; in fact, a letter stating the adoption is final would be sufficient at much less cost to all concerned. However, the event is one to be heralded. The child is yours . . . no one can take it back!

Roughly then, this is how the adoption process progresses with an adoption agency. There are several ways you can approach this process. You can be absolutely truthful and revealing, holding back nothing. Or you can be selective in the amount and content of the information you provide. Or, you can present yourself in a way that is most likely to get you the child you want.

Ideally, the approach should be honest, open and forthright. This should be an opportunity to explore all of your feelings about what you bring to this potential parenting experience. You should be able to discuss your limits with respect to the child you want to adopt with the potential for enlarging them. You should be able to explore flaws in your marriage in the hope of gaining insight into how to better deal with the problems. You should be able to reveal your resolved and unresolved feelings about your inability to have a biological child and in the process understand and live with them more comfortably. You should be able to deal honestly with the support systems you wish you had but do not have and to make the adjustments necessary to remedy whatever difficulties exist. You should feel the agency is one hundred percent behind your efforts and is working with you toward your parenting goal. This I believe is how adopting through an agency should be and could be. Unfortunately, this is not the way it is in the real world of adoption agencies.

Your second option, and probably the most frequently used option, is to be selective in what you say to the adoption agency. You are well aware that the adoption agency has the prize you want, so you do some cautious and judicious editing. You neglect to tell them of your husband's anger when he comes home tired. You decide not to tell them about your mother-in-law who believes that "illegitimate babies come only from lower-class people and are basically inferior." You decide it isn't important to tell them that you still cry each month when you have your period, when they ask you how you feel about your infertility. You take a basically honest approach, but you remember that these workers are judging you to see if you fit into their preconceived ideal of a parent for one of their scarce and valuable children.

The third choice is a further extension of the previous option. However, this time you seek to find out what the adoption agencies are looking for and you give it to them. You find out as much as possible about their methods of selection and their reasons for turning people down and you act in response to this information. Of course, adoption workers are appalled at the mere suggestion of acting in this way. They would obviously say the first option of honesty and openness is the only way to approach the process. For them it would be. For you who want a baby, I'm not sure. If you really want a baby, you go about getting a baby in the best way you can. If you know you will be eliminated if you tell them that you, the wife, love your job and want to work throughout the new child's growing years, what do you do? Some people would choose to say you intend to stay home with the child and you do so until you go to court and finalize the adoption. After that, the agency has no say in how you lead your life. If you know you will be eliminated if you tell them that you really would have great difficulty having a child who is from a mixed racial background, what do you do? Again, some people would choose to say you are open to the possibility of accepting a child from a mixed racial background and hope that it never comes to the point you have to say no to a child that is offered to you. You don't have to take any child they offer. Obviously, you lessen your chances when you turn down a child, but at least you have a chance as long as you are being considered for a child by the adoption agency.

What would I tell you to do? I don't know. I believe the way you approach the process of adopting through an agency must be thoroughly, thoughtfully and individually considered. I believe the more you know about the procedures of the agencies and all the alternative means of obtaining a child, the better choice you can make for your best way to approach adoption.

Criteria for Selecting Adoptive Parents

Now that you are familiar with the general procedures for adopting a child through an agency, I believe it is important to look at the specific criteria the adoption agencies say they are looking for in prospective parents. You know in general terms the areas they will cover in their interviews. Now you need to look at the specific qualities they deem desirable in adopting parents. In contacts I have had with agencies throughout the United States, the agencies state they are looking for specific characteristics in the people who want to adopt a child.

Financial Status The primary factor the adoption agency looks for when examining potential parents' financial status is stability. All things being equal, the agency would obviously prefer that the adoptive parents be in the best financial situation possible. Fair or not, the more money and job stability, the better your chances are to win a baby.

More and more subsidized adoptions, especially for children with special needs, are available. Adoption by foster parents, at times, is made possible through subsidies, especially if the child is a hard to place child. As long as the parents remain foster parents, they receive state aid. The moment they adopt the same child, they lose all state support. Some families would be unable to handle the financial burden this might involve, especially since the medical expenses of some of these children are very expensive.

Most agency adoptions are not subsidized and the agency is looking for couples who demonstrate their financial stability. At times the agency will look for adequate housing as a means of determining financial security. Checking out employment records also helps to determine the stability of the financial situation of the family. Agencies look for a couple whose income allows one of the parents to remain at home with the child.

Many agencies maintain sliding fees as a means of providing adoption for people of modest incomes. Private agencies are limited in the percentage of their cases where lower fees can be used. At the same time, agencies are looking for families who can provide financial security to a potential child. In order to provide a happy, healthy home, the family in financial difficulty at the time they seek a child is a poorer risk than a financially sound family. In the war between love and poverty, poverty usually wins. Poverty causes so much anxiety that good marriages rarely survive. This is not the home environment the agencies want for their adopting families. Money cannot be a stated criteria, but there is no question that it is.

Age Recent court cases involving age have significantly changed the adoption agencies' ability to use age as a criterion for acceptance. Some agencies admit they still use age as a factor in selecting adoptive parents. Some say you must be over twenty-one, others say over twenty-three, some say over twenty-four, and others say over twenty-five. Obviously, no one knows which minimum age is the "correct" one.

The primary concern of agencies is on the other end of the age spectrum. While unstated by many of the agencies because of the violation of federal civil rights, most agencies will place children with adoptive parents who would be the normal age for a parent of the child who is placed with them. Generally, this would be less than a forty year difference between the parent and the child. Some agencies believe it is permissible for the father to be older, with a greater age difference than the mother. Currently, with older children needing homes, older applicants can be considered.

As in all of the requirements put forth by the adoption agencies, people in the middle range of the requirements stand the greatest chance of selection. If you are about forty, you just have less chance of adopting through an agency than a couple of thirty, if all of your other attributes are equal. Linda and Sam found out about age as a deterrent to adoption. Sam had been married and divorced after two children. He married Linda when he was forty-two and she was thirty-eight. She had never been married, nor did she have children. When she was not pregnant after eighteen months, they sought to adopt a child through their local adoption agency. They were unsuccessful. The reason for their rejection by the agency was her age, but even more important was the fact that at her age she had never had any children. The agency was concerned about her adapting to a child, even an older child at such a late period in her life. Her age and her childlessness worked against her. They were told they should consider being foster parents, but they were not approved to be adopting parents.

Educational Background Educational level is not usually a stated criterion by adoption agencies to adopt a child. Its influence is more subtle. While some agencies state they want their parents to be the kind that "will provide a stimulating environment" or that "will provide a positive cultural environment," few will go any further.

However, education in our society is highly valued. Since all the social workers share a college background, it is not surprising to find this same college background an asset in your application. The higher the degree the better, especially if the man is the highly educated one; the woman's high degree (M.D. or Ph.D.) at times causes the agency to question her commitment to children as a high priority in her life. Martha and Charles found their education was a door opener for them with the adoption agencies. Martha and Charles had a fairly distant relationship in their marriage and that was fine for each of them. They were both bright people who had a tendency to be very intimidating to many people they met. While the agencies saw their aloofness, the fact that he was a physician made a big impression. Agency workers, like many other people in our society, can be awed by physicians. The verbal ability of both Martha and Charles also made a good impression on the agency. His financial ability was also viewed very positively. They received a baby with little difficulty. Soon after they received the baby, Charles became involved with another woman and Martha found out. She was enraged and blamed his infidelity on the new child. Their aloofness allowed them to get by this period until they went to court without the agency knowing of their marital difficulties. Their personal qualities were not the kind the agencies say they want in their adoptive parents. In fact, many of their acquaintances were surprised they even got a child from the agency. The primary factor that set them apart from others was that he was a physician; so they got a baby. Education makes a difference.

Medical History A medical history is required in virtually all adoptions. The results are expected to indicate that each person is in good health except in terms of the infertility problem.

Infertility is an asset. In fact, many agencies will not consider your application without a fertility problem. The adoption agency wants you to have resolved your feelings about the infertility, but this single medical deficiency is a requirement for acceptance.

Health does not fit neatly into good or bad, so how does health fit in as a criterion for becoming a parent? The answer to the question depends on which agency and which worker you are asking. In general, the more serious the medical problem, the more it will affect your chances to adopt.

People who weigh more than average have had difficulty being approved for adoption by the agencies, since children have become more scarce. With thirty percent of the population of the United States overweight, this obviously places greater restrictions on the overweight person who also happens to want to adopt.[1] Barbara and Gordon Ray gained considerable notoriety in the media over the refusal by the Wisconsin State Department of Health and Social Services to allow them to adopt a child because of being overweight.[2] The Rays were told to lose weight or no child. They sought help from their state senator in getting a child. The agency says the refusal is based on insurance company's preferred height-weight charts. The Rays objected to this discrimination because their doctors certified they were in good health. They maintained there was no proof that a problem existed, but it will be difficult to get the agency to change its stand. To deny someone a chance to adopt a child because they have a weight problem is unfair, but the agencies make the rules; it's their game.

To my knowledge, smokers and drinkers have not experienced the same discrimination as have overweight people. If someone who applies is an alcoholic or even a reformed alcoholic, this would be grounds for their elimination. It is unlikely that the smoker, whose life span is significantly shortened, will be given any special scrutiny. The one exception to this might be the chain smoker. The worker who sees this behavior might feel that the smoking he or she exhibits is a symptom of great stress and that might work against the couple's adopting a child.

Physical handicaps are seldom discussed in the criteria adoption agencies use to determine qualifications for adoptive parents. Mostly they are ignored, at least verbally and in writing. An adoption agency would have to be legally quite naive to ever state that the reason a couple is not accepted is because one of the parties has a handicap. A lawsuit would be immediate. Sally and Matthew ran into the agency's subtle discrimination after they applied to adopt a child. Sally met Matthew after he was a quadraplegic. He had been fine until being wounded in Vietnam. When they married, she knew he could not father any children and she just assumed they would adopt. After they were married for six months, they approached the adoption agency. They were told they would have to wait until they had been married two years before they could apply. So, they waited the specified time, then applied and were turned down. No one from the adoption agency said it was Matthew's confinement to a wheelchair, but that was the reason. Everyone who knew how much they both wanted a child knew that his handicap was the reason for the denial. I remember being very moved by Matthew when he said, "I can hold a baby and I can love a baby . . . I just can't play ball with a child." I believed him. The adoption agency, faced with a choice of many healthy fathers, would reason, "Why choose one with limited fathering capacities when we can simply choose someone else?" I understand their reasoning; I just can't accept their solution or their delaying these people for two years when they had no chance to be accepted as adoptive parents.

Race and Nationality As with other criteria I have mentioned, race and nationality cannot legally be stated as a method of selecting potential adoptive parents. Legally, however, these factors have been used as justification for denying a child's placement in a specific home. The case of Timothy that was reported in the media was a case in point. Timothy, who was partly black, had been raised in a foster home since he was one month until he was two and a half. At that point his foster parents sought to adopt him and were denied by the adoption agency because they were white. The foster parents fought to keep Timothy, but their legal appeal was lost on the grounds that "adoption agencies have a right and responsibility to take racial questions into account when matching a child with prospective parents."[3]

Black social workers have taken a strong stand against black children being placed in white homes. They believe, as do many blacks, that the white family cannot help the child identify with his or her cultural heritage.

A judge in Pennsylvania agreed that race should be a consideration in adoption, but from a different perspective. The judge said he would no longer allow white families to adopt black children. His reason was that, "It's great when they're little pickaninnies. They're cute and everybody is a do-gooder. But what about when they're children."

Large groups of parents who have adopted children of other races and nationalities believe these adoptions have been successful. The adoption agencies, mindful of the position of the black social workers, discourage many couples from adopting children from a race that is different than the parents.

Religion Most adoption agencies do not have specific requirements for religion unless they are private religious agencies. The religious requirement from these specific agencies is obvious. Catholic and Jewish agencies are the most common among religiously oriented agencies.

At times, the biological mother has specific criteria she sets forth. In that case, the adoption agency is likely to honor her request. Her request may be quite general such as, "I want my child to be raised by people who believe in God" or, "I want my child to be raised in a home where religion is a significant part of the family's life." Some mothers may want their children specifically raised Catholic or Methodist. Since the biological mother may know the histories of several families seeking to adopt, her religious preferences may enter into her decision of which family she prefers.

The one area mentioned at times about religion are those religions that prevent the child from receiving medical care. Agencies do not specifically prevent people from any faith from adopting children, but under circumstances where religion affects the medical care, the agency will consider the case specially. Again, since it does not fall into the normal range which is sought by the agencies, a less popular religion is likely to be considered a disadvantage in a prospective adopting family.

Marital Relationship Length and strength of marriage are criteria used to select most parents chosen to be given a child to adopt. The length of the marriage is easy to measure; strength of a marriage presents some real difficulties.

Some agencies specify how long a couple must be married before they will consider their application for adoption. Most agencies require between one and three years. Usually this requirement has three purposes. One is to ascertain the stability of the relationship. The second reason for this requirement is to preserve the stability of the relationship by not having a child placed too early. This reason has much less validity now that there is such a long wait to have a child placed after the application is accepted. The third reason is to determine with certainty the fact that a fertility problem does exist. Sometimes the stress of trying to have a baby will cause fertility problems that go away without treatment. Almost anyone can tell the story of their friend who got pregnant right after they adopted a baby. This is not as common as it seems, but it does happen.

At times adoption agencies have different length of marriage requirements if one of the partners was previously married. Any couple who has a history of a previous marriage is given extra scrutiny. Despite the large numbers of people in our society who have been divorced, it is still viewed negatively by most adoption agencies. The agencies are unlikely to eliminate you for that single factor alone, but it is one more mark that works against you.

When the adoption agencies attempt to determine strength and stability in the marriage, they work from a precarious position. Who knows what makes a good marriage? Some marriages that one couple would evaluate as strong and secure are relationships I would not, under any circumstances, consider satisfactory for me . . . but they work for them. Our society doesn't have one good kind of marriage; but for some reason, if you are seeking to adopt a child, your marriage has to meet a certain set of criteria.

Characteristics exemplifying marital strength vary with the agency. The agencies are usually positively influenced if the marriage seems to show "communication between the partners," a "sharing relationship," or "being committed to the marriage." One agency looks for a "growing" marital relationship. I certainly think all of these marital characteristics are worthy, but they cannot be reliably assessed by the agency. Even if they could measure whatever criteria they feel creates a good marriage, it is obvious that some marriages can and do work successfully without all of these factors present or maybe even without any of them present.

Employment of the Mother Adoption agencies have varied on how critically they view the working mother. When babies are plentiful, the employment of the mother has been more acceptable. With the current scarcity of babies, most agencies want the mother home. Some agencies specify that one parent must remain home. While more and more people are recognizing that the male is quite capable of being the primary parent, it is a rare case where an adoption agency will place a child in a home where the father is planning on being the one left to care for the child. Again, this does not fit into the normal pattern. Strong questions would be raised about the adoptive mother's ability to mother. The possibility of the father being the primary parent would lessen a couple's chances of having a baby placed with them.

Other agencies have criteria which state that "acceptable arrangements be made for the care of the child." Marie and John found that sounded better than it turned out to be in reality. Marie was a doctoral candidate in chemistry and very excited about lots of things in life. She was thirty-two and felt she had to go ahead now if they wanted to adopt. She also loved her work and had several exciting opportunities coming up. To pass them up now was to pass them up forever. She wanted it all and she had the energy and drive to do it all. John fully agreed. The adoption agency didn't. Their application was denied until she felt that a baby pre-empted her desire for a career. For the agency it was one or the other. Despite the large numbers of working mothers in the United States, the agencies want it the way *they believe it should be* . . . a full-time mother. Any other arrangement does not qualify. They have the babies and they make the rules.

Involvement with the Adoption Agency Many agencies look for potential parents who have "an ability to work with the agency." I am sure this helps the agency, although I have difficulty seeing how this evaluates potential parenting qualities. This very fact, however, may account for the reason that more adopted children are seen by mental health professionals for psychological problems than non-adopted children. After working with the medical profession on infertility problems and the agency adoption worker on getting a baby, these people are accustomed to asking for help and admitting problems. The adoptive parent sees a problem and assumes they need professional help in solving it.

At times adoption agencies become quite competitive. I recently heard from a social worker in one adoption agency that if a couple tells their agency that they had previously applied to another adoption agency that this alone would eliminate them from consideration. This particular agency wanted complete loyalty and dedication to their agency and no other. Perhaps the feeling was that if the couple was not good enough for another adoption agency they were not good enough for this one either.

On the more positive side, the agency is also trying to generalize. If people cannot work with them, can they work with others in their life? How do these potential parents get along with others? How do they relate to the people in their lives?

Flexibility Flexibility of attitude is a characteristic that entered the selection process only as children replaced babies and scarcity replaced abundance. This characteristic—flexibility—is the single most frequently mentioned characteristic that agencies cite as an ingredient they look for in prospective parents.

Flexibility primarily concerns what type of child you can accept. The agencies are seeking people who are willing to take older children as well as infants. The adoption agencies are screening in people who will take physically handicapped children and screening out people who want only physically healthy children. The agencies are eliminating people who would not consider an emotionally disturbed child in favor of those people who would consider this possibility. The agencies are searching for potential parents for children of mixed racial backgrounds and are reluctant about people who will only consider Caucasian children. The more demands you place on the agency for what you want, the more your chances decrease for a baby. The less flexibility, the less chance of adopting through an agency.

Personality Factors If you describe an emotionally stable mature person, you have just included the personality factors the adoption agencies are seeking in their potential adopting parents. Statements the agencies use to describe the people they choose for parents include the following:

—Is emotionally mature
—Is stable
—Has sense of humor
—Is warm
—Deals well with others
—Is loving
—Expresses affection
—Is sensitive and caring
—Is accepting
—Is committed to whatever he or she undertakes
—Has problem-solving ability
—Is secure within self
—Has good self-image
—Succeeds with struggles
—Is optimistic about life
—Has ability to cope with stress and change
—Can handle whatever comes along

—Is well integrated
—Is open
—Is able to accept responsibility
—Is wholesome
—Is understanding
—Is able to see small gains and not take everything personally
—Is empathetic
—Is realistic in expectations
—Admits imperfections in self and can handle them
—Is self-aware
—Has ability to delay gratification
—Has common sense
—Is motivated
—Handles frustration and anger
—Has character
—Has ego strength
—Is able to relate positively and grow
—Is sharing
—Establishes meaningful relationships
—Is able to turn to others for assistance if needed
—Does not need neighbors or friends for self-worth
—Has support of extended families
—Has high expectations of life, of themselves, and of others
—Has stable relationships
—Is aware of each individual's dependency needs

What then does this lengthy list of characteristics tell us? It means if you have everything really together, the adoption agency will consider you normal and will see if they have a child for you.

Parenting Skills Parenting skills, above all else, are what the agency wants to find in the potential parents they are trying to evaluate. As with the more abstract criteria we have discussed, parenting ability is also extremely difficult to predict and to evaluate. The best predictor of parenting ability is "successful" parenting, but the agency is usually seeking people without children. Evaluating what constitutes quality parenting is like evaluating what makes a good marriage. We do not have the knowledge to say that, if you do this, your child will turn out well-adjusted. We simply do not know what makes good parents.

Given these rather serious limitations, the agencies set out to do exactly what no one has shown they can do: to evaluate what will make a good parent. While their task is impossible, their intentions are admirable.

With this goal in mind, they search for potential adoptive parents who can "love and accept a child they did not produce." They want "parents who can be open about the biological parents" and who can be "understanding of their adoption decision." "Respect for the biological roots of the child" and a "willingness to discuss the child's adoption with him or her" are some of the ingredients they seek to find in the people wanting to adopt.

Beyond the adoption issue of parenting, the basic skills of raising children are characteristics the adoption agencies look for in the potential parents. They want parents who can allow a child to grow to his own potential, who are able to give and receive love from a child, who can meet the needs of a child, who have a realistic approach to parenting, who are accepting, nurturing, supportive, understanding . . . basically the agencies seek parents with good, healthy child-rearing skills.

The adoption agency uses several methods in evaluating these skills. What the potential parents say, what experience they have had with children and what experiences they have had in the homes in which they were raised all feed into the evaluation of the parenting skills of the potential parents.

The agency listens carefully to the statements of the people seeking a child. The prospective parents must convey their *strong* desire for a child to the agency's social worker. The agency has to believe that having a child is exceptionally important . . . a high priority in these people's lives. Without this intense feeling being conveyed, they won't get a baby. The Brunsons were a good example. Bob and Eileen Brunson were quiet people who were not very demonstrative or expressive. They each came from homes where self-sufficiency, not vulnerability, was valued. They had not responded with outward emotion to Eileen's fertility problem, nor did they respond with any intensity in their desire for a child. They knew they wanted a child and their lack of intensity in expressing this desire did not lessen the wish. Their low-keyed, quiet approach to life was interpreted by their social worker as meaning a child was not very important to them. They were rejected because their inability to fully express their desire to have a child left their adoption worker unconvinced that it was really a critical goal for them. The agency didn't hear the statements which indicated, to the social worker, how important a child was to Bob and Eileen.

The second method the adoption agency uses to evaluate your skills is your experience with children. The worker wants to know of all of your contacts with babies and children . . . the more the better. If you have had none, the adoption agency will feel you lack the skill necessary to parent versus some other potential parent who has had this experience. Search your background. Remember every baby-sitting experience, the Christmas with your sister's family including her three children, the day at the zoo with the neighbors and their children, your airplane ride and discussion with the four year old who ended up in the seat next to you. You are proving parenting skills to the agency worker.

The other method used to determine your potential for parenting is what kind of parenting you had. The agency wants to know about how you were raised because that frequently predicts how you will parent. When Lori and Scott went to adopt they did not know that their childhood was one of the areas in which they would be evaluated. They were both proud of the fact that Scott had overcome a very difficult childhood. He had been badly neglected as a child and was eventually sent to live in a boys' home from the age of twelve until he was on his own. He had really pulled himself up on his own and had established a close and loving relationship with Lori, whom he married when he was twenty-five. Now to be turned down by the adoption agency because he lacked the proper parenting model was a great blow to them. After the rejection, they knew they had made a mistake in even telling the agency about it at all.

The agencies, seeking the best possible home for their limited number of adoptable children and trying to make the best placements possible, have an extremely difficult job. They necessarily work in the dark because of our lack of knowledge about which homes will be the best homes for the available children. Unfortunately, many fine people are turned down by the adoption agencies because they do not adequately fit these undocumented criteria for becoming good parents.

Fighting the Adoption Agency's Rejection

If you go through part or all of the adoption agency process and are rejected, is that it? Are there ways to fight the agency decision or to get them to change their minds?

The place to begin to try to reverse the adoption agency's rejection of you is to find out the cause of the rejection. This sounds easy but that is not always the case. Many times the agency will be vague and not specific with statements that they have simply too many applicants for the number of children they have to place. For some reason you were eliminated so there is some cause for this rejection. Try to get them to be specific but be tactful; you are still trying to work within their system. Annie and Ed decided to fight the rejection they received from one agency. They were a fine young couple who seemed as though they would be ideal parents, but they made several tactical errors with the agency. They waited until they had been married nine years to seek a child, so the agency felt this indicated a child was not too important to them. Annie worked as a teacher and loved it, but the agency felt this could be a problem if she decided to go back to work. Annie and Ed thought they could ask for a baby, since that was their first choice, but the agency believed this demonstrated their lack of flexibility. They led a busy, active life, but the agency felt it would be difficult for them to incorporate a child into their life style. So the agency said no baby. They were crushed. They went back to find out the reasons for their rejection and if the agency would reconsider. Of course, this effort alone indicated to the agency a greater desire by Ed and Annie for a child than the agency had previously believed. So the agency, knowing Ed had a very powerful position with a television station in the community, decided to allow them to be evaluated by an agency psychologist for their potential parenting ability. Ed and Annie were bright enough to know you do not let the person who has rejected you send you to his or her colleague for a second opinion. They asked if they could have a private evaluation from another psychologist and the agency agreed. Their own psychologist gave them a glowing evaluation, which they well deserved. The agency reconsidered their rejection and within six months they had a darling baby boy. They fought and won.

Marian and David fought the agency in a different way. They were an older couple seeking an older child. They had been approved for adoption but waited and waited and waited. After two years they were not even being contacted by the agency any longer. The adoption agency worker suggested they withdraw their name from the agencies' waiting list but they refused. They could not understand how articles could appear in the local newspapers about the older children in need of homes that were not available. They were available and they wanted one of those children. In fact, they would even take older siblings as well as only one child. They called the newspaper and questioned the validity of the agencies' "propaganda" about the children needing homes. The newspaper, recognizing a controversial, newsworthy story, interviewed them and published their plight. The agency has never contacted them since their story appeared in the newspaper. The likelihood that they might get a child or children from that agency is very slight. (At the same time Marian and David were not making headway with the adoption agency, two young children, aged four and six, were being evaluated by a committee that was to decide what was in the best interest of this older brother and sister who had just been made available for adoption. The committee consisted of a psychologist, two social workers from the adoption agency and the supervisor of the local center which screens problem children. It was decided that these two children, who had been together since birth and who represented the only stability they had ever known in each other's lives, would be put into separate homes because there was no one who would want to take both of them at the same time. The protest of the psychologist that this would seriously harm the two children was ignored because it was "impossible" to find a home which would take both of these children.)

Your chances of fighting the adoption agencies and winning after you have been rejected are not good. However, it's better to fight than to do nothing. Remember, the people who get the children today are those who really know how to go after them. They know how to work within the system and they know how the system works.

Creative Flexibility Needed Within the Agencies

Everything is changing and the adoption field is no exception. In order to keep abreast of the needed changes, adoption agencies need to look at their deficiencies from a position of hope, not from a position of defense. The areas in which the agencies are weak are areas that should become vital, new and alive with change.

The adoption agencies have been able to respond with a vital, creative approach to change before. When the supply of available infants diminished, the agencies put additional emphasis on the "special needs" child. Partly this was altruistic, partly it was for the agencies' survival. An adoption agency must provide children to adopt if it is to remain in business. The adoption agencies, as a positive response to the lack of children, found themselves in the unique position of at last being able to place children who were previously unadoptable. They developed new criteria for parent selection and moved right along with the trend.

In placing children with special needs, the agencies recognized the need for conducting group parent meetings after the adoption placements. The agencies knew there was a need for broader support systems for the families that adopted "special needs" children. They responded to this newly created need.

As "special needs" children were frequently more expensive to raise, the adoption agencies approached the problem creatively. Frequently, financial assistance is given to the families that adopt children whose medical costs alone might have prevented their adoption.

The adoption agencies are beginning to respond to the potential opening of the adoption records as the adoptee becomes an adult (See Chapter 11). While some adoption agencies fought and continue to fight this possibility, others are creatively making plans for its eventuality. Letters from the biological parents are being enclosed in the records in case the adoptee wishes to know, on a more personal level, the biological mother or father. Some adoption agencies are currently taking an active role in reunions between adoptees and their biological parents. The role of the adoption agencies sometimes has been that of communicator between the biological parents and the adoptive parents without identities becoming known. Some adoption agencies have shown that they are able to respond to the needs of all of the people so personally involved in adoption.

The needs of the biological parents became more important as the supply of infants dwindled. The biological parents had a product the adoption agencies wanted, so the parents had more negotiating power. In response to this shift in power, the adoption agencies allowed the biological parents to have more say in the placement of their child. The biological parent, usually only the mother, was allowed to read case histories of several families being considered for their child. She then could choose the family she liked the best. This was a marked departure from the past. This could become even more responsive to the wishes of the biological parents through direct parent-to-parent contacts without names. There is no question this is a creative step for the adoption agencies.

The adoption agencies have also exhibited delayed creativity. While delayed creativity is not as desirable as timely creativity, it at least indicates a willingness to try new things. Let me give you two examples of the creativity the agencies have reluctantly demonstrated.

In the peak years of baby availability, the adoption agencies did not know how to cope with the overabundance of children available for adoption. At the end of this period when there were fewer babies, the agencies finally utilized the powerful medium they had so long neglected . . . television. In limited numbers, the children who were hard to place were shown on television and the response from the public was extremely positive. You still hear on television or radio of the children who are available. Since the supply of children is so limited, it seems we should now be advertising the waiting parents who are now so abundantly available. This positive approach when there were too many children should be a shining example now that there are so many available prospective parents. So far the agencies have not generalized from the one effective solution to a problem to the new problem.

Another example of the delayed creativity of the adoption agencies was the situation involving too few adoptive homes for black children. For years the adoption agencies bemoaned the fact that blacks adopted fewer babies than were available. Frequently, blame was placed on the black culture for their non-acceptance of adoption as a means of parenting. The agencies failed for too many years to look at what they had neglected to do that could have improved the situation. As the agencies developed more outreach programs and hired more blacks to work for them, the black community responded positively and increased the number of babies they adopted. The white agencies finally began to meet the needs of the black community.

These examples of creative responses and delayed creative responses from the adoption agencies clearly demonstrate the ability of the agencies to make changes when necessary. Since these changes have been instituted they have continued to utilize them and to slightly modify them, but still the picture changes. The response time of the agencies is too slow. The agencies need to carefully scrutinize the ways they are not meeting the needs of adoption participants today. To continue what was innovative yesterday is to be inflexible today.

The adoption agencies have, for some reason, chosen not to participate in some other creative concepts that have emerged from the related helping professions. One of the most remarkable changes that has occurred in the helping professions in current years has been the advent of free or low-cost medical care and counseling through community outreach programs. It was clear that minorities and, especially, young people did not feel welcome or comfortable in the normal, organized health settings. As a result, free clinics developed. These clinics, staffed primarily by volunteers, became the direct health service provider for a significant segment of our society. The facilities were not glamorous, in fact they were austere. The volunteers were not the bejeweled member of the auxiliary society. Instead they were young people, blacks, or Chicanos with whom the individuals seeking services could identify. The professionals who participated in the free-clinic movement were a special group who also identified with the needs of the community they served. As a result, adoption agencies who had normally provided service to these people found their client base eroding. Many women get pregnancy tests and pregnancy counseling about their unwanted pregnancy at a free clinic from volunteers who know little about adoption. Abortion and keeping a child are freely discussed, but seldom is adoption even mentioned. I believe that a significant number of potentially adoptable children have been lost to the adoption agencies and to the people seeking to adopt because the adoption agencies have failed to participate actively in the free-clinic movement.

I am not saying that the free-clinic movement created the problem. In fact, I believe the free-clinic movement has been exceptionally responsive to the needs of the group they serve. The adoption agencies have never, to my knowledge, seen fit to participate in this modern health provider setting. The adoption agency workers have no contact with the free clinic workers . . . no exchange of information is provided. The adoption agencies may have lost a significant source of potential clients through their hesitant approach to change.

Power of the Adoption Agencies

Social workers from the adoption agencies, as with all helping professionals, have a difficult problem to surmount. They offer to help people, but frequently they exercise control over those they seek to help. Social workers suffer from the power that they wield and the godlike feelings the power engenders.

There is no question of the power that the social worker has over all of the people involved in adoption. The biological parents are at the mercy of the social worker. The social worker controls the destiny of their child. Based upon how the biological parents present themselves to the social worker, the future of the child is cast. The control of the biological parents is ultimately the control of the child. The judgment of the worker extends most profoundly to the potential adoptive parents because here we are not only involved with presenting a "good" image, but also in being chosen. The social workers from the adoption agencies get to decide if you will or will not be chosen to get a child. You can't get much more godlike than that.

Unfortunately, at the point when social workers become fully aware of their power, they become less effective in helping their clients. Their emphasis switches from helping others to controlling others. Adoption workers need to help their clients, not to be their judges.

The only possible reason to trust a worker from the adoption agency is if you believe she is working for you. Social workers who are seeking ways to eliminate people cannot possibly be working for you. To even pretend that the social worker is there to help you is a misrepresentation.

The adoption agency states who their primary client is. The only client the agency says they are seeking to serve is the child. The agencies make it abundantly clear that the "best interest of the child" is their primary concern.

This single representation is truly unfortunate. There is no reason that the agency would be in any conflict if they sought to serve the biological parents, the adopted child and the adopting parents equally. Serving one segment of the adoption triangle does not preclude serving all segments.

To thoroughly serve the biological parents, the social workers from the agency should seek to clearly understand all the ways they can help either of the biological parents. While in most cases the biological father is not as involved as the mother, all of the suggestions I make are applicable to him as well as to her. The agency needs to meet her needs of knowing about the family with which her child will be placed. At times she may want to meet the new parent. Fine ... if it's agreeable to both biological and adopting parents, then why not? The agency needs to set up a regular communication system with her if for no other reason than to update medical records. It is possible that she might wish to keep up with the child's progress. Again, if it is acceptable to everyone involved, the role of the agency would or should be to facilitate these requests. If the biological parents are open to contact with the child when the child becomes an adult, the agency should help in whatever manner makes it easiest for all of the people involved. Basically, the role of the agency should be to serve and to help each of the biological parents as much as possible. This service should be available to the biological parents even after the child's relinquishment has been obtained.

To adequately help the potential adopting parents, the agency should seek to serve the adoptive parents in whatever way possible. This should include trying to find a child for them. The agency would then be involved in recruiting babies to help serve the people who wish to adopt them. If the interest of the parents who wish to adopt was a high-priority item for the agencies, the problems and concerns the adoptive parents encounter with infertility, with parenting and with raising an adopted child could be freely explored. The adoption agency would be there to serve, not judge, the potential adoptive parents.

To thoroughly serve the child who has been adopted means to provide service after placement. This could only be done if all parties are openly served by the adoption agencies. The child, who is now given the primary emphasis in placement, is done a disservice by the lack of concern for the other parties involved. The child whose adoptive parents are having difficulty with him cannot now consult with the adoption agency for help for fear it might indicate weakness and jeopardize the legal adoption. This is not in the best interest of the child. The older, adult adoptee who seeks information about his biological parents is not served by the agency which tells him there is no way they can help him and that he should be grateful for the adoptive parents he has. Even the teen-age child who seeks information about his or her adoption could benefit from some careful counseling, taking into account the current concerns being expressed. To thoroughly serve the child necessitates current updating of the medical records so that newly found medical problems for the biological parents can be told to the adoptive parents. In this way the health of the growing child is protected. Adoption is healthiest for the child when the needs of the child are given equal priority with the needs of all the people involved in the adoption picture.

The adoption agencies have a long way to go to make adoption a healthy, viable alternative for those who are involved: the biological parents, the child and the adopting parents. The base is there ... the potential is there. In this time of scarcity of children for adoption, the goal should be to serve all those who have a need for help in the adoption process. This is not a time for defensive retrenching on old lines but for new, creative, open approaches that take into account everyone's importance.

Summary
People who want babies are going to find them somewhere, somehow. They will find them even if they would be borderline parents or even if they are seriously disturbed. To work with these people and all of the people who really want a child within the framework of an organized adoption setting would increase their potential for raising happy, healthy children. To force these people out of the system only causes them to look elsewhere and to not have the support systems that could exist through the adoption agency.

Many advantages are available to those people who work within the adoption agency system. The biological parents receive more pre-relinquishment counseling here than anywhere else they may give up a child. The biological mother has all the medical care provided from the time she enters the system. If she or the father wishes not to be identified, they have the greatest chance of anonymity in the adoption agency system. The biological parents know the child they relinquish to the agency has a greater choice of homes than if they place the child privately. Frequently the biological parents become involved in a group-counseling session where they share a common bond with others in the same predicament.

Advantages to going through the adoption agency system exist for the adoptive parents also. The adoption agency system offers the greatest source of children available for adoption. By going through an agency, the adoptive parents know the child they receive has been fully relinquished before they receive the child. They can be confident that the child has been medically screened and that known medical problems are evident to all. The adoptive parents do not have to deal directly with the biological parents, so they can remain anonymous if they wish. The adoptive parents are aware that the child placed with them is likely to be a child that has been screened as to how appropriately this child will fit into their home.

The adopted child also gains advantages by being adopted through an agency. The child has the chance of being placed in a home that most fits his or her needs. A child whose biological mother and father had demonstrated superior intelligence might experience great difficulty being adopted into a home with less-than-average intelligence parents. The child with special needs will best fit in a home that can accept his limitations.

While the advantages to adopting through an agency are significant, they have the potential for becoming far more significant. This means greater advantages to everyone if the adoption agencies can make the necessary and timely alterations of the adoption agency system. But for now, no matter how great the advantages might be, if you aren't accepted you have to choose another direction.

The best way to increase your chances of winning the adoption game with the adoption agencies is to thoroughly understand their method of operation. It is important that you understand who their primary client is and where you fit in the current adoption picture. If you understand what the adoption agencies are looking for in the parents they choose, then you stand the best chance of getting your baby. I wish you luck!

6
YOUR
OWN GAME

Horror stories are told and retold of babies being taken back from their adoptive homes, babies being sold to be sexually abused by those who adopt them illegally, babies being taken from their adoptive homes by judges who uncompassionately say the adoptions were illegal. These tales are usually told to discourage non-agency adoptions. Similar tales that have occurred in agency adoptions are rarely heard. Great efforts seem to be made to discourage and discredit and placements of children that are not controlled by an adoption agency.

At the same time, terms such as gray market adoptions, black market adoptions and agency adoptions are bantered about in the adoption scene. Exactly what these terms mean and what things are legal or illegal in adoption is not always clear. All adoptions, even most illegal baby placements, ultimately become agency adoptions. In actuality, there are no private adoptions; there are, however, private placements of children. The one exception to private adoptions ultimately becoming agency adoption occurs when children are adopted in other countries (See Chapter 8).

In the United States, three alternatives exist to agency adoptions. Each of these three alternatives is considered a private adoption since an agency did not place the child.

1) Private Adoptions (Independent adoptions)
2) Family Adoptions (Step-parent adoptions, grandparent adoptions)
3) Black Market Adoptions (Illegal adoptions, baby selling)

The way a couple obtains the child is different in each of the above methods. However, after a couple has the child, they usually then go through a formal adoption proceeding through some state-designated adoption agency. *Private adoptions are legal adoptions in most states*, although some states have specific provisions that must be met for the adoption to be legal.

Confusion exists about the difference between black market adoptions and private adoptions (gray market). The primary difference between these two forms of placements is the exchange of money that takes place. The laws regarding the exchange of money in adoption cases is ambiguous from state to state and many people circumvent the law. What expenses can be legally paid in a private adoption are sometimes difficult to define. In a regular private adoption no money is paid to have a child placed. However, the line between black market babies and gray market babies is not at all distinct.

Private Adoptions
Private adoptions are legal in most states despite attempts to discredit or to make private adoptions appear shady or illegal. Most private adoptions fall into the category where no one receives money for the child being placed for adoption; therefore, they are not black market adoptions and they are legal. Most private adoptions go smoothly with no problems.

Adoption agencies over the years have attempted to have private adoptions ruled illegal; in most states they have been unsuccessful. The agencies maintain that private adoptions should be illegal to protect the welfare of the child. The adoption agencies say these adoptive homes have not been investigated prior to the child's placement and, therefore, might be inappropriate or unsatisfactory. Could this be carried to the extent that the state would license married couples to allow them to conceive and raise children?

If the adoption agencies could clearly demonstrate a higher quality of parenting in agency-chosen homes compared with private placements, they might have some reason to advocate only agency adoptions.[1] Yet no research has shown that agency-placed adoptions are any more or less "successful" than private adoptions. Certainly with all of the screening that occurs in agency adoptions, they should be better; yet they are not.

Another reason adoption agencies want private adoptions stopped is that they cut into their business. Adoption agencies across the country have been severely threatened by the lack of available children for adoption. Many adoption agencies have closed because the commodity they deal with, namely children, is no longer available in sufficient numbers for adoption placement. A child placed privately might have been, under other circumstances, a child placed through an adoption agency. Sometimes, birthparents deliberately choose private adoptions so that they can be intimately involved in choosing and knowing the home into which their child goes. At other times, a birthmother might decide how she wants her child placed more on the basis of who talks with her first.

The adoption agencies maintain that the interests of all of the people are not met in a private adoption. They claim that anyone who has been rejected by an agency, with all of its wisdom, can still go out and adopt privately. They claim that counseling is not provided the woman relinquishing her child and that the child is a pawn in the process. At times these criticisms are justified. However, the same criticisms can properly be directed toward adoption agencies as well.

There are several advantages to using an adoption agency to find a child to adopt. The primary advantage of adoption agency placements over private adoptions is that the agencies have most of the babies. They may not have many babies, but they have more than anyone else. Therefore, if you are in the market for a baby, the adoption agencies are probably the best place to start looking. The second advantage in going through an agency is that most of the legal hassles of adoption are taken care of by the agency. The third reason to go through an agency is if you feel you would be uncomfortable with the exchange of names that usually occurs (but not always) in a private adoption. With the possibility of records becoming open to all adult adoptees, (See Chapter 11) the emphasis on maintaining anonymity becomes less important. The fourth reason is that there can be greater matching of qualities of the child with the adoptive parents because an agency has a greater number of both available.

Despite all of the above, many people still adopt privately. Some people adopt privately because they are turned down by the adoption agencies.

Other people adopt privately because they believe that the advantages of this type of adoption outweigh the risks. At times people adopt privately because they believe this will get them the child they want fastest.

Before you become involved in private adoption, learn the difference between private adoption and agency adoption. You should clearly understand how a private placement works. It is also important to understand the risks and the advantages of adopting a child privately.[2]

How Private Adoption Works
All private adoptions are similar . . . even those that involve monetary transactions, as in black market adoptions. You need a general understanding of what goes on so that you do not get bogged down by lack of knowledge of your next step.

Making Contacts In order to adopt privately, you have to find someone who has, or who knows about, a child that is available for adoption. This is the main difference between private and agency adoptions . . . *you* have to find the contact who can provide the child.

Historically, the primary contacts for potential children to adopt, outside of adoption agencies, have been physicians and lawyers. This is still probably true, but these groups, like the agencies, have seen availability of children decline in recent years.

Many other potential sources of contact are available for the resourceful person who tries to find a child. These potential sources are discussed in detail in the next chapter. *You* are the only limit on the number of possible contacts. Children are available for adoption if you search long enough and thoroughly.

In each of the contacts you make, tell the person about your situation and about how they might be of help to you. Find other leads from each person you contact, so that even if they don't personally know of a child for you, they can suggest someone else who might. You are attempting to contact a wide range of people in the hope of finding one child. The more people who know of your situation, the greater the chance of finding the one child you want.

Once you begin your search, you have to be prepared for what happens when you find a contact that pays off. What do you do when someone says "I heard about this baby I thought you would be interested in knowing about?" Then what?

Contacts with attorneys are sometimes easier than other contacts. They know the next steps (or at least they should know), so it makes it a bit easier for you to proceed if an attorney is the one who tells you about a baby. Just because this is an added advantage, in no way does it mean you should limit your contacts to attorneys. You can and should hire an attorney to handle the legal side after you have found a child . . . you don't necessarily have to have one to *get* that child.

Hiring a Lawyer After you have found a possible adoptable child, you need to find an attorney fast. Preferably, while you are still looking for the child you should also look for an attorney so he will be available when the child is found.

No matter what your present problem, all lawyers are not equal. If you have a legal problem related to a business contract, you want a lawyer who has expertise in business contracts. If you are planning to adopt a child, you want a lawyer who knows something about private adoptions. Some lawyers know little or nothing about adoption . . . you don't want to hire one of them.

You need to assess the level of knowledge of your potential lawyer. In effect, you need to interview lawyers to find the one who seems best for you. Ask the lawyer how many private adoptions he or she has handled. How many agency adoptions has he represented? The legal side of agency adoptions is far simpler than the legal side of private adoptions. What has been the outcome? What are the laws under which you will have to operate in this particular state? In general, you are trying to figure out if he knows what he is talking about. As you interview several attorneys, you will see very quickly which ones know most about the subject.

If you don't even know where to begin to find a lawyer, call any lawyer you know and ask for a suggestion. If you have read about any controversial adoption proceedings in your local area, find out who represented the adoptive parents. If someone teaches classes on adoption, ask the instructor for recommendations. If none of these suggestions works, call your local bar association and ask for names of lawyers who know something about adoption. But, after you have any of these potential sources of legal help, you still need to determine if they are the best for you. You still need to interview them to make certain they know enough to handle your case. You want to be sure.

After you have settled on a lawyer, you need to be positive that you are going about this private adoption in a legal way. Your lawyer should be able to tell you exactly what is legal in your state. The laws pertaining to adoption and their degree of enforcement in your state may vary; your lawyer should be able to answer any questions you may have about the laws.

Even if this book were longer, it would be difficult to clearly relate specific laws from state to state in a manner that you could know exactly what you might encounter. Some laws in each state are not enforced, while other states with less specific laws may enforce them far more stringently. The law is not known for its consistency of application.

Five general trends and documents seem to be setting legal precedent in adoptions. More states seem to be encouraging adoption through agencies rather than private adoptions. Frequently the states are looking at the Revised Uniform Adoption Act as a guideline, though few states have adopted the Act in total. The United States Senate hearings on baby selling have had considerable impact on the interpretation of adoption laws. The Supreme Court ruling on *Stanley* v. *Illinois*, which ruled that all parents, legitimate or otherwise, are entitled to a court hearing before their children are taken from them, has had a strong legal impact on the rights of the birthfather. Another document that has had considerable impact on adoption is a book called *Beyond the Best Interests of the Child*[3] which has set the precedent for what is termed the psychological parent. The informed potential adoptive parents who are considering private adoption should be familiar with each of these items, as should their attorney.

The legal aspects of private adoption are critical. It is imperative that you get an informed, competent lawyer to advise you on what is or is not possible in your state. No lawyer can decide if you should go ahead with an adoption placement or not, but a lawyer should be able to tell you exactly what the potential legal risks are. Then you should be able to decide if you choose to go ahead or not.

How great a legal risk would you be willing to take in order to adopt a child? That question is difficult for anyone to answer with certainty, but it is only for you to actually decide. If you have had great difficulty finding a child and you are strongly motivated, you might be willing to take a reasonable risk if a child were available. Most people who really want a child will take some legal chances rather than give up a child they might be able to adopt. Obviously they need the best legal help they can get.

Determining the Amount of Contact   One of the primary deterrents for couples seeking a child is the potential contact they might have with the birthmother. Without question, you are more likely to have contact with one or both birthparents in a private adoption than in an agency adoption. How much contact you might have will vary from situation to situation. The contact may be as minimal as an exchange of names or the contact may exist as long as you raise the child.

The amount of contact you might have is difficult to predict. At times, you start out with one level of contact, but the birthmother, who is usually in control, may decide to change the amount. Wendy and Mickey found this out. They had waited a long time for a child. They were delighted to hear about a pregnant woman who wanted to place her child privately for adoption. They agreed to pay medical and other expenses incurred by the pregnancy in exchange for the child. The birthmother was satisfied with the arrangement and she chose not to have any direct contact with them. She wanted to know a lot of details about the adoptive parents from the intermediary, but she did not want to meet them. That was fine with Wendy and Mickey, who kept their fingers crossed as each month, week, then day rolled on in the pregnancy. At last "their" baby boy arrived. Everything was great. The birthmother never wavered in her decision to let them have the child, but she did decide to meet them. After her son arrived, she decided she wanted to meet and talk with Wendy and Mickey. The news of this meeting was met with great uncertainty by Wendy and Mickey . . . they were scared. What if after finally getting this close, she changed her mind? What if she didn't like them? However, the birthmother had what they wanted, "their" baby, so she could call the shots. They arranged to meet her at the hospital. Wendy and Mickey left the meeting in a very different frame of mind than when they entered. They were absolutely glowing about the meeting. They really liked her and felt she liked them. They had a long, meaningful talk and left feeling grateful that they had met her. She, too, felt that way. She said any doubts she previously had were gone after meeting them. She said she felt she was doing something that was really important and that made her feel really good about herself. She felt her baby was going to have an excellent home and she was absolutely certain that she had done the right thing in meeting them. Everyone felt good about the meeting.

While Wendy and Mickey's experience went very well, not everyone would want to have contact with the birthmother or the birthparents. In a private adoption you have to remember that the birthmother is pretty much in control. You will probably have to do it her way because you want her to give you the baby. You have much greater control of the contact after you have legally adopted the child, but by that time you will be less concerned about contacts. Some adoptive parents maintain contacts with the birthparents throughout the entire growing-up period of their child. Jim and Barbara send pictures of their daughter to the birthmother regularly. They also tell the birthmother about the child's development and interests and they are not the least bit worried about the contact. Since they have two other children, they make a point of sending a family picture each time a picture of their daughter is requested; they want the birthmother to think of their daughter as part of a family. Another couple, Patty and Andrew, take their son to the park so that the birthmother can watch the growth of the boy she placed for adoption. The birthmother never makes contact with the boy, but she is able to see for herself that he progresses beautifully in his family.

In "olden" days, if you could maintain anonymity in an adoption, it would make it difficult for the birthmother or for the adopted child to ever make contact. If no one ever knew the other's name, no contact would be possible. The illusion that this was an ordinary family was able to be maintained. Now, this illusion is recognized as just that ... an illusion. This is not a regular family. This is a special family that stays together by its history, not by its blood. This in no way lessens the family ties. At some point the child becomes an adult and may seek to know more about his or her blood ties. The trend is toward making identifying information available to the adult adoptee and thus anonymity becomes less important. Contact between the two sets of parents seems less ominous.

Paying Pregnancy Costs The main differences between black market adoption and private adoptions is the financial arrangement. In a private adoption no one makes a profit in the transfer of a child from the birthparent to the adoptive parent. The medical costs of the pregnancy, other expenses resulting from the pregnancy and legal costs are the only expenses allowed in a legal, private adoption. Some states require a full disclosure of funds that the parties have exchanged in relation to the pregnancy.

Because expenses can vary a great deal, it is not always easy to determine if the fees being charged are legal fees. Don't hesitate to ask for itemization of all monies paid to make certain that the adoption remains legal. Inflation quickly dates money figures; but in general there are some guidelines you can follow. Adoptions that cost over $15,000 are likely to fall into the category of being questionable. One can expect medical costs of several thousand dollars. In deliveries where there are complications, these could easily double. Legal costs should usually not be more than $1,500 but may be slightly more if the lawyer also makes the placement arrangements.

The fact that a baby is being sold on the black market will not be identified to the potential adoptive parents. No one says "Do you want to buy a baby?" Adoptive parents must be able to identify the circumstances that would result in a black market adoption. Allison, a single woman who wanted a baby, found out that it isn't always easy to distinguish a black market baby from a private adoption. She wanted a baby but she wanted it legally. A friend told her about a lawyer who knew of a woman about to deliver a child. She had her friend call the lawyer to find out some of the details. The lawyer, with no prior knowledge of the person to whom he was speaking, told Allison's friend that he had this baby who was born yesterday. The couple who was going to take the baby backed out at the last minute but he knew it would be no problem to find someone else to adopt the boy. The friend asked what kind of costs were involved. The lawyer said it would be $12,500. The friend gasped and asked why so much. He said it was $3,500 for the medical costs, $2,500 for psychotherapy because the woman had been raped, $3,000 for expenses for the woman to "relocate" and $3,500 for the legal fees. The longer they talked, the more uncomfortable the lawyer became with Allison's friend's comments and questions. He finally said "I think you're right . . . this sounds too sticky and I don't want to be a part of it." They hung up. Allison then had a lawyer call the lawyer with the baby. It was apparent the lawyer with the baby still *did* want to be involved. The total fee was the same although the itemization was different from the day before. The lawyer told Allison's lawyer to act quickly because several people were considering this child. As you can see, the lawyer made the fees not too far out of reason. Someone would obviously pause and consider this baby even though they would not consider an illegal adoption. It is not as obvious as the situation where a baby is offered for $40,000 and is unmistakably illegal.

The usual costs covered in a private adoption are medical costs related to the pregnancy, such as prenatal care and hospital costs. You can also reasonably expect to pay costs for prenatal vitamins or other tests necessary for the pregnancy. You can also pay a reasonable legal fee for the lawyer's time. Other expenses become more questionable. Counseling or psychotherapy for the pregnant woman would probably be permissible in most states . . . especially since one of the major criticisms of private adoptions is that the pregnant woman does not receive adequate counseling about her decision. Dental care to some extent might be related to the pregnancy. Cost for food to make certain the woman is adequately nourished would probably be acceptable. So you can see "other" expenses can add up rather readily.

Private adoptions are usually more expensive than agency adoptions. It is worthwhile to formalize in the early stages exactly what expenses you, the adopting parents, will pay. It is very difficult to say no as the delivery of the child approaches. You also need to have an agreement as to what happens financially if the birthmother changes her mind and does not relinquish the child for adoption. This is a very sensitive area.

Securing Medical Consent Forms One of the first things you should do if you adopt privately is to have the birthmother sign a medical consent form so that you can legally treat the child when necessary. This is the type of document you don't have to be concerned with in an agency adoption. In a private adoption you should be cautious about taking the baby until this document is signed.

You can ask the birthmother directly for her signature on the document you have ready. Your lawyer can also prepare one and have her sign it before she turns the baby over for adoption. When possible it is worthwhile to have the document notarized, although this is not always critical. The most important thing is that the birthmother sign it.

If for some reason the form is not available, should you not take the child? Again this is your choice. You increase your risks, but you also have the child. It is better to have the medical consent and the baby.

Working with the State Agency After you have had a child placed with you privately, you now begin the formalized proceedings of adopting the child. In most states, a court representative, or an agency delegated by the state, investigates the adoptive home and makes its recommendation to the court.

The emphasis in the state's study is far different and more superficial than the home study done by adoption agencies to determine if they will place a child with you. In some cases, the state worker assigned to you will have far less training than regular adoption agency employees. The state is merely trying to make certain you are a fit home instead of trying to

YOUR OWN GAME   113

decide if you are the best home available. The burden of proof is on them, not on you. One private adoption agency in Ohio is using an interesting approach in cooperation between prospective adoptive parents and a private adoption agency. If an adoptive family locates a potential child for adoption, this private agency will do all the investigating, counseling and legal steps. This increased involvement of an adoption agency with private adoption cases has some excellent possibilities. Seldom is this level of cooperation seen.

The usual six months probationary period ordinarily starts at the time the petition to adopt is filed in court. This means that after your lawyer files the necessary papers you still must wait approximately six months before the adoption is finalized. It is during this period that the relinquishment papers are signed by the birthmother or, when necessary, by both of the birthparents.

Signing Relinquishment Papers The signing of the relinquishment or consent-to-adopt papers is the *crucial* point in the adoption process. In agency adoptions, the relinquishment papers are usually signed *before* the child is placed in an adoptive home. In a private adoption the relinquishment papers are usually signed *after* the child has been placed with the new adoptive family. In neither case do the adoptive parents obtain the consent to adopt from the birthparents. In an agency adoption, the agency obtains the relinquishment, in a private adoption the state-designated agency obtains the relinquishment or the private lawyer does. The consent or relinquishment is the major legal problem involved in adoption.

Actually, consent of the adopting parents is also obtained in an adoption. They give their consent by filing the petition to adopt. It is possible that adoptive parents can be unhappy with the child placed with them or feel they were not fully told about the child's background or medical history. They, like anyone unhappy with the adoption, can ask to have the proceedings stopped or declared void even after the adoption is finalized if they can prove fraud occurred.

At times the consent of the child is also necessary. This is usually the case only if the child is around twelve years of age or older. Usually this consent is given at the court hearing for finalization of the adoption. At this time, the judge will ask if the child agrees to the adoption.

In some states, the consent of the foster parent is recognized in the adoption process. The foster parents' rights have actually increased in recent years. At times the foster parents are allowed to contest the adoption if they believe it is not in the best interest of the child.

The single most critical person involved in consenting to the adoption is the birthmother. In the case of unmarried parents, the birthmother must consent to the adoption even if she is a minor. The only exceptions would be if, 1) the birthmother is legally incompetent and, therefore, unable to give consent, 2) the birthmother has had her legal rights to the child terminated because of abandonment, or 3) the birthmother has already relinquished the child to an adoption agency.

The laws governing the consent of the natural father are less clear and less consistent in cases where the child is illegitimate. The landmark Supreme Court decision in the case of *Stanley* v. *Illinois* has had a significant impact on the rights of the unmarried father. The court ruled that all parents, legitimate or not, are entitled to a court hearing before their children can be removed from their custody. This decision was based on the case of a man and woman who had lived together out of wedlock for a long period of time. They had several children, but after the woman died, these children were taken from the father on the grounds that he had no rights to his illegitimate children. The major impact of the court's decision was that it was based on the man's rights as a father and not on the basis of the family unit that had been established.

With this decision, adoption was given a severe jolt. Up until then, the father's consent if he was not married to the mother of the child was hardly ever considered necessary when a child was relinquished for adoption. As a result of this decision, some states established what is called the Uniform Parent Act. This, in effect, says the father must be notified before the child is adopted. The father must either sign consent forms for the adoption or he must be legally deprived of his parental rights. Some adoption agencies publish notices of a pending adoption in the newspaper stating that the father should claim the child if he wishes to exert his rights. If no one comes forth to acknowledge fatherhood, the father's legal rights are severed and the adoption can proceed without the father's consent.

On the less stringent side, the 1978 Supreme Court upheld a Georgia law which said the consent of a father is not a requirement for adoption. This decision indicates that perhaps the *Stanley* v. *Illinois* decision was interpreted too broadly and that the consent of the unmarried father may not always be necessary. Reading through the tremendous variety of decisions from state to state leaves one feeling the courts are inconsistent on how they view the unmarried father's role and at what point the father has or does not have parental rights.

The birthmother's legal rights and responsibilities in relinquishing the child for adoption are much more clearly drawn than those of the father. It is important to understand exactly how your state operates and to act within the law in obtaining the consent of the birthmother. One of the few reasons for courts nullifying or voiding an adoption is when it can be proven that the consent of the birthparents, especially the birthmother, was obtained by fraudulent means. Some states will not allow birthmothers to sign relinquishment papers until at least three days after the birth of the infant; this is to avoid criticism of pressure or charges of too hasty a response in an unduly emotional time.

Some states do not look favorably on private adoptions even though they are legal in their state. These states will pay particular attention to the consent of the birthparents. The courts want to make absolutely certain that no coercion was involved in obtaining the consent. These states, to have the utmost control, frequently insist that the relinquishment be obtained by an authorized service agency representing the state.

Usually, once a consent has been signed it may not be withdrawn without the approval of the court. If the birthparent can prove that the consent was obtained by fraud, misrepresentation, or coercion, the court may decide to cancel the consent. If the parent has merely changed her or his mind, the case will depend on the individual circumstances. The overriding factor in these decisions is what the judge deems to be in the best interest of the child. The longer the child has been in the adoptive home, the less likely the child will be removed. The courts more and more are recognizing the concept of the psychological parent of the child. This concept is clearly spelled out in the legal precedent.

Even in cases where fraud was involved in obtaining consent of the birthparents, they must act within a "reasonable" length of time in order to have the adoption set aside. The same is true if the adoptive parents believe they were not fully informed of pertinent facts at the time of the adoption. The courts expect a person to act promptly if they believe a problem exists.

In most private adoption cases, the consent of the birthparents is rather routinely obtained. All of the parties believe that what is being done is in the best interest of the child and of each of the other people involved in the adoption. However, because this is not always the case, it is important to have the best legal advice possible. Your lawyer should be able to inform you how best to keep within legal bounds in order to keep the adoption completely beyond question.

Going to Court States vary in the manner that court proceedings are conducted in adoption cases. Some adoption proceedings are conducted in Superior Court, others in Circuit Court, Surrogate Court, Domestic Relations Court, County Court, Orphan's Court, etc. Your lawyer knows the court in which your adoption will be conducted.

All the people involved in consenting to the adoption must be notified of the court hearing. Again, your lawyer will know how this notification must be made.

The actual court appearance will probably be in a judge's chambers or in a private session with the judge. The hearings are informal even though they sound very formal. Usually the adoptive parents and the child, especially if the child is older, will appear for the hearing. Sometimes the lawyer must attend. Some states do not require anyone to be there.

In general, the court hearing is an informal session that signals the formalization of the adoption. It is a jubilant time for the adoptive parents because it means the child is now theirs legally as well as psychologically.

In some states the court hearing occurs at a different period in the adoption process. At times the hearing is merely a probationary hearing that declares the home is now open to be investigated. At other times, if there is some question about the fitness of the adoptive parents, the judge may require a probationary period to examine the qualifications of the adoptive parents.

The role of the state-appointed agency which has conducted the home investigation is important in this court hearing. If the agency says the adopting home is not a good home for the child, the judge will probably not approve the adoption at this time. The weight of this agency recommendation is important. If the judge has questions about the home, the usual course is to have a longer investigation of the adopting home. Remember though ... the agencies must prove your unfitness. The investigation is seldom thorough and seldom goes against the adopting parents.

Following the granting of the final adoption decree, an amended birth certificate is issued for the adopted child. The new birth certificate lists the adoptive parents as the parents of the child and the child's name as that of the adoptive parents. In California, the adoptive parents may request deletion of the birth city and county of the adopted child. These are details you need to be aware of so that you can decide how you want them handled. Your lawyer should be able to keep you advised before you face each of these steps in a private adoption.

Basically, this is the general framework in which a private adoption operates. The person who enters the process understanding what to expect makes the fewest mistakes. The importance of the legal help you hire cannot be underestimated, especially in an adoption where there are any unusual circumstances.

The Risks of Private Adoption

Certain risks occur in private adoptions. These very risks strongly support the use of adoption agencies whenever possible. However, many people will not be given a child by an adoption agency. The agency, seeking ways to eliminate excessive applicants, is forced to use arbitrary and unvalidated criteria to eliminate some of the people applying to adopt. Therefore, for some couples, no matter how great the risks of private adoption, it is their only potential avenue to a child.

Certainly the investigation of backgrounds,—whether it is the child's, the birthparents' or yours—is much less thorough in a private adoption. In an agency, some attempt to match the child's background or the child's potential to that of the adoptive parents is made. Your opportunity to have the best child selected for you is not available in a private adoption. If you hear of a child available privately, that is likely to be the child you will get. There is little selection. At times, you may know less about the background of this family than if you had gone through an agency.

The risk of identities being exchanged is significantly higher in private adoptions. You are likely to know the birthmother's name and she is likely to know yours. If the birthmother seeks to regain her child, it is much easier for her if she knows who has the child.

The legal risks are significantly higher in a private adoption than in an agency adoption. In an agency adoption, most of the legal problems are handled by the agency and you won't even be aware of them. The relinquishment by the birthmother is usually obtained before the child is placed in your home. This decreases the chance that the birthmother will change her mind, even though it delays early placement of an infant into the adoptive home. You also have to anticipate far more legal steps in a private versus an agency adoption. The adoption agency tells you each step you need to take. As a consequence, your lawyer plays a much more important role in a private adoption: *it is more important to have a knowledgeable, competent lawyer if you are adopting privately than if you are adopting through an adoption agency.*

The potential risk of having an adoption declared null and void is higher in private adoption than in an agency adoption. The risk in private adoption is very slight if the necessary legal precautions are followed. The primary reason that this occurs is if the consent-to-adopt forms are not signed by the birthparents or if they are not properly signed. Hire a qualified lawyer and you will not have to worry.

The biggest single risk in private adoption is that the birthmother will change her mind and ask for her child to be returned. (A similar risk exists in agencies but it would be the adoption agency that asks for the return of the child.) In an agency adoption, the relinquishment of the child is done fairly early and then the child is in the custody of the adoption agency. In order for a birthmother to regain custody of the child she has relinquished to an adoption agency, she must go through the agency. The birthmother who changes her mind in a private adoption has to merely request the return of the child if she has not signed the relinquishment papers. If she has signed the papers, it is harder to change her mind but at times it is still possible. Even if she has difficulty regaining custody, the amount of identifying data she has about you could cause you great concern.

Does this mean the risks in private adoption are too great to take a chance? Definitely not! Most private adoptions are successful and proceed without a problem. Out of a group of 3,722 independent private adoptions in California, only 250 complaints were received. Figures like these testify to the safety of independent adoption.

The Advantages of Private Adoptions

The biggest single advantage to adopting privately is that this may be the only way you can get a baby. Currently, most people who adopt privately are people who cannot, or believe they cannot, adopt through an agency. The supply of infants available through agencies is seriously limited; the primary children being placed for adoption by the agencies are older children and children with special needs.

Even if it is possible to adopt an infant through an adoption agency, the waiting period is a long process, perhaps several years. In all likelihood, the waiting period will be much less in a private adoption.

The usual immediate placement from birthparents to adoptive parents is an extremely significant advantage in private adoptions. Agency adoptions emphasize the conservative side so placements usually do not occur until all relinquishment papers have been signed. This approach may offer the greatest legal safeguards but it is definitely not in the best interests of the child or of the adoptive parents. The importance of the early bonding between parents and child cannot be overestimated . . . *it is critical.* In some private adoptions, the adoptive parents are allowed to spend time with the newborn within hours after the child is born. Psychologically this is a distinct advantage to the adopted child and to the adopting parents. It is also to the advantage of the birthmother concerned about the child fitting in with the greatest ease in the new family.

The lack of prying by the agency is considered an advantage by many people who select to adopt privately. Forced counseling is seldom fruitful. The forced counseling for birthparents and for adoptive parents may be considered intrusive by some people.

Control of the process in a private adoption is also an advantage for both the adoptive parents and the birthparents. The adoptive parents are actively involved in finding a child to adopt. They are involved with making the contacts and the actual search for the child. The birthmother and perhaps the birthfather can be directly involved in the placement of their child. As one woman stated, "I could never just give my child away to an agency; I want to know exactly where she is and whom she is with or I would be uncomfortable for the rest of my life."

Another big advantage in private adoption is the personal knowledge about each other you can gain. While some people talk of the disadvantages of meeting the birthparents, this can be a most important advantage. To be able later to tell an adopted child personally about his or her birthparents can be extremely positive for all concerned. To be able to have personal knowledge about the people who will be raising your child makes the letting-go easier. *You can learn many facts about each other if you go through an agency to get your child. But if you meet one another personally, you know each other.*

Private adoptions have their risks and they have their advantages. You need to look at both to see if the advantages outweigh the risks. You also need to look at your options. The fewer options you have for obtaining a child make the risks of private adoption seem less monumental and the advantages seem more positive than ever.

Many of the alarmist views and negative statements about private adoptions come from adoption agency representatives. In actuality, the adoption agencies are the newcomers to the adoption scene. As the agencies have become larger and larger, the only method of supporting their programs has been to have a bigger segment of a continually diminishing pie. One of the ways they seek to get this larger segment is by initiating state laws to drive the competition out of business. Monopolization of adoption gives agencies all of the pie.

Private adoptions keep the proper checks and balances on the adoption agencies. It also offers a choice to people who would have difficulty meeting the rigid system the agencies frequently run. The other reason private adoptions should be maintained is to put an appropriate amount of pressure on the adoption agencies so that the latter will examine the relevancy of their methods in today's society. Private adoption offers another way that is neither better or worse than adoptions through agencies . . . it is merely a different way!

Family Adoptions

Adoption of a child by relatives is a type of adoption that presents little difficulty. In fact, about half of all adoptions are of this type.[4] As long as the adoption is agreed upon by all of the individuals, it is relatively simple. Usually no home study of suitability for parenting or probationary period is involved. While the same consent forms are necessary, the courts at times waive other restrictions that otherwise might be imposed.

The main concern in family adoptions is the potential for fights over the child. To have an aunt and uncle or grandmother and grandfather raise the child sometimes sounds good to the young woman until she sees her relatives being "parents" to her child. Legalization of this arrangement prevents the moving about of the child following family feuds.

The other form of relative adoptions is stepparent adoptions. Particularly in our society where divorce has become so common, there has been a significant increase in this type of adoption. The primary requisite in stepparent adoption is obtaining consent of the parent abdicating his or her parenting rights; generally, this is the father. In California, if the parent who does not have custody of the child fails for one year or more to pay child support or to visit the child, his or her consent to the adoption is no longer required.

Family adoptions are mentioned here only because they are one other form of adoption. Since the primary focus of this book is not on this type of adoption, it is discussed only to complete the picture of what kinds of adoptions are available that involve children. However, even in this type of adoption, it is worthwhile to hire a lawyer to make certain you proceed in a legal manner. Adoption is too important and too permanent to let anything be overlooked.

Black Market Adoptions

Of the several kinds of adoptions available, no other kind elicits more emotional response from the public than the concept of baby selling. These are the tales that cause people to question the entire idea of private adoptions. These are the adoptions that are big money for those involved. But, these are also the only ways some people have to get babies in this time of baby scarcity.

Black market adoptions are not legal because in every state there are laws against people profiting unduly from the placement of children for adoption. We have no way of really knowing how many babies are placed in this manner. It is estimated that between 5,000 to 10,000 babies are placed each year where a significant sum of money is exchanged through intermediaries to pay for the child.[5] No one is really sure.

Why would any couple pay $20,000 or $30,000 for a baby when they could go to the local adoption agency and get a child at a fraction of the cost? Why would anyone risk getting involved in an illegal arrangement to get a baby when they could go to an adoption agency and legally have a child placed with them? The answer to both of these questions is, they wouldn't. Couples seeking a child would go to an adoption agency if they could. Illegally obtaining a child is not the way they would choose the situation to be, but this is their reality. These are couples who probably can't adopt from an agency not because they are unfit or wouldn't be good parents, but rather because they don't fit the image of a parent the adoption agencies are seeking.

Black market adoptions thrive under certain conditions. Those conditions exist right now. There is a scarcity of infants available for adoption. There is a need for someone who cares about supplying what these couples dearly want . . . a baby. The current adoption agency system does nothing to remedy the scarcity, nor does it do anything about taking care of the potential adoptive parents' need for a child. As a consequence, a different group has emerged to handle these unmet needs . . . people who sell babies.

Why Not Sell Babies? Selling babies would not work if there was not a need and demand for these services. People are quick to criticize the people involved in selling babies, but the ones who would come to their defense, those who have obtained children from them, are necessarily quiet. The question needs to be asked, "Why are people upset about baby selling?" If it is meeting a need and no one is hurt, why not sell babies? Is it the profit being made by the intermediary? Does baby selling sound like slavery? Will selling babies cause women to get pregnant just for the money? Are babies more of a commodity this way than through an adoption agency? Are we concerned that the birthmother is being taken advantage of or do we object to the birthmother making a profit from her nine months labor? Just exactly what upsets us about black market adoptions?

The profit being made on black market adoptions seems to be one of the main areas of concern for some people. These people argue that intermediaries or baby brokers shouldn't profit from people's miseries. That sounds correct but in reality many people profit from other people's miseries. The brain surgeon operates on your brain tumor for a fee, the dentist charges you for the tooth he pulls, the mortician profits from the death of your loved ones, the psychotherapist charges you for listening to your problems. Even adoption agencies make enough money in their "non-profit" organizations to have nice facilities, good salaries and pleasant working conditions. Our society is set up in such a way that you pay for the things you want, even if you need them very badly. We obtain these services only if we cannot provide them ourselves. Many people in our society profit from the needs of another person, but for some reason, to do this by selling babies really upsets people.

If the profit is what most upsets us in black market adoptions, perhaps the way to solve the problem is to figure out how to decrease the profits. One of the age-old ways to decrease profits is to allow supply and demand to equalize. Currently there is a great demand for babies. If we remove the legal restrictions from people profiting by selling babies and allow the supply to meet the demand, the cost of buying a baby would go down radically. The profits being made today in baby selling would be cut drastically. Perhaps all the legal restrictions we put on baby selling are creating the very problem we deplore . . . large profits in the selling of babies.

People get very upset when they think of an unwed mother "selling" her baby. After all, they believe it is horrible that she got pregnant in the first place and bad enough that she would consider giving it away, but for her to make a profit is deplorable. Perhaps the reason people are so against the mother making a profit is that they really want the mother punished. If we pay her for her transgressions aren't we rewarding evil? Are intercourse and pregnancy really evil? She may not be doing a good thing for society but she certainly is doing a fantastic thing for the childless couple who has been stopped at each turn from finding the child they want so much.

If it isn't the profit that we worry the birthmother will make from her illicit sexual behavior, perhaps it is our fear she will be exploited. By offering her money for her baby, is it possible she isn't doing the right thing for herself? Maybe she should have an abortion or maybe she should keep the baby. Maybe she needs counseling to decide what is the best. If there is any possibility she is being exploited, it is most likely to occur while this process remains illegal and underground. If a woman felt she was doing something worthwhile in placing her child for adoption, she could freely choose which alternative would be best for her. Yet if the attitude of everyone is to punish her for what she has done, even in subtle ways, she is much more vulnerable to being exploited. All businesses, even baby selling, are easiest to regulate if they are not driven underground. Prohibition taught us this most vividly.

The criticism that baby selling is a form of slavery is difficult to substantiate. Perhaps all forms of parenting are a type of slavery. (I'm not certain for whom: the parents or the child.) Certainly, any form of adoption would be subject to this same criticism. It would be difficult to say whether more slavery is involved when a child is bought for $30,000 from a baby broker or when we negotiate a baby with a social worker for $3,000.

Another complaint raised by critics of black market adoptions is that the fitness of the parents who are seeking to adopt has not been verified. Sex perverts and child abusers can get children by this unscrupulous means. Why any sex pervert or child abuser would go to all this trouble is beyond me . . . especially when it might be easier for such persons to have their own children and not have to pay so much for them. No one makes us pass any tests for parenting unless we want to adopt a child. Just about anyone, no matter how unfit for parenting, can have a baby. *Only the infertile must offer proof of parenthood fitness.*

Another objection raised about black market babies is that they take away potentially available babies from legal adoption sources. An opposing criticism is raised when the critics say that young girls are hired to get pregnant so that large profits can be made from the babies they produce. Obviously if this second criticism is true then the first one is not. If it is possible to take potential children from adoption agencies because of the profit to the mother when she sells her baby, then we should examine how we can learn from this. Should we offer greater incentives, better living conditions, a financial allowance, and, consequently, less feelings of guilt to the birthmother who elects to place her child with an adoption agency? Again, instead of expecting penitence from her, let us demonstrate to the woman that her pregnancy is not such a terrible thing. Someone is going to benefit from her mistake and inconvenience.

People will respond that the approach just described would encourage women to have babies for profit. The feelings of remorse that are an inherent part of placing a child for adoption and the length of time it takes to produce a child will ultimately limit and discourage this practice. However, if someone is really good at making babies and can make them for others who are not, then why not?

One of the most poignant arguments against black market babies came from a pregnant woman about to give her baby up for private adoption. She said she could never sell her baby because she was sure that someday her child would find her. How then could she explain selling her baby? As long as making a profit on giving up a baby for adoption is so condemned, she is right. Ultimately, the birthparent and child may realize that, regardless of money, the most worthwhile situation occurred, a loving mother and father raised a loving child. That should be the focus in the debate over selling babies.

Another argument used against high-priced black market adoptions is that it discriminates against the poor people who cannot afford to participate. This argument is a strong one only if you believe that black market adoptions are worthwhile. Again, if supply meets demand, the cost of buying a baby would be more affordable to people with less money.

Obviously, the stand I an taking on black market adoptions is not the usual stand. One writer on adoption boldly stated, "Baby selling is abhorrent to all civilized people."[6] I believe we should consider changing current adoption laws to allow the mother and those involved with arranging adoptions to make a profit. I take this stand for several reasons. I have known the pangs of infertility. I have known the intensity of the desire to have a child. I have met couples who desperately wanted a child they could not find. I have known women who loved being pregnant, but who did not want to be mothers. I have seen poor women struggle financially with a pregnancy that would eventually become an adoption, fearful of taking any money because it might look like a black market adoption. Somehow there should be a way to accommodate all of these people in their times of need.

People will say, "What of the abuses?" But the abuses will always be there. They are there now in parenting by birth, in adoption through adoption agencies, private adoptions, stepparent adoptions, grandparent adoptions and in black market adoptions. The abuses are least likely to occur when the system can be scrutinized ... the system can be scrutinized when the system is legalized.

The Risks in Black Market Adoptions Certainly risks are a significant factor in why a person should be very careful about getting involved in black market adoptions. As in all illegal business, unscrupulous people can be involved. Illegal business is unfamiliar to most of us, so we don't know our way around in this system.

The biggest single risk in black market adoptions is the possibility that the adoption decree might be set aside if the illegality of the procedure is discovered. As a consequence, people adopting in this way live in fear for several years with the thought that someone can take their child from them. Of course, this fear diminishes over time. At some point, even if it were found out that you had paid $25,000 for your child, the judge is unlikely to take your child of five years away from the only home he or she has ever known. Living with this secret fear for years, however, is bound to take a toll on you. It also makes you vulnerable to threats of blackmail.

The financial risk in black market adoption as it is currently practiced is significantly greater than adoption through an adoption agency. The first figure quoted to a couple is not necessarily the end cost to them. As with private adoptions, it is important to have an agreement before you begin. After you have agreed to pay $25,000 and you have paid it, it is difficult to say forget it when the baby seller says he needs $5,000 more. You can't say that's not fair or I am going to report you. Remember, the law does not look upon your baby transaction with favor.

Another problem associated with obtaining a baby by the illegal black market is that when you go to court to finalize the adoption, you have to commit perjury. When the court requests a recounting of the expenses involved in the adoption, you obviously cannot tell the truth. The lie you tell, if discovered, could cause the adoption to be set aside.

As black market adoptions are currently done, the rights of the father are frequently ignored to expedite the adoption. If the birthmother indicates the father is unknown when he is really known, she is depriving him of his rights to his child. If this is later discovered, once again, the adoption could be set aside.

At times in black market adoptions, the woman originally agrees to place the child for adoption and later changes her mind. In a reputable adoption, whether through an adoption agency or a private adoption, the adoption proceedings should stop at that point. In a black market adoption, the woman might be pressured into continuing with the adoption. Threats of having to pay back money already paid toward prenatal care or "damages" to the adopting couple who are waiting for her baby might intimidate the woman into signing relinquishment papers she would not otherwise have signed. If it can be proven that the woman was coerced into signing consent forms to the satisfaction of a judge, the finalized adoption can still be nullified and the baby returned to the coerced birthmother.

At times in black market adoptions, the birthmother enters the hospital and registers in the name of the adoptive mother. When the birth certificate is filed, the adoptive parents are listed as the birth-parents. Obviously, this is illegal and it, too, is grounds for taking the child that is not theirs because it has not been legally adopted.

One other technique used in black market adoptions may in fact be the primary way of legalizing this process. A child is born in the United States, bought by a couple, flown to Mexico and adopted legally in Mexico. At times, the birthmother is represented by an attorney who formally acts in the interests of the mother in relinquishing the child.

As you can see, there are definite risks in black market adoptions. Because of the risks and mostly because these adoptions are illegal, I would be hesitant to recommend adopting a child in this way. On the other hand, there is much to be learned from the successes of these operations. If this type of adoption were legal, I see nothing wrong in people making a profit from meeting a definite need that currently exists in our society.

Very few differences, other than what have already been mentioned, exist between private adoptions and black market adoptions in relation-ship to the adopting parents. The primary difference is how you obtain the baby. You need to make contact with someone who knows about a baby that is available for adoption for a sum of money. After that, the investigation and the legal process are usually the same in terms of the finalization of the adoption. Most black market adoptions go rather smoothly and most of the children adopted in this manner remain in the home of the adoptive parents just as in any other adoption.

Black market babies are a response to an unmet need in our society. Emotional arguments against this form of adoption fail to explore why this type of adoption exists and why black market adoptions elicit such a strong response. Perhaps it is time to overhaul antiquated laws that might be creating the only negative side to profitmaking by meeting a need ... baby selling.

Summary

Adoptions which involve children being placed privately constitute a significant number of adoptions in the United States each year. Some of these are children being adopted by relatives. Others are children being placed privately. The last group are children adopted through the black market where money is exchanged for placement of a child.

The primary difference in these non-agency adoptions is the control that the birthmother has in determining with whom her child will be placed. Although this will frequently be determined by an intermediary, the birthmother has the opportunity to say yes or no. This is especially true now that there are so many potential adoptive homes for so few babies.

While adoption by relatives occurs, it is less the concern of an infertile couple seeking a child than other kinds of adoption by private placement. Most couples would probably choose agency adoptions if that choice were open to them. Agency adoptions are easier, cost less, involve less legal knowledge, are legal and offer the greatest choice to a couple seeking a child. But too many couples are eliminated by the agencies' rigid rules, arbitrary requirements and non-creative approaches to adoption. The second choice of most couples is a private adoption. The biggest difficulty here is in making the contacts that will produce a child (See Chapter 7). Sometimes, during the course of seeking a child privately, a couple will encounter an opportunity to buy a child. A couple who has been rejected by the adoption agencies and who has been having difficulties finding a child to adopt through regular private means is likely to consider a black market adoption. Black market adoptions are not good places to seek a child but they are all that is left for the desperate. It is difficult to find fault with the people who are driven to this point by the inability of our system to allow them the child they so much want.

Private adoptions, no matter how the placements occur, offer infertile couples a choice. The need for the choice is apparent by the number of people who adopt in this way. Private adoptions and intercountry adoptions (See Chapter 8) are the only opportunities left for the people whom the adoption agencies see as less fit for parenting. In no way does this make these people lesser parents. It only makes them parents by a different method because the adoption agencies did not choose to help them become parents.

7
LOOKING ELSEWHERE AND EVERYWHERE

You say you want a baby. How much time, effort and creativity are you willing to put into finding your baby? One test of your desire for a child is how far you are willing to go. It's one thing to go to an adoption agency and wait for them to give you a child; it's a whole different matter to go *find* your child.

Many people have never before considered *finding* a baby. The approach is radical. The approach may be necessary for some people and impossible for others. The only way for you to evaluate its merits for your own use is to study its advantages and risks. How does it feel to you? Are you uncomfortable? If so, why? New approaches may take some testing before they fit well into your life. Our attitudes change when we experience more familiarity with a new idea. Look back on ideas about which you were intolerant a few years ago and see how familiarity has changed your attitude toward them. In the same way, consider some of these approaches, discuss them with others, become familiar with them and *then* see how they seem to fit for you.

. Searching for a baby takes time, lots of time. The more time you spend, the greater likelihood of your success. The more people you inform, the more people there are who know of your desire to find a baby. You may be lucky and learn about an adoptable baby after a contact or two. On the other hand you may have to talk to dozens of people before you get even a trace of a lead.

Patience is a critical ingredient in a baby search. Many leads will turn up nothing. But remember, you are only looking for one baby so don't give up . . . be patient. It is easier to be patient when you are actively working on a problem. You are not waiting for a call from the adoption agency that may or may not come. You are an active participant in deciding your fate.

Skill is also important in your search. You need to know what you are doing. You need to understand why you should approach this group or that person. You need to know who gets pregnant and why, in order to understand where you are most likely to find a baby. With a clear method of searching and a clear goal, the hunt beccmes easier.

Develop your creativity as you begin your search for a baby. There are probably all sorts of innovative approaches to finding a baby that you could try. With an understanding of who gets accidentally pregnant you simply have to figure out how to reach them. We are all creative in a pinch. You merely need to develop that creative approach because, right now, you are in a pinch.

Openness is essential in searching for a baby. If you would have difficulty contacting the biological parents or knowing anything about them, you will have difficulty with this approach to parenthood. The more open you can be, the greater are your chances of success. You need to be open with lots of people about your feelings of being childless. You need to be open to leads people suggest and to where these leads might take you.

Above all, in a baby search you must be bold. Believing that there is a child out there for you, you must be willing to venture forth to find him or her. Timidity will leave you childless. The people who will find a child are those who boldly go after one.

All of these qualities are within each of us. You may not see yourself as bold or creative but check it out . . . maybe you really are. The desire to have a baby is very powerful. The strength of this desire may cause you to discover characteristics you didn't think you had. Give it a try. What's the worst thing that can happen? It is simply that you may end up without a baby and that's where you are right now.

Potential for Finding a Child

Before you begin your baby search, you have to believe that there is a potential for success. If you don't believe the potential is very great you won't put your heart into the search. There are several reasons why I strongly believe that a child is out there for you now.

America is a society influenced by fads and cycles. The world of fashion is an example. Fads and cycles also exist in family size, sexual behavior, contraceptive practice, unwanted pregnancies and babies available for adoption. Over the years the pendulum swings back and forth.

The figures I have received from adoption agencies across the country indicate a slight trend toward more children being placed for adoption than five years ago. Part of this increase is attributable to fewer agencies handling more babies as others close. While this trend is not marked, it does refute the idea that there are few adoptable babies as is sometimes presented. It is possible we have seen the depths of this cycle and are now on an upswing of adoptable babies.

The increased negative publicity given to abortion as a solution to unwanted pregnancy argues positively for adoption as an alternative to abortion. Abortion may also be experiencing a peak in its cycle. The number of abortions has leveled off in recent years and may be beginning a downward trend. Fewer abortions does not necessarily mean fewer pregnancies; it could mean that other options to those pregnancies are being used with greater frequency.

Another reason I believe that a child may exist for you is related to the trends I have just been mentioning. Statistics can be very misleading. Statistics from adoption agencies cite the huge numbers of people waiting to adopt, but anyone wishing to adopt has also consulted with every other potential agency in town. They are probably being counted two, three, or four times. We really don't know how many people are trying to adopt. Every doctor and lawyer you approach has a list of people who would like a baby, but again these lists overlap and re-count people many times. I know of dozens of people waiting right now for a baby, but if I had a baby available today for adoption many of these people might no longer be looking for one. Some would have moved, some would have just gotten a child, some would not want this particular child because they would not like his background, some would just want a girl and this is a boy, and some would just get scared off when actually confronted with the possibility that they are about to have a specific child. Therefore, my list is much shorter than I would report to you if you asked whether I knew someone who wanted to adopt.

Another reason I strongly believe there are babies who potentially are available for adoption is the number of "accidental" pregnancies that may at some unconscious level be deliberate (See Chapter 2). Some women want to be pregnant and therefore purposefully allow themselves to be exposed to an "accidental" pregnancy. If these same women knew of someone who really wanted to adopt their baby, they very well might choose adoption, not abortion. If women really don't want to be pregnant today, they have the means to prevent it. If they choose not to use these means, it is possible they really *do want* to be pregnant.

Additionally, adoption is not a well-known or common choice for women who become "accidentally" pregnant. If you can reach women who are "accidentally" pregnant, but who had not previously considered adoption as an alternative, you reach an entirely new group. These are women from whom the adoption agencies should be recruiting babies. Lisa represents this potentially untapped source of biological mothers. Lisa was a bright young lady who knew about contraceptives but found them "inconvenient" to use. She came in to make plans for her second abortion. She was nineteen. I asked her if she had considered adoption and she said she hadn't. She reasoned very clearly, though incorrectly, that there are already too many unwanted children in the world and she wouldn't want to contribute another. She was not at all aware of the current lack of adoptable babies. Lisa and the thousands of women like her are an untapped source of adoptable babies.

Supporting the contention that babies are available out there for those who search is the changed attitude of young people toward openness. Many young women would not consider placing their child with a monolithic and impersonal institution such as an adoption agency. Adoption agencies and their aloofness are looked on with disfavor by large numbers of young people who want to be personally involved with the event. To give a baby up to an adoption agency would not be comfortable for them, but to give a baby up to "real people" would be worth considering. Amy was going to have an abortion until she heard about a couple who desperately wanted a child. The more she learned about their long wait and their strong desire for a child, the more sure she became. She said she could never give her child up to an adoption agency where she "wouldn't be sure what happened to it." So she chose private adoption over abortion because she believed she was "doing something significant for society" by helping this childless couple. It gave her a reason to feel good about herself and her decision about her unborn child. The personal details about the couple who wanted the child gave her positive involvement with adoption as an alternative. To have waited for her to decide between abortion and adoption might have altered her choice. Amy needed personal knowledge about adoption in order to fully consider it.

All of these reasons support the theory that babies are there . . . you just need to find them. But any searching needs a plan. Where does one begin a baby search?

Beginning Your Baby Search
You believe you are capable of trying to search for a baby; you have looked within yourself and believe you have the patience, the openness, the boldness and the creativity to find your own baby. You also believe there is a distinct possibility you *can* find one. Now you need an understanding of how to approach your undertaking.

Limits for Your Search Everyone has limits on what he or she will accept. Before you begin to search for a baby in a random manner, it is essential that you understand your own limits. If you definitely don't want a child from a Mexican background, don't approach Mexican people with your plight. If you would find it extremely uncomfortable to have the mother live with you prior to giving birth to the child you want to adopt, make certain this doesn't occur. If you would have difficulty meeting the biological parents, indicate this so that it does not become an issue; you can use an intermediary. Each limitation you put on yourself also limits the options open to you, but limits are important in making the situation comfortable for you. The critical matter is not the limits you set but knowing, at least in general terms, what your limits are before you begin your search.

One area of limitation is in the amount of contact you are willing to have with the birthparents. People differ in the amount of contact they would be willing to have with the birthmother or the birthfather. Some people would feel comfortable in having only knowledge about the biological parents, but would want no contact. Other people would feel that it is extremely desirable to meet the biological parents. Maura and Jon, who had previously adopted through their local adoption agency were extremely open to contact with the biological parents. In fact, they felt it would be beneficial for all of them, including their four-year-old adopted son, to become more personally involved with the biological mother and/or father. With this willingness to have contact with the biological parents, they met Debbie, who at nineteen was getting ready to have her second abortion. Maura and Jon really liked Debbie and expressed their desire to raise her child if she would let them adopt it. Debbie was flattered at their interest in her. She also liked many things about both of them. She was, however, confused about what to do because her boyfriend, the father of her unborn child, wanted her to have an abortion. Maura and Jon told her she could come to live with them until the baby was born. They told her how good it would be for their adopted son to see a mother who really loved her baby and who would place it for adoption. Debbie really wavered and said she would love to do that if only she could convince her boyfriend. She tried, but to no avail. He stood firm and told her that he would never see her again if she placed his baby for adoption. Through tears for both Debbie and Maura, it was confirmed that Debbie would have an abortion. Maura and Jon both supported her decision. Soon thereafter, Debbie broke up with her boyfriend, but at the time of her decision he was too important in her life for her to ignore his wishes. Maura and Jon continue to have contact with Debbie because they shared a very important time in each other's lives.

Some people would limit their baby search to areas where they could be sure of no legal difficulties. Others are more willing to take legal risks. Carly and Jake did not feel threatened by the possibility of legal difficulties when they had a chance to adopt. Carly and Jake were at the older limits of the age group that the adoption agencies were willing to accept. Coupled with this was the fact that this was a second marriage for each of them and Carly had a strong desire to continue working. They knew they had little chance with the adoption agencies long before they were given their rejection. They were disillusioned because they really felt they would be good parents, but they were undeterred in their search. They sought help, advice, ideas and directions from anyone who might possibly help them. One of their contacts heard about a twenty-three-year-old pregnant girl who wanted to place her baby for adoption privately. Their contact called them because of their strong desire for a child, their inability to get a child from the adoption agency, their willingness to have contact with the biological parents and because they were willing to take a chance. When Carly and Jake heard about the woman, they decided to approach her, despite the fact that she might change her mind. Additionally, the father of the child was considering fighting for custody of the child in court. They could lose any financial support given her during the pregnancy. They decided they had to take some major risks if they were to achieve their desired goal. They also reasoned that if the worst thing happened and they did not get the child, at the very least they would have served society by helping this woman with her prenatal and birth expenses. Their open manner was of prime importance to the biological mother who strongly disliked secrecy and red tape. She occasionally tested their support by making additional demands, but they were unwavering in helping her in every legal way possible. Their limit to getting a child was that it had to be legal; they would not waiver on this area. They were willing to face the father of the child in court; to them that was no big problem. They were willing to take the risk he might even win. Ultimately, the biological father relented in his attempts to gain custody of the child when it turned out to be a girl. Carly and Jake stayed with the biological mother via an intermediary who was their contact person and someone the biological mother trusted. They found out many positive things about the way the mother cared about the child she was carrying. The adoptive parents felt they would be able to discuss the birthmother with their daughter in the coming years because she had loved and planned for her child, even though she could not keep her. This was what the birthmother wanted. She won, they won and the little girl won.

One of the issues that at times causes couples to put limitations on the choice of the baby they are searching for is the drug involvement of the biological mother. People seeking babies at times become alarmed over the potential drug use of the biological parents and how it will affect their newly adopted child. How alarmed you might be will tell you how far you can go in this area. If you want a child whose mother has never experimented with drugs, you might find yourself very limited in today's drug-oriented culture. On the other end of the spectrum, however, are mothers who are addicted to heavy drugs like heroin. The chances are you would know this before the child was born. In fact, the greater the contact between you and the biological parents, the more likely you are to know all these kinds of personal things. You are certainly in as good a position to find out this information as any social worker with an adoption agency. I think prospective adoptive parents should seek information about drug use, alcohol use and tobacco use, all of which may be harmful to the child. Would you eliminate a child if you discover that the mother used marijuana regularly? Would you eliminate that child if the mother smoked a pack of cigarettes a day while she was pregnant? Two packs a day? I don't know what your limits are, but you need to know what they are. You will also find that they change with time and disappointment.

Intellectual limitations are another factor about which people are frequently concerned. If you feel it is extremely important for you to have a child who is likely to be bright, how can you go about searching for that kind of child? As with all limitations in what you can accept, this also limits the potential for finding a child. On the other hand, if you feel strongly about it, you should limit where you search for a child. Maybe you should seek a child from a woman in college. You should also make it clear to those you contact that this is an important criterion to you. This doesn't assure you the child will be bright . . . neither does having your own biological child. This merely *increases* the chances of your child being bright.

Some kinds of situations that might produce a child for you are predictable and you know they will be acceptable. These are easy to define ahead of time. You won't be able to anticipate every situation, but if you are comfortable about your ability to solve problems as they arise, unexpected situations won't become major problems for you.

Mary Lou and Greg were delighted when they heard from a physician about a young girl who just had a baby and would be willing to give it to them. They tried to keep calm by talking about their "maybe baby" in case the whole deal fell through. They did not want their other adopted child to be too disappointed if the plans did not work out. They entered the situation very confident of their ability to handle an independent adoption. The biological mother wanted to nurse the child for a couple of weeks before she gave it to them; this obviously, created ambivalent feelings for them. It was nice for the baby but caused fear for Mary Lou and Greg, who worried that the bonding might cause her to change her mind. Then the biological mother became ill and she asked them to come early to get the baby. Naturally, Mary Lou and Greg were more than willing. They drove the one hundred and fifty miles in a state of joy. But as the end of the journey approached, the pending meeting with the biological mother began to concern them. What if she didn't like them? What if she changed her mind? What would they talk about? They finally reasoned that the only way to solve their fears was to confront them. The biological mother had something they wanted, a baby, so she was in a position to call the shots. They decided they would just have to take whatever came. After meeting the biological mother and their "maybe baby," they wanted to grab the baby and run. Instead, they handled the situation with what appeared to be relative ease. When they heard that the mother had named their baby boy they said nothing, because that could be dealt with later. When the biological mother offered them numerous items for their new son, they graciously accepted them even though they wanted nothing but their child . . . everything else seemed to make their son more hers. They handled each unanticipated surprise from her smoothly, much more smoothly than they thought they could. They were taking care of things that they could never have anticipated. They did not anticipate a visit from the maternal grandparents the second week they had their son at home, but they weathered that potential crisis also. They found the limits that they had set were helpful in many ways, but many issues they were forced to confront were unexpected. Later, as they reflected on their son's adoption, they expressed the opinion that some aspects made it better than their previous agency adoption. The secrecy was gone. Everyone felt good about everyone else. The weaning process for the biological mother seemed healthier than for her having to give up the baby to an agency worker. The magnitude of the emotional response from the grandparents seemed lessened by their chance to meet the people who would be raising their first grandchild. The biological mother knew what kind of a home Mary Lou and Greg had, knew the town her child would be raised in, knew about the sister her child now had, and she could feel comforted in her knowledge. People ask Mary Lou and Greg how they would feel if the birthmother stops their son some day after school and tells him she is his mother. They answer that he would be curious but it would not be any big issue because he already knows about her and he knows his "real" mom and dad are the ones who adopted him. They are secure in their relationship with him. They don't feel they own him; they just have had a fantastic opportunity to borrow him and raise him. They feel very fortunate. They are.

One of the primary advantages of having significant interaction with the biological parents is that you grow to know them. One mother of two adopted children, one a private adoption and the other an agency adoption, discussed what this interaction had meant to her. She said she knows more specific details about her first child, a son adopted through the adoption agency; she knows all sorts of medical and historical information about his family. She continued by saying that she knows far more about the parents of her daughter who was adopted privately because she met them. This adoptive mother says, "I can tell my first child facts about his parents, but for my second child, I can really tell her about her parents because I know them as people and I can pass on feelings to her about them. I wish I could give this same advantage to my son."

Most of us know we can significantly improve the health and maybe even mental state of our child if we can control certain prenatal factors. Nutrition is one essential ingredient in the health of an unborn child. If you could choose the mother of your child, I am certain you would hope that she eats properly during her pregnancy. If you have to choose, however, between a child whose mother ate poorly during her pregnancy and not having a child, which would you choose? It is well known that good prenatal care decreases the potential problems of the unborn child. If you could choose the mother of your child, I am certain you would hope she gets regular prenatal medical care. If you have to choose, however, between a child whose mother did not receive any prenatal care and not having a child which would you choose? Increasingly, evidence supports the belief that the mental state of the mother during her pregnancy can affect her unborn child. If you could choose the mother of your child, I am sure you would want her to be as relaxed and at peace as possible during her pregnancy. If you have to choose, however, between a child whose mother was under great stress and duress during her pregnancy or not having a child, which would you choose? Your choices are limited. Compromise is essential. Compromise only as far as you are reasonably comfortable, but strict limitations, no matter how well placed, are limitations on your finding a child.

Establishing Priorities Establishing priorities in your search is essential. This is, of course, closely related to limits. The priorities really tell you what your choices would be, while your limitations tell you how far down your priorities you can go. As you go down your priority list, you are likely to enlarge and expand the kinds of situations you are willing to experience to get your child. As you go down your list of priorities, you are likely to expand your limits.

People can set priorities for different reasons. They may be set by how likely that area of search is to yield a child or may be related to how likely you are to get a specific kind of child. Again, you have to decide what you want, which then determines how and where you start to look.

In setting priorities, you set up what it is you most want if you could choose. Then you work down the list until you reach what would not be comfortable with any of the choices left.

One of the areas discussed later in this and the following chapter is kinds of places to search for children. In order to begin your search, you need to determine which of these suggestions are the best ones for you. You can begin once priorities are established.

Presenting Yourself Now you know what you are looking for, how far you will go and what you would most like in a child. The next step before you actually start making contacts is to prepare something to leave with each of the contacts you make . . . an information sheet about yourselves.

Resumes have been proven effective in employment searches. There is every reason to believe they would be helpful in a search for a baby also. A resume or information sheet shows the people who are evaluating you not only how serious you are, but it also serves to remind them of who you are. The same logic applies if you want a baby. You want the people to remember who you are and to have some way to contact you if they hear of any potential children. Your contacts might also choose to pass your information sheet along to others, which of course would enlarge your number of contacts.

Ideally, your information sheet will have a picture of you on it. Let the picture truly represent you. The formal picture represents a formal person. The serious picture represents the serious person. Choose your picture carefully, keeping in mind how you want people to remember you as well as how you would best come across to the pregnant woman to whom you are trying to appeal.

To leave a document like this with numbers of people obviously destroys your chances of remaining anonymous. On your information sheet you should have a name, address and phone number. You should indicate your willingness to receive collect calls. You see how vulnerable you are becoming. Be prepared for some calls you may not like. You can, if you wish greater protection, leave the number of an intermediary. Lawyers, for a fee, are willing to do this, but this could turn off some good sources.

Your information sheet should include something about your interests. Do you ski? Do you play the piano? Do you like camping? What do you do for a living? How far did you go in school? You want the interests you list to appeal to the group to whom you are trying to sell yourself. Again this argues for understanding the population group you are trying to convince to place a child with you . . . usually this means young people.

Worth reporting on your information sheet is how long you have been searching, how important this is to you, or why you can't get pregnant. You are trying just a bit to tug at the birthmother's heartstrings. You want to consider her emotional side and convince her that as a pregnant woman she would be doing a service for the world or for you by giving her child to you. Don't be maudlin but don't be too aloof. People open their hearts to other real, down-to-earth people in our society.

With this sheet in hand, you are ready to begin making contacts. Emphasis so far has been on the fact that someone out there has something you want. Remember though, you too have something important. You have love and a home to offer to some child.

Contacting Everybody

Now your work begins, but this can also be fun. You are about to meet many new people in a way you are unlikely to have met people ever before. You are about to boldly ask a lot of people to help you with your problem.

Everybody you meet is a potential contact for a baby. Everywhere you go, you need to figure out a way to bring this subject into your conversation. Every time you talk to someone you should leave your sheet about you with them; just because they don't have an immediate suggestion for you doesn't mean they won't have one in a week or two. Everyone you talk to is a source of other contacts. Ask people for suggestions of others to contact.

While any of these random contacts might possibly result in the lead you need, there are some specific places that you are most likely to find a baby. These are not presented in any special order, but rather you should put them in the order that seems appropriate to you and your priorities and limitations. The places suggested are places that are likely to have contact with young people, pregnant women, women in trouble and women with financial problems. These are the places you are most likely to find someone who would consider your proposal of adopting her child.

Physicians Historically, physicians, especially obstetricians and gynecologists, have been sources of potentially adoptable babies. This has significantly changed in recent years and adoption has been replaced by abortions and the keeping of babies in unwanted pregnancies.

The fact that there are fewer babies available from physicians should not eliminate them from the sources you contact in your search for a baby. You are only looking for one baby. Any potential source is worth exploring.

The best way to approach the physician is through a personal contact. Certainly if you know any physicians, tell them your story. Ask them to talk to their physician friends. Ask your friends to mention your adoption desires to their physicians. Basically, any way to make the contact personally increases its effectiveness for you. You probably can't contact every single physician in your city in a personal way. Contact as many as possible personally and just write to others. Go as far as you can.

With each of your contacts, be sure to leave your information sheet. If your contact mentions they might know of someone they could speak to about your case, leave them an extra copy or two. Ask them if they would suggest anyone else in particular whom you might contact. Ask for their help.

Lawyers Lawyers are basically in the same category as physicians. They used to know about adoptable babies. With the decreased supply of babies for adoption, they have found themselves much less involved in adoption placements. However, from time to time, lawyers still have a child for whom the biological parents say they want a lawyer to find a home.

Again, the personal approach in making contacts with lawyers is the best way. Contact every lawyer you know. After you have contacted the lawyers you know, try to make personal contacts with as many others as possible. You should be certain to contact any lawyers you hear about who have been involved in any adopted children placements. Try to find the names of lawyers who work a lot with the groups with whom you are trying to make contact. Lawyers giving seminars on college campuses, lawyers serving in free clinics, lawyers who work with poorer people, these are the lawyers most likely to hear about a child who might be available.

Tell each of the lawyers you contact of your circumstances and ask them to help. Ask them to pass the word along so that they, hopefully, make contacts for you also. Be sure to leave your information sheet with them.

Some lawyers will have suggestions about babies that sound more as if they are being sold than that they are being placed for adoption. This is an area you will have to explore carefully and cautiously.

Lawyers are always involved in adoption. At the point the adoptive parents go to court to finalize the adoption they are represented by an attorney. The involvement at that level has nothing to do with contacting a lawyer to find a child.

As with any of the contacts mentioned, the more the better. Your information sheet, mailed to many of the local attorneys may be all it takes to find the baby you want.

Groups of Adoptive Parents While it doesn't seem that adoptive parents would be a source of adoptable babies, they certainly can be. Once you are involved with adoption you seem to remain involved. People who have adopted children, who have gone through the agony of infertility studies, and who have shared the excitement of getting a child through adoption seem to be eager to help others.

Virtually all major metropolitan areas have "parents of adopted children" groups. These groups usually meet regularly as a social group and to offer a support system for adoptive parents. You can get names of these groups from your local adoption agencies by simply calling and asking for the names from the switchboard operator or the receptionist. At times these groups are specialized like the Open Door Society—a group of parents of children from mixed racial backgrounds.

"Parents of adopted children" groups will be one of the most understanding of all the groups you might contact ... they know the desire to have a child. They will be able to tell you of contacts they have found helpful. They also have an exceptionally large, informal network. Adoptive parents have a great deal of information on adoption. Most people who have adopted a child would love to help you adopt a child.

Be sure to leave your information sheet with strategic members of the group. Ask if you can check back with them from time to time. The groups change, so each meeting may be attended by a different nucleus of people. At times, the groups will have speakers on topics pertaining to adoption. The speakers are also potential contacts for you.

This is an excellent source group to ask for names of others to contact. Find out how each got their children. Some of them will have ways you had not thought of that might work for you.

Infertility Groups Most infertility groups would not be a good source for children to adopt; they are, however, a good source of information. They are also a good source of support for people experiencing difficulty accepting their infertility.

You can locate infertility groups in your area in several ways. Sometimes the adoption agencies will know the names of people who are active in infertility groups. RESOLVE, Inc. (P.O. Box 474, Belmont, Massachusetts 02178) is a national group with local chapters throughout the United States. If you write them they will tell you of groups in your area. Large metropolitan areas are likely to have groups like the Infertility Association of San Diego. You can even contact the local medical association and get the names of doctors working in the area of infertility or ask your own doctor if any groups of people experiencing infertility meet with regularity in your area.

Not everyone in an infertility group is in competition with you to adopt a baby. Some people who experience infertility will choose to attempt to correct the problem or they will remain childless. They do not necessarily consider adoption. So at times, your contact with members of these groups might lead to information about an adoptable child.

The primary reason for contacting an infertility group would be to enlarge your contacts. The more people who know of your desire, the greater your chances of finding a baby. Leave your personal information sheet with some of the group members. Don't hesitate to call again to let them know how important this is to you.

Free Clinics One of the best available sources for potentially adoptable children is the free clinic. Free clinics are a relatively recent health care delivery service designed to appeal to groups of people who might not use the regular health services provided by private physicians. The free clinics are used especially by young or poor people, both groups which are likely candidates to consider placing a child for adoption.

I use the term free clinic as a concept of health care . . . not all of the groups are called this. Included in this large group would be Planned Parenthood, Birth Control Institute, Birthright, Women's Clinic, Feminist's Clinics and Free Clinic. Each town has a different list of names, but they are groups which provide contraceptive information, pregnancy testing, pregnancy counseling, vasectomies, venereal disease testing, pelvic exams, pap smears, alternative life style counseling, general health care sevices and counseling to young people, minority groups and poor people.

You can find out the names of individual groups like these in your town by checking several sources. Check with young people, they know the names . . . it's probably their source of the pill. Another way is to check local newspapers under the personal section . . . frequently you will find ads for free pregnancy tests or birth control information. A third source of information to identify these local clinic groups is the newspapers which are designed for young people. College newspapers or counter-culture papers frequently have advertisements or articles about these groups.

All of these groups are similar, and they are usually staffed by volunteers. Since they use volunteers, especially for the information and counseling services they provide, they have a great deal of turnover and numerous part-time staff members. Their survival depends on bringing in large numbers of people as volunteers. A lot of information is shared from one group to another. In some areas they have interagency council meetings to share what they are doing and as a result, this further increases their similarities.

Few of these agencies understand the difficulties encountered by the couple wishing to adopt a child. The volunteer workers have a tendency to view adoption as a bleak alternative to an unwanted pregnancy which is much more difficult and time consuming for a woman to follow than having an abortion. As a result, the volunteers seldom mention adoption to the woman who says she wants an abortion. The volunteer doesn't even think about abortion as an alternative. This is the attitude you need to change. You want to help the volunteer think about adoption as an alternative.

You need to talk personally to as many volunteers in each agency as possible. Tell them about your problem. Inform them about adoption. Let them know personally of someone who desperately wants a baby. Then the next time they give an unhappily pregnant woman her positive pregnancy test results, they can discuss with the woman this neat couple they met the other day who really has been searching everywhere trying to find a baby to adopt. That approach is so much more effective than giving them statistics on the lack of available babies for adoption.

It will help to have the supervisors in these groups learn about adoption and about you. But to really make the potential contacts, you need to talk directly with the workers who are dealing with the pregnant women. They are the people who need to know about you personally.

Planned Parenthood is probably the best known of these type of groups. I have talked with many of their volunteers who never even thought about adoption as a viable alternative to an unwanted pregnancy. Yet they are providing pregnancy counseling daily for thousands of women with unwanted pregnancies.

As you finish talking with each worker, leave your information sheet with her. She can help spread the word for you. Many of these volunteers are young people themselves. Contacting these volunteers becomes a double contact. They will pass your information along to the clients they serve and they will also tell their friends. Your sheet may be given out to the next pregnant woman they counsel or it might be taken home to their roommate.

Of all of the most likely sources of finding a baby, I think groups like the free clinic provide the greatest potential for success. This is especially true if you are the kind of person who would appeal to young people or if your story is especially appealing. Check out the local groups in your area and spend some time there.

High Schools Many pregnant women are young; therefore, it is worth your time to contact schools who work with this age group. At times this might even include junior high schools, but pregnant girls are more likely to be found in high school.

The schools may or may not be aware of the numbers of their students who are pregnant. Certain staff members, those who relate well with young people, are most likely to know. Schools are under considerably greater restraint than free clinics in dealing with matters such as pregnancy. How openly pregnancy and other personal matters are handled greatly depends on the individual staff members of the school. I remember one school counselor who said he would never let a pregnant girl leave his office until she had called her parents and told them of her predicament. He would probably not have this problem often because pregnant girls would learn this and never come to him. What you need to find out is to whom the young people in the specific school talk. One way to find out who these staff people are is by asking some of the students who the best teachers and counselors are. They will tell you. The school personnel they tell you about are excellent contacts.

Besides the people the students talk to when they are in trouble, other staff members are sometimes in a position by nature of their specific assignment to know of pregnant girls. Physical education teachers are frequently the first ones to realize a young girl is pregnant. Make contact with the physical education department in as many schools as you can. The school nurse knows about anyone getting sick, even with morning sickness. She is worth contacting. These are both sources found at any high school.

Another source worth checking is the high school pregnant minors program. These are special programs (usually held at only one school in each district) that are designed to keep the pregnant girl attending school rather than dropping out. Young girls who have elected to abort their pregnancies will not be in these programs, but most of the young women in the programs are planning to keep their babies. Occasionally, a pregnant girl may be planning on placing her child for adoption or a "keeper" may change her plans.

The teacher of this kind of class is usually specially selected for the ability to work with these young women. The school, recognizing that these young women are very prone to drop school, tries very hard to find teachers who relate well with youngsters in trouble. These are certainly teachers worth talking to about your problem.

At times teachers invite couples in to speak with their classes about trying to find a child to adopt. The teachers are usually careful to balance these presentations with talks by young women who keep their children. These presentations are made to help all of the pregnant women in the class consider fully the reasons they are choosing the alternative they have selected. Some women will change their minds as they continue with a pregnancy. They may change their minds after they hear about someone who wants a baby or maybe they will change their minds after they hear about the problems of raising a child when you are still in high school. The fact that this important teacher knows about you, or the fact that this young pregnant woman heard you talk in her class, might result in your getting a child. You are trying to be in the right place at the right time.

A source similar to pregnant minors programs are the continuation high schools that many school districts have. These are schools where students who are not doing well in the regular high school are sent. Usually each school district has one continuation school. The staffs of these schools are also selected to work with students who have problems and who, without special treatment, are likely to quit school. These are good people to contact.

Since these classes are very small and frequently are run on a one-to-one basis, the teachers usually know the students very well. They not only know how the students are doing academically, but they also know a lot about the student's personal life. The teachers often know about pregnancies. Students are likely to seek out teachers they know on a personal basis to discuss their problems with and to seek advice.

You are not only telling each of your contacts in the schools about you, you are also telling them about the whole adoption picture. These school personnel to whom students go about their pregnancies need to know about adoption if they are to talk knowledgeably about pregnancy alternatives. You are helping them to understand the current picture of adoption through a personal perspective.

Schools are a potentially great source of contacts for you if you get to the right people. Some members of the staff would be of no help to you. The teacher who hid his own niece for the last five months of her pregnancy is unlikely to be a good contact. The teacher who believes that school personnel shouldn't be involved in a student's personal life and that school is only a place to learn is unlikely to be a good contact. Find the right members of the staff or your contacts will be very discouraging to you.

The place to start to make contacts in the schools is *not* at the top. Don't contact the superintendent or the principal to ask permission to do something they would rather not know about . . . many of them would rather be in the dark. Contact individuals, not schools. This is a personal matter between you and another individual. No one needs to approve or disapprove of your conversation. If you go to the superintendent for permission, you will be refused because this is not a matter in which the schools want to be involved. If the school finds out what you are doing, they may tell you to stop. Fine, stop, but hopefully at this point you will have contacted several people. You may have contacted the very one you needed to find your baby.

With each of your personal contacts, leave your information sheet. They need something by which to remember you. It is not enough for them to remember your story . . . that's easy. But if they have a potential child for you, you want them to have your name and phone number or some way to contact you. Remember to ask everyone to keep your information sheet. A note on the sheet would help, like "Please don't throw me away."

Another worthwhile piece of information to get from each contact you make is whether they would have any suggestions of people you might contact. Maybe they can give you the name of the next teacher you should talk with or maybe they know a minister or doctor to call. Have everyone you contact be a source of further creativity of where you might find a baby. The other reason to ask for suggestions is to involve them on any level with helping you. You want your contacts to be interested in your search. You need their help.

Colleges Working with the staffs of higher education institutions is slightly easier than working with high school staffs. These people are no longer working with minors and, as a result, they are less restricted by parents and fear.

Work in the same way as you did with the high schools. Find the staff members who talk to students on a personal level. Being eighteen and older does not preclude students from seeking help from their teachers. Teachers are one of the adult groups students know about so they sometimes seek help and advice if the student trusts the teacher.

Colleges also have counseling staffs. If the pregnant woman doesn't know where to go, she may seek help from the counseling staff. This, as always, varies with how good a job the specific counselor does ... the word passes quickly on every campus.

One new possibility in colleges is the health services center. The high school had its nurse who was limited to providing a place for the sick student to rest. At the college level some of the health services are extensive—some colleges do pregnancy testing and counseling right on campus. Of course, these are valuable staffs to contact.

Tell each of your contacts your story, enlist their help, get new names for further contacts and leave your information sheet. You are getting this down to a science. None of the individual contacts takes a long time but all of your contacts can be very time consuming. Don't give up ... all you are looking for is one contact to succeed.

School-Age People While contacting school people is a good way to find out about pregnant young women, so is contacting young people directly. Young people are very open. Subjects that adults may hesitate to talk about are casually discussed between young people who barely know each other. Young people can also be very open with adults, too.

Talk to any young people you know. Ask them if they know about anyone who is pregnant. Tell them about your problems finding a child to adopt. Enlist their help.

You can find young people to talk to all around you. Besides the ones you know well, extend yourself and talk to those you don't know very well. Talk to the adolescents or the twenty year olds who live on your street. Think of which of your relatives have children who fall into the right age category. Talk to your best friend's young baby sitters. All of these are people with whom it would be worth discussing your problem.

Specific places where young people are likely to be are good places to go to meet them. Go to some of the concerts that appeal to young people and try to talk with the people who sit next to you. Go to the ski movies or the surfing movies and be friendly with those around you. When you eat, go to the restaurants that adolescents or young adults frequent and meet people. The ice-skating rink, the billiard center, the youth-oriented dress shop are all potential sources of contacts.

Another potential source is hitchhikers who are the right age. You have the advantage in this situation of talking on a one-to-one basis with a young person who might give you a lead. The open response might surprise you. When I was doing a study of teenagers' emotional responses to their abortions, I regularly stopped to give hitchhikers a ride and asked them if they knew of anyone who had an abortion. I told them about my study and how I wanted to interview teenagers who had obtained abortions and to talk to them about their responses to the procedure. Without hestitation, I got the names of other young women who had abortions. When I called these complete strangers and told them what I was doing and how I heard about them, every one of them was willing to be interviewed. I was really surprised. I found that I was more reluctant to ask them to help than they were to respond.

Again, be sure to leave your information sheet with each person. If they don't know anyone who is pregnant now, ask them to keep it in case they hear of someone later.

Those most likely to succeed in this approach are people who can readily talk with young people. If you feel this is impossible for you, try to find someone who would be willing to make some of the contacts for you. That isn't quite as effective as doing it yourself, but it is far more effective than not doing it at all.

One million young women between the ages of fifteen and nineteen get pregnant each year. You are trying to get your information and your story to some of these women at the right time so they will consider adoption as an alternative to their unwanted pregnancy. One of these million babies is all you are trying to find.

Friends, Neighbors, Acquaintances and Everyone Now, if you have exhausted the method of direct contact with young people, it is time to begin to check with your friends, relatives and acquaintances. Here you are probably aiming at the parents of pregnant girls more than the pregnant girl herself.

Many times the mother of a pregnant girl is very involved with her daughter and her pregnancy decision. To find out that a daughter is six months pregnant would be startling to most parents. At that point, the parents may inform their pregnant daughter that they will not raise her child for her. The daughter, who may have been counting on this arrangement, may now consider adoption where before she was planning on keeping her baby with Mom's help.

You are trying to make contacts with parents or friends of a pregnant woman. This means that contacts with lots of people have the possibility of paying off. Talk to everyone. Your neighbors are a contact. They have relatives and friends to whom they will spread the word for you. People you meet at the coffee shop or at the bus stop are contacts. The clerk at the maternity shop where you are shopping with your friend is a contact. Your grocery clerk and the person bagging your groceries should all hear about your efforts. The lady with the little girl who sits next to you on the airplane; tell her how cute her daughter is and how much you are hoping to find a child. If nothing else, you will find people fascinated to hear how you are going about trying to find a baby and they will also learn about the current state of adoption. Hopefully it will also lead you to a child.

In Southwestern communities bordering Mexico, there is a large Mexican population that at times knows of available babies. For people wanting to adopt children with a Mexican background, this can be an excellent source. The fact that most Mexicans are likely to be Catholics who disapprove of abortion makes this group a likely place to hunt for a child to adopt. Mexican women may know of people who have chosen not to abort but who are financially unable to raise a child. You may be just the right solution for someone's pregnancy problem. To hear of the right people at the right time might work out to everyone's advantage.

Friends or strangers, it doesn't matter; you need to spread the word about your search. Leave your information sheet and your personal story with people. Any contact has the possibility of being the one you need. Since these contacts are all so varied, you have to modify your approach depending upon whomever you are contacting. Perhaps it is clearer now why it is important to start with a knowledge of capabilities, limits and priorities for your search. Knowing where you are on a search gives you the basis to know who to approach and how to approach them . . . it is your framework for looking everywhere.

Advertising

Advertising for a baby may seem like a radical approach to finding a child, but is it really? You are trying to contact as many people as possible. The media is one method of doing this. Fifty years ago you hung a notice in a conspicuous place and everyone for miles around knew exactly what you were hunting for. Today it would be almost impossible to contact everybody in a radius of so many miles. As a result, newspapers, radio and television seek to inform people. We have of necessity modernized our methods or we would not be able to communicate effectively. All advertising is a means of communicating. You are trying to tell people in a specific area what you want, so you advertise.

If you want money for your business, one way to get it is to advertise. If you want a new partner to come into the business with you, you might find one by advertising. If you want a wife, you might find one by advertising. If you want a baby, you might find one by advertising.

There are many kinds of advertising you might use. You can type a card and put it on the bulletin board at Safeway and the laundromat; they will let you keep it there for a specific length of time. You can take out an ad in the local newspaper or in a specialty advertising supplement that is mailed to every house in a certain area. You can have flyers printed that you distribute to sources you think might get you a child. You can advertise in magazines that have national distribution. These are all ways of advertising.

If you want to advertise for a baby, some states have specific laws about how it may be done. You should check out the laws in your state. Some states will allow written or typed advertisements that are personally placed as long as they are not printed; other states have no objections to the concept of advertising as long as you do not become involved in "buying" a child. The laws pertaining to advertising are not always clear-cut, nor are they always enforced.

Two couples in one area of California elected to advertise for a child. Their methods were different and so were their results. Pat and Ray had two adopted children and were told by both of their local adoption agencies that they could not adopt another child. Pat and Ray were both very open to having contact with the biological parent(s). Pat was also a school counselor who had a lot of experience talking with young people and she felt she would be at ease interviewing women who might be the birthmother of a child she would raise. So, they decided to advertise for their baby. They chose the local university as a place to put their ad because they reasoned it could increase the chances of finding a child from bright parents. The university newspaper unhesitatingly accepted their ad. They placed their ad after a long vacation period when they felt more young women were likely to be pregnant. Their ad ran for only one week and they heard nothing. In the meantime, one of their other contacts paid off and they found themselves adopting a baby after all. They canceled their ad and never found out whether it would have gotten them a child. They still believe it eventually would have.

Another couple, Heidi and Joe, had a different response. They too were turned down by both of the local adoption agencies. They also had circumstances they felt could appeal to young people. They placed the following ad:

Paralyzed Vietnam veteran and his wife really want to adopt a baby. Would you consider helping us? Call Heidi or Joe. Phone Number --- ----.

They chose the Pennysaver newspaper—an advertising supplement sent to all homes in a given area. They had a call within the week from someone who asked if they would be interested in a baby from Mexico. They indicated they would and within three months they had legally adopted a newborn baby boy. Right after they got their call about the Mexican baby, they received a second call. This call came from one of the supervisors who had turned them down when they applied at one of the local adoption agencies. She called to tell them that to advertise for a child was illegal and to query why they didn't apply for a child through legal channels by contacting an adoption agency. Heidi told her of their experience with the agencies. The supervisor told them that even if they had been rejected, they could not legally run printed ads for a child and so must stop. Heidi told her they would. Their ad, however, still got them their son.

Another couple in Florida recently published the story of their successful experience in advertising for and getting a baby. They pointed out the problems of crank calls they had to deal with and the long days (not months or years) of waiting they endured. They discussed their fears that it wouldn't work until the time they actually held their new baby. At that point, of course, the adoption agencies become involved in the legal proceedings but the couple had their baby. All they then needed to do was to go through the formal adoption process. They took a chance because they felt they had no other choice if they wanted a child.

Advertising is just another way to find a baby. It is simply a way to get people who want a child together with someone who has a child they don't want. Some people would feel comfortable advertising for a child and others wouldn't. Where do you fit in? You should do what you feel is right for you. There is no effective model as to how to advertise for a baby. This is a new way to find a baby that few people have used, so you must set up your own rules. You must be sure of yourself and your goal as you break new ground because some people will be critical of your method. It is easy to be critical of people who want a child so much that they would advertise for one; it is especially easy to be critical for people who already have the children they want.

Summary

Most people who want children would not as a first choice elect to go out and find their own child. Your first choice would undoubtedly be to simply get pregnant. Your second choice would most likely be to go to an agency and have them cooperate with you in finding a child for you. But if neither of these choices is open to you, you need to find another choice that is open and that choice is to find your own child to adopt. Despite the fact that finding your own child is probably your choice of last resort, there are some extremely positive benefits for you in adopting this way.

What a fantastic story to tell your child as he or she grows up! To share with her the tremendous desire you had for a child that you would go this far to find one. To share with him how much you gained from meeting and learning from others and from finding him. You would really have a special story to share.

Obviously there are risks involved in seeking a baby in this way. You have the same risks anyone has who is involved in a private independent adoption. You have the risks of being contacted by people who are upset with your method of adopting. You have the risk of not finding a child. You have to evaluate the risks versus the potential results. Not everyone should try this method. I don't know whether you should. I do believe searching for your own child is a method seriously worth considering. It may be the *only* way you will get a child.

Along the way you will find people who say you can't do this. Maybe you can't. If that is the case, stop. If you go out looking for all the things you can't or shouldn't do, you will find your options limited. It is one thing to set your own limits, but don't let others set your limits, at least not initially. Go as far as you want and if someone says you shouldn't go that far, you may have to revise your plan. Your other option is to not go very far at all. You may avoid all possible criticism . . . but you may miss your baby.

8
FARAWAY BABIES

Americans have always been a group to rally behind countries in need. Following World War II, Americans adopted many European orphans. More recently, after the Vietnam War, planeloads of orphans were flown to the United States for adoption. The adoption agencies handling these foreign adoptions were flooded with inquiries from people wanting to know how these children could be adopted. After earthquakes and other natural disasters, American couples seek ways to bring the orphans of the tragedies to this country for adoption.

The countries of the world respond differently to the generosity of the Americans. Some countries in need welcome the people who want to provide homes for children who would otherwise be a burden. At times this view changes radically as the foreign country is better able to provide for their homeless children. Then countries make adoption by foreigners much more difficult and sometimes impossible. At times, the only children allowed to leave are handicapped or sibling groups, while children who are easier to place are assimilated into families within the foreign country.

Some countries view adoption of their children the same way that some black people view adoption of black children by white families. They believe it undermines their pride and is, in effect, an insult. Americans pursuing adoption in foreign countries need to be cautious in approaching foreigners to avoid insulting their national pride.

International Adoption: A Changing Scene

International adoptions do not account for a very large segment of the children who are currently being adopted. We hear of it more today because of the scarcity of available infants and because of the publicity generated from the Vietnam baby airlifts. While the number of international adoptions is increasing, it still is only a small proportion of the adoptions in this country.

International adoptions are a constantly changing part of adoption. The rules and regulations regarding adoptions continue to be changed by each of the countries involved.[1,2,3] Individual states within the United States also change their rules regarding adoption of foreign children. It is hard enough to keep up with the state laws let alone trying to keep current on the numerous countries from which one might want to adopt.

A good example of the international changes in adoption is Korea. Korea allowed a significant number of children to be adopted following the Korean conflict. These were frequently children whose birthmothers were Korean and whose birthfathers were American. These racially mixed children had great difficulty being accepted into the Korean society. These children were adopted privately by people who knew of their situation in Korea and wanted to provide homes for them. The adoption of Korean children was significantly altered by Henry Holt, who later founded the Holt Adoption Program. His program significantly increased the number of children from Korea who were being placed in American homes. He publicized the plight of the children and began screening potential homes that wanted to take racially mixed children and children who had been orphaned by the war. As his group became more and more active in adoptions in this country, Korea went from allowing primarily private adoptions to adoptions involving agencies. Most of the Korean children now placed are entirely Korean and no longer racially mixed. Adoption has significantly changed over the years in this one country.

At times, countries will allow children to be adopted because they are unable to care for them. As "have not" countries gain greater economic stability, they are better able to care for all of their children and there are fewer to be adopted by foreigners. It is possible that large-scale international adoptions will eventually be a phenomenon of the past.

Changes are occurring in the United States in international adoptions. Up until 1978, international adoptions were frequently handled under the Department of Immigration. A private, cursory home study for those people who wanted to adopt a child from another country was often the result. A recent change in the law mandates that all international adoptions must have a home study by a state-designated agency. As a result, adoption agencies are usually taking over this function.

This change is good and it's bad. No one can fault a change based upon need. If unqualified families were adopting foreign children, extensive home studies would be indicated. However, there has been no indication that this was the case. There were criticisms of the Department of Immigration for its slowness in adoption proceedings and its lack of background for doing this type of work. If, however, the law was changed only to give additional power and control to the adoption agencies, I question the validity of the change.

Up until this law was passed, international adoptions were a viable alternative for getting a child if you were rejected by the adoption agencies. Now this new law puts prospective adoptive parents back with the adoption agencies who have already rejected them and this means that one alternative way of getting children has been taken from them. Once again, people who cannot meet the "ideal" requirements arbitrarily established by the adoption agencies are driven out of the mainstream to seek their children elsewhere.

A Different Way for Different People

International adoptions have historically been an alternate means of adopting children. The rules and regulations, while hard to follow, have usually been fairly easy to meet. The flexibility of the couple seeking to adopt internationally was met with flexibility in the screening criteria for choosing who was allowed to adopt internationally.

The trend toward tightening this screening is evident and alarming. For the most part, agencies are looking for couples to meet the same criteria they use for screening any other couple who wishes to adopt. The only visible difference seems to be that many times the adoption agency will allow people to adopt even if they already have more than two children. In general, adopting internationally follows many of the philosophical requirements as adopting a "special needs" child. Obviously no one can fault careful screening to make certain that people will be good parents. Unfortunately, we just don't know how to do it . . . neither do the adoption agencies.

Because the institutional criteria are becoming more rigid, it is likely that an increasing number of people will seek to adopt internationally, but privately. There are two ways one can adopt internationally . . . through an agency or privately. At times, in both types of adoption, the help of an additional private agency with international contacts is used.

There are some private agencies, developed over the years, whose goal is to find people to adopt homeless children from foreign countries. These groups are not like the regular adoption agencies who place many different kinds of children; they are only involved with international adoptions. They are like international contacts to find children to adopt. They help people deal with the international complexities of the process. A few of the groups that specialize in this service are:

Holt Adoption Program
Post Office Box 2420
Eugene, Oregon 94707

Families for Children
10 Bowling Green
Pointe Claire
720 Quebec, Canada

David Livingston Missionary Foundation Adoption Progam
Post Office Box 232
Tulsa, Oklahoma 74101

Los Ninos International Aid and Adoption Referral Center
919 West 28th Street
Minneapolis, Minnesota 55408

Friends for All Children
445 South 68th Street
Boulder, Colorado 80303

The Foreign Adoption Center, Incorporated
2701 Alcott Street, Suite 471
Boulder, Colorado 80211

If you want to adopt privately it is worth contacting these groups to see if they can help you. If you want to adopt internationally but through an adoption agency, the agency will tell you about these groups and will have you make contact with them at the same time you are working with the adoption agency. In order to work with these groups, you have to meet their criteria as well as that of the foreign country, your state, and the adoption agency if you are working with one. As you can imagine, it is a complex process.

With all this knowledge of the complexities involved in international adoption, you may still want to adopt a child from another country. Now you need to know how to do it. You need to have a thorough understanding of the process both for an agency adoption of a child from a foreign country and for a private international adoption.

International Adoption Through Adoption Agencies

Adopting a child from a foreign country with the help of an adoption agency is very similar to a regular agency adoption. Many of the criteria listed in Chapter 5, "The Adoption Agency Game," are applicable to couples wanting to adopt internationally. There are some differences in procedure, costs, criteria for selection and type of children available that you should be aware of before you begin. You also need to understand the difference between international adoptions involving an adoption agency and those which are privately arranged.

Procedures for International Agency Adoptions Adopting internationally isn't easy. Sometimes it's difficult to even know where to begin. If you are planning on going through an adoption agency, you first need to learn which agencies handle foreign adoptions. In order to obtain this information, you can call any adoption agency in your community. They should be able to tell you who is doing all of the foreign adoption home studies. Then you make the call to find out how you begin.

Every agency will be different, of course. In general, however, most adoption agencies will follow somewhat the same pattern. You are likely to have a group intake meeting, followed by a meeting between the agency worker and you and your spouse, then with each of you alone, ending with a meeting in your home. It is worthwhile to familiarize yourself with what the agency social worker is looking for in any adoption; therefore, carefully read over the "Agency Process" section in Chapter 5.

During each of the meetings you will have over the next several months, the social worker will be attempting to do two things. She wants to make certain that in her mind you will be appropriate parents for a child from another country. The second thing she is trying to do is to educate you about the adoption of a child from a foreign country.

Adopting internationally sounds very romantic. A beautiful foreign child arrives for you to save from his or her terrible fate. In reality, the children you receive are usually fearful, not grateful. Sometimes these children are not the beautiful children you have pictured in your mind but at times are undernourished, unhealthy, and may possess defects that look worse than they had sounded on paper. The child you hope will love you doesn't even understand the language you speak. The social worker is trying to help you to be realistic about what your expectations are for this foreign adoption and what the potential problems are that you must be prepared to confront in an adoption of this sort.

As the process continues, you will be encouraged to contact one of the international agencies supplying children to adoption agencies in this country. The adoption agency you are working with will tell you which agencies they have successfully worked with in the past and which agencies get children from which countries. Since you are going to be put on the waiting list of this international adoption agency as well as the waiting list for the adoption agency you are working with, you want to move ahead rapidly.

After you have met the criteria of both groups, you wait. In this interim, after you have been approved but have not yet received a child, some adoption agencies have monthly group meetings. This enables couples to meet others who are waiting or who have recently had children placed with them. These meetings can be a useful source of information to help you avoid problems that others have had when their child arrived. It is difficult, however, not to feel that you continue to be on trial to see whether you can win a child from the adoption agency which holds your fate. Screening continues until that child is not only here but is legally yours.

At some point, which is never as soon as you would like, the agency worker will tell you about a child who seems appropriate for you and that they are considering placing the child with you. Background information that is available to the agency will be given to you concerning the child. You are likely to hear far less in this type of adoption than in an adoption that is within the United States. This is one of the reasons that couples are carefully screened for their flexibility.

After you have approved the child on the basis of the information that is available, the process can take many different turns. Some countries at this point insist that one or both of you go to the country to formally adopt the child. Other countries let an intermediary, usually a lawyer, act in your name. In other cases, the guardianship of the child is given to the adoption agency. The agency holds it during the probationary period and until the adoption is finalized in the United States.

After guardianship is established, the child must get a visa to enter this country legally. His or her status gives the child a preferential treatment in this process. Even with this special status, all of the steps continue to take more time than you would like.

At last the child arrives. Undoubtedly, the child looks older than you thought because time has passed since the description of the child was made or the photograph was taken. Hopefully, at this point, all the education the adoption agency has given you, the meeting with others who have adopted internationally, and any material you have read about international adoption will have prepared you to handle this new child. Yet nothing can completely prepare you . . . this is something only you can experience.

Unfortunately, once you have your child you must wait again. The adoption agency continues to study you for your suitability for parenting. Adoption agencies maintain that this is to offer you support in a period of adjustment, but the possibility remains that your child could be taken away if you don't stay in the agency's favor. The only remedy is the finalization of the adoption in court. The adoption agencies seldom hurry this process.

The procedures to adopt internationally are complex. This is a long process that no one but you seems anxious to hurry along. There are some very positive benefits to be gained in this period. The educational process is extremely valuable. The amount of red tape that the adoption agency is handling for you is significant. But the continual screening and the necessity for you to meet unspecified and undocumented criteria for parenting causes confusion, dependency and mistrust. More importantly, it prevents feelings of security from developing between the child and the new parents.

Criteria for Parenting International Children The adoption agencies are looking for specific personality characteristics in the parents they approve for international adoptions through them. Most of these criteria were discussed in detail in Chapter 5. Along with these traits, they also want some additional characteristics demonstrated by parents who want to adopt children from other countries. International adoptions usually fit into the category of "special needs" children (See Chapter 9). They are frequently older children and many times they have "special" problems. The couples who can demonstrate a flexible and open approach to the child they might receive are the most likely ones to be approved.

In screening parents adopting normal Caucasian children from this country, the agencies want a childless couple or at a maximum, families with only one child. In international adoptions, couples with parenting experience are considered some of the best candidates to handle the "special" problems of these children. In fact, adoption agencies believe the couples best suited for these children are couples whose lives revolve around their existing children. This also fits in with the view that these international children are "special needs" children who will take a great deal of time and energy to raise properly because of their backgrounds. The optimistic view of most people adopting special needs children is another characteristic found in many of the people who successfully adopt children from foreign countries through adoption agencies.

Basically then, you stand the best chance of passing the adoption agency screening if you know what they are looking for in the parents they choose to receive their children. Do not pretend to be something you are not, but if you do not present that which the adoption agencies believe is necessary, be prepared to look elsewhere.

The Costs of International Adoptions The cost of international adoptions varies. Some agencies charge a percentage of the family's gross annual income up to their regular fee for an international adoption through their agency. The home study alone, which is necessary if you are going to adopt privately from another country and find your own child, is still several hundred dollars. These costs vary from state to state. Adopting internationally is not a bargain way to get a child.

One International Agency Adoption The Worth family is a good example of the kind of family that adopts internationally through an agency. The family consists of the parents, Doug and Janine, and their two children, Marni, eight, and Mike, seven. Adoption had never been an issue to them until they went to a program put on by their church one Sunday evening that discussed the plight of homeless children from different nations being adopted by American couples. This program, put on by a representative from the Holt Adoption Program really impressed the Worth family. They felt they had ample love and money to provide for a child from another country, so they made contact with the agency in their state which took care of international adoptions.

They went to the group meeting of all the couples interested in finding out about international adoptions. There were eight other couples who showed up out of an expected fifteen. The woman who gave the presentation sounded extremely discouraging about adopting from another country . . . in fact, more discouraging than encouraging. She seemed to imply that any couple who proceeded in trying to get a child from another country should be prepared for the very worst. The Worths left the meeting surprised because this wasn't quite what they had heard about international adoptions from the representative of the Holt Adoption Program.

They discussed the matter thoroughly with each other and with their children. They decided to go ahead despite the presentation of the worker from the adoption agency. They regained their enthusiasm and called the agency to begin the next step.

They met with another worker from the adoption agency who was only slightly more positive than the first worker. But by now they knew for sure this was something they intended to pursue. The worker liked them very much. They personified just what the agency sought from the couples with whom they wanted to place children. They were loving, optimistic and flexible. They had a stable marriage and sufficient income. They had many friends. Their religious background, while not an essential factor, was an additional plus. They were willing to take any child the adoption agency felt they could help. Their relatives supported the idea of an international adoption. Their neighborhood, which was primarily white, did have about twenty-five percent mix of different races; it would be easy to accommodate a racially mixed child into this kind of situation. Their children were as eager about the pending adoption as Doug and Janine were. This was just about all any agency could ask for.

Because the Worths so ideally fit into the agency's criteria, it was easy for them to work together. The Worths felt everyone went out of their way to make the procedure simple for them. The procedure went exceptionally smoothly for them.

Eight months after they heard the man speak in the church, the Worth family heard about the Korean child who was to be theirs. He was six years old and an orphan. He had been crippled at birth and walked only with the aid of crutches. The orphanage where he lived believed this handicap might be correctable. In Korea, however, there was no chance for him to have this corrected. He spoke no English. Everything seemed fine to Doug and Janine and they wanted to proceed.

Two months later their new son arrived. They were delighted. The boy wasn't too sure.

The first months weren't easy with him. He was quiet and seemed moody and unhappy. He didn't eat very much, but he did sneak food when no one was watching him. He slowly began to open up to them, but it wasn't instant family or instant love.

Within three months he was an active playmate for Marni and Mike who thought he was great fun. Surgery was delayed for at least a year to help him make an adequate adjustment to this country and his new home before he was put into another strange situation. They also did not enroll him in school because they felt it would be difficult for him to adjust to too many new things at one time. However, after several months, Doug and Janine decided he was ready to try.

Doug and Janine are really glad they heard the man from Holt. They don't plan on adopting any more children, but this additional bonus to their lives was just what they wanted. To them, the adoption was a complete success. They fit perfectly into the system so it was easy to feel comfortable with the fit.

Using an adoption agency can smooth out many of the complexities in adopting internationally. While the agency helps with the procedure they conduct an educational program on the cultural differences your new child will experience. This helps make adoption easier for you and for your new child.

At times the adoption agency's educational approach may discourage couples. People must be dedicated to the idea of adopting internationally and committed to proceeding despite the discouragement they will receive from many people, including the adoption agency. This ultimately becomes one of the ways people who are not certain of their course of action get eliminated.

The other way couples are eliminated is in their inability to meet the screening criteria of the agency. Even with the relatively small number of children who are adopted internationally, the adoption agencies have far more applicants than children. Ways are sought, even in international adoptions, to eliminate potential parents who apply. You significantly increase your chances of getting a child if you know what the adoption agency wants before you begin the process of trying to adopt a child from another country.

Private International Adoptions

Private international adoptions are similar to private adoptions within the United States. The variety of rules and regulations found from state to state in this country are similar to the confusion and differences among different countries. You will find many people who will discourage this type of adoption. These are the same people who discourage private adoptions in the United States. If you are easily put off with confusion and ambiguity, this type of adoption is not likely to appeal to you.

In a private international adoption, you need to do many of the same things you must do in a private adoption in the United States. You must find the baby. You must meet your own state's regulations and the regulations of the country from which you want to adopt. To do this you will need legal help in the other country as well as in this country. Besides legal help, you need a contact in the foreign country who will do the searching for a child to adopt. Unless you can go to the country, you will not be able to make all the necessary arrangements to find a child to adopt . . . that is why you need someone to help you in this critical area.

State Regulations The regulations pertaining to private international adoptions are different from state to state. Some states, in fact, do not allow private international adoptions. The only way you can be certain about your own state is to check.

Find a lawyer who knows about international adoptions. This is a very specialized area, so many lawyers will know very little about it. A good way of finding knowledgeable lawyers in the area of international adoptions is to get names from anyone who has adopted internationally. If you do not know of anyone who has adopted a child from another country, ask a lawyer you do know for names of lawyers who would know about international adoptions.

A qualified lawyer should be a valuable source of information on all aspects of international adoption. However, a lawyer should not be considered a substitute for what *you* need to know. When you have a fair understanding of what is involved in international adoptions, you will find the input from the lawyer is much more valuable to you.

Understanding Private International Adoptions It is very simple for me to say you *should* understand as much as possible about private international adoptions. To gain that knowledge isn't quite so simple. Yet there are many sources from which you can learn about adopting internationally. Even though we are discussing private international adoptions, you can profit from learning about any kind of international adoptions.

One of the ways to understand about private international adoptions is to make contact with others who have adopted in this way. The Organization for a United Response (OURS) (4711 30th Avenue South, Minneapolis, Minnesota 55406) has numerous chapters in the United States. Their major emphasis is on educating parents about adopting children from foreign countries. They also publish newsletters which are one of the best sources of current information on the rapidly changing international adoption scene. The Foreign Adoption Center, Incorporated (Post Office Box 3158, Boulder, Colorado 80302) is actually a licensed child placement agency, but it also provides information about foreign independent adoptions. There are also many agencies that help in making contacts; many of these operate in only one or two states and sometimes these groups come and go. Since many of the people working for these various groups are volunteers, there is a tremendous turnover in personnel. You need to check within your own state to see what groups are helping in the international adoption scene. The state agency that handles international adoptions can tell you of groups in the local area who will help people seeking to adopt internationally. These groups are usually made up of people who have adopted internationally and who are happy to help you in your adoption. These contacts with groups in the United States will be some of your most valuable sources of information. Explore them all!

Another source of valuable information is to read about others who have adopted internationally.[2, 3, 4, 5, 6, 7, 8] While each person's experience is different, learning how they handled the problems they had to confront can help you a great deal. Learning too, about the cultural adjustments of the child will help you to minimize the problems the adopted child will have. Many of the books on transracial adoptions are applicable to international adoptions also.[9, 10, 11]

Making International Contacts As you continue to increase your information on private international adoptions, you will learn of many ways to make contacts with people in foreign countries who might be able to help you find a child to adopt. If you already have a contact, it is much easier. Other people who have adopted internationally are also excellent sources of information about potential foreign contacts.

Your foreign contact person can be anyone who has the potential of getting you in contact with someone with a child to adopt. Americans living abroad or working abroad sometimes become contacts for people in the United States who are hunting for children to adopt. Foreign lawyers and foreign physicians at times act as contacts just as they do in the United States. Contacts who work in orphanages or with poor people in foreign countries also become involved in international adoptions and become contacts for people wanting to adopt a child internationally. People involved in religious work sometimes know of children needing homes and who are available for adoption.

You need to be able to trust the person who becomes your foreign contact person. It is somewhat like being able to trust your lawyer ... you depend on the accuracy of the information this person gives you. The best basis for trust is to have someone recommend a person to you. If others have used this person before in adopting, you know more about how this person operates and if he or she is honest.

If the intermediary you make contact with is not someone you know about, check with the United States Bureau of Consular Affairs staff in the country with which you are working. You may be able to at least eliminate known disreputable people who prey on people trying to adopt from a country that is foreign to them. The United States Consular staff is a good source to keep in close contact with throughout your adoption process.

The reason a couple will pick a specific country is frequently based on having a contact already there. This can greatly help in securing a child to adopt. Mel and Becky were helped in adopting their daughter by one of Mel's students. Mel taught college and became close to one of his students from Colombia. In having Juan come to their home for dinner several times, Mel and Becky were able to talk with him about one of their dreams ... to adopt a child from another country. Juan became actively involved in their dream. His family in Colombia located a four-year-old girl at an orphanage in a small town. She was available for adoption. Juan's family helped Mel and Becky make contact with a reputable lawyer who took care of all of the legal work for them. Mel and Becky went to their local adoption agency for a home study for this specific little girl. Everything went smoothly and because of their contact through Juan's family, all they had to do was pay the legal costs and send money for the child to come to this country. They also sent part of the fare for someone to accompany their new daughter and two other Colombian children who were also being placed for adoption in this country. Juan, Mel and Becky met the tired little girl at the airport. Juan helped bridge the language barrier for her and allayed the fears she had in this new country with these new parents. Juan also was a tremendous help in giving Mel and Becky an understanding of the cultural conditions in the country where this little girl had been living. Juan's knowledge of Colombia helped Mel and Becky avoid overwhelming their new daughter with new foods, new language and new customs. Juan and his family, in effect, took on the role that many agencies perform in international adoptions.

The importance of your contact person cannot be overstated. He or she is selecting a child for you and doing it in a country about which you know very little. You need to be able to trust and to depend on this important person.

Risks of Private International Adoptions The risks involved in adopting privately in an international adoption are greater than if you adopt internationally with the help of an adoption agency. The agency does a lot of work for you. They know ahead of time what to do to minimize problems. The adoption agency has lots of children they are working with and lots of couples so they have greater flexibility in meeting any specific demands you might have. However, the adoption agency approach also takes longer and you must take a more passive role in the entire procedure.

The risks also are greater in international private adoptions than in private adoptions in this country. Four reasons account for this increased risk. The first is the language barrier. The second factor is the meeting of international rules and regulations in addition to your own state's regulations. The lack of knowledge about your contact person also increases your risk in private international adoptions. And finally, the lack of ability to exchange information is also greater in this type of adoption.

The language barrier that must be surmounted in a private international adoption is significant. All information exchanged will need to be translated. When an adoption agency is involved, they do this for you. In a private international adoption, this is up to you. Literal translations will not substitute for someone who has a working knowledge of the language and who can help you understand the intent of the messages. It is always helpful to have someone who is thoroughly familiar with the language and the country with which you are working to assist you in the process.

Dual regulations of both state and foreign country involve risks. The risks can be minimized by using a lawyer, but it does add to the complexity of the adoption process. Before you begin an adoption of this kind, be sure that you are completely familiar with or advised about your own state's regulations. You will save yourself time and frustration if you do this at the outset.

Unfamiliarity with your contact person is another risk in private international adoption. In private adoptions in the United States, if you don't like what is happening you can fire your contact. In private international adoptions though, you probably won't even know what the person is doing. It is important that you obtain information about your contact person before you begin. In any private adoption, unscrupulous people can take advantage of people who want something very badly. Make certain you know with whom you are working.

The difficulty of having information exchanged about the child you are adopting is another risk that should be taken into account. In private adoptions in the United States, you may learn a great deal about your child. You may meet birthparents or even grandparents. In international adoptions involving agencies, they are likely to be able to give you some specific information about the child you are adopting. At a minimum you are likely to know about this child's medical background before you agree to the adoption. In a private international adoption, you may not know much at all about the child. Your contact might be able to get information but it may be minimal. The child is likely to have had at least some kind of medical checkup but it is difficult to anticipate exactly how healthy the child will actually be. You probably will not be able to learn any of the birthparents' medical history.

There are many unknowns in this type of adoption. Couples adopting internationally, but privately, have to maintain a flexible approach to the child they are going to receive.

One Private International Adoption In order to help you understand some of the complexities of international private adoptions it seems worthwhile to relate one couple's experience in some detail. This couple's adoption of their son is not typical because every international private adoption is different. The experience of Harold and Nina does, however, give a picture of what private international adoption is like.

Nina and Harold were a couple who inadvertently learned about private international adoptions. Nina and Harold were turned down by both public and private adoption agencies in their local area. Still, they were certain they would make good parents and they wanted a child. They decided they would try to adopt privately. Then they read a newspaper article about couples adopting in Mexico and contacted the woman the article mentioned, Helen, an American contact. Helen told Nina and Harold she would be glad to tell them about adopting a Mexican child and they agreed to meet. She explained how the adoptions worked, how long the wait generally was, the costs involved and what they would need to do to proceed. Nina and Harold were excited about the possibility and they eagerly began the process that would lead them to their son, Aaron, within six months.

They first wrote to an American woman who was the contact person in Mexico. They asked how they could get on her waiting list for a baby. She wrote back explaining they would need to send copies of their birth certificates, a copy of their marriage license, four letters of recommendation, pictures of each of them, and a letter from them explaining why they wanted to adopt a child from Mexico. All of these had to be translated into Spanish; they needed to send the original English copies as well. After these papers were received, she said she would contact them and tell them how many people were ahead of them on the list.

Harold and Nina moved ahead rapidly. Everything was mailed to the woman within six weeks. Three weeks later they received a letter from her saying that their papers had arrived. Since Nina and Harold had indicated their willingness to take either a girl or a boy, the woman from Mexico said their chances of an early placement were increased. She told them there were five couples ahead of them for a girl and only one couple ahead of them for a boy. She told them they currently had three women who were pregnant and planning on giving up their children for adoption. She explained that sometimes more women came in unexpectedly so that the number of potential babies at any time was difficult to predict. Nina and Harold were told they should prepare immediately for a trip to Mexico.

Their American contact woman, Helen, kept in touch with Harold and Nina throughout the entire process. They were invited to potluck dinners where many of the couples who had previously adopted children from Mexico proudly displayed their beautiful children. They discussed the problems of getting the babies, the waiting period and how to get the children back into the United States. The information that was passed from one family to the next was very helpful to Harold and Nina.

In the meantime, Harold and Nina contacted the state agency that was supposed to do a home study before they brought a child in from another country. They filled out the papers and waited for the agency to begin the study. Two months passed. In this period they moved up to the number one place for a boy. One couple on the list for a girl dropped out because they got a child through someone else in the United States. Things were moving right along for Nina and Harold in Mexico and the time for getting a child was rapidly approaching. This same rapid approach did not happen in the state agency that was supposed to do the home study for them. Helen reassured them they would be able to continue with the adoption even if the home study was not finished in time. That is just what happened.

Two days after their home study was finally started, the Mexican contact woman called to say another baby boy was born. Did Nina and Harold want him? They did. They flew to Mexico two days later to adopt their new son. They met the Mexican contact woman at the airport and she took them to their new son, Aaron, with whom they were delighted. His abundant dark hair was beautiful despite the constant look of dishevelment. They thought he was absolutely wonderful.

They had a chance to meet many other people who were actively involved in Mexico in trying to find homes for children whose birthmothers could not keep them. They met the doctor who delivered most of the babies and the lawyer who handled the legal matters. The personal approach each of the people took in the adoption of each child was impressive.

The procedure for them to legally adopt Aaron was very different than adoption in the United States. Fortunately, the Mexican contact woman was able to prepare them and inform them about how things were done in Mexico. The lawyer whom they had met was prepared to handle the case in court. He was also the one who was to give some extra money to the judge to make certain the adoption was expedited. This same lawyer also had the birthmother sign the relinquishment papers. At the last minute the birthmother said she wanted something in exchange for relinquishing the baby. This was expected. The lawyer and the birthmother agreed that a sewing machine would be a fair exchange and Nina and Harold readily agreed. The payments made to all of these people are highly irregular to our way of thinking ... it makes the adoption sound like an illegal or black market adoption. Yet in Mexico there was nothing irregular at all. Since Nina and Harold had already heard of the differences in Mexico they were not shocked. They felt the entire procedure was a bargain. In fact, it cost them less, including their airfare, than if they had adopted through an American agency. Besides that, they had a wonderful vacation in Mexico. In the four-day vacation in Mexico they had legally adopted their son ... in the United States that would have taken them over six months of waiting before the procedure could have been legally completed.

The primary flaw in Aaron's adoption was that because his home study had not been completed, Nina and Harold did not have the proper papers to bring him into this country. This had happened to many other couples so they knew what to do. It was legal for Aaron as far as the Mexican authorities were concerned . . . he had all the proper papers to leave Mexico. He had been legally adopted and everything else was in order but it was necessary to smuggle him across the border and they knew that this was illegal. They felt they had no other choice since the system was not set up to function in a way that could accommodate their circumstances. They knew when they went to get him that this was necessary and they were prepared.

Smuggling a baby into the United States sounds so undercover . . . it wasn't. They simply drove up to the border with him, were waved on, and they drove through . . . it really didn't turn out to be very exciting. One of the women who had previously adopted a child from Mexico had met them at the airport in Tijuana. The woman, a dark-haired woman, bundled Aaron up and held him as Nina and Harold drove across the border. Aaron slept through the entire operation.

They eventually completed their home study in the United States and Aaron received his proper papers to be here. Nina and Harold are not lawbreakers by nature . . . they wanted Aaron here legally.

The story of Nina, Harold and Aaron is an exciting account of a Mexican adoption. Their case may be different from others but it has some of the ingredients found in many private international adoptions.

—They had tried to adopt with the local adoption agency and were rejected.
—They didn't exactly know what to do next to get the baby they so much wanted.
—They stumbled onto the possibility of adopting internationally.
—They decided why not try something different since the other way hadn't worked.
—A lot of caring people gave them supportive help and information.
—They were adaptable to a different kind of culture.
—They flowed with the process.
—They could afford to go this route.
—They took the necessary risks and they got a baby!

Nina and Harold learned a tremendous amount about private international adoption. Since they adopted Aaron, they have helped dozens of others adopt. They didn't know when they began the process how much Aaron's adoption would change and open their lives. Not only did the experience of a new child change their lives, but their future involvement in helping others adopt has had a profound and permanent effect on them. They found themselves open to different experiences they never thought possible. The risks they took to adopt Aaron taught them about taking other risks also. Adopting Aaron changed their lives as much as it changed Aaron's.

Health of the Child Adopted Internationally

The health of the child you adopt is not always as clear-cut or medically sound as that in Aaron's case. He was delivered by a physician who provided some degree of prenatal care and care after he was born. This is seldom the case in internationally adopted children.

Since the children being placed for adoption are frequently from poverty-level parents, many of them are malnourished. You should assume that the medical care the children have received is minimal . . . in fact, it may consist of an individual check when preparing them for adoption.

You may have no way of knowing exactly what has occurred in the background of a child whom you are planning to adopt. When many of these children's birthdates are not even known, how can you expect to know medical and health histories? Once again, the couple's flexibility is essential.

In an international adoption handled by an agency you are likely to be told ahead of time about known medical problems . . . that health history is likely to be more complete than in a private international adoption. In private international adoptions your entire process is heading toward adopting a specific child that you may or may not know very much about until you are committed to the adoption. For many people, maybe for you, that poses no problem at all.

Private international adoptions are not for everyone, but for some people they are the best way to get a child. How comfortable you feel about this prospect, only you can tell. Babies are out there in the world to be adopted. If you want one and have decided this is a good way for you to proceed, go find one. Find the child you want, it's worth it.

Summary

Adopting internationally is probably not the adoption of first choice for most people. Ordinarily people adopt internationally because they have been unable to adopt through the ordinary ways in the United States . . . maybe because they were not qualified to apply or maybe because they were rejected by the adoption agency. The procedure to adopt internationally is more complex than adoption in this country, yet this way may be the only way a couple gets a child, especially a young child.

International adoption is a radically changing scene. New laws which differ from country to country constantly keep international adoption in a state of change. Recent trends seem to indicate that more regulations and restrictions seem to be closing off international adoptions as a good alternative means for people to adopt children.

Adopting internationally necessitates that those seeking to adopt this way are prepared for multiple demands. They must meet their own state's demands, the immigration department's demands, the foreign country's demands, the adoption agency's demands and the demands imposed on them by a new "special" child from a different culture. Only the hardy should apply.

9
THE
SPECIAL KIDS

No one has gained more from the current bleak picture in adoption than previously unadoptable children. "Special needs" children had little chance of being adopted only a few years ago. Couples who adopted had a choice and wanted "normal" babies and "normal" families; that left the "special needs" child languishing in the foster care system indefinitely.

In a similar way, "special needs" parents (See Chapter 10) were seldom considered as potential adoptive parents. If an agency had a choice between "normal" parents and "specials" they went with the former. Now that the adoption picture has changed, "special" children are available. At times, these "special" children fit best with "special" parents.

Does this mean that all the handicapped children are now being placed for adoption? No. Does this mean that all the handicapped parents seeking children are being accepted? No. But what has occurred in the changing adoption scene is that significantly more hard-to-adopt, "special needs" children are being placed than ever before. All that has changed for "special" adopting moms and dads is that they are sometimes considered "good enough" to handle some of the "special" kids who need a home.

Enough talk about "specials"! What does it mean? "Special" is a euphemism for hard-to-place, unadoptable, handicapped, mentally retarded, emotionally disturbed, racially mixed, previously unacceptable people. In the past, these children and these parents were shuffled aside so that large numbers of easy-to-handle, easy-to-place adoptions could go through the system. There was simply no time to get involved in the unusual and unfamiliar kinds of adoption cases.

Today, when you go to an adoption agency and you want to adopt a child, the children most available will be "specials." If you are willing to consider one or more of the "special" kinds of children available in the category of "special needs" children, you will be kept on the active list. This is true sometimes even if you, too, are a "special" potential adoptive parent.

Five groups of adoptees constitute the "special needs" children. Handicapped children are one group of "special needs" children. This includes physically, mentally and emotionally handicapped children. A second group would be those children who are harder to place because of their age; they are generally over three. A third group are those children from mixed racial backgrounds. The fourth group are sibling adoptions. Here there may be difficulty in placing two or more siblings in a single home. Finally, the fifth group are children who have been unsuccessful in a previous placement for adoption. At times these groups of "special needs" children overlap and you may have a child who falls into more than one category.

Most of the children considered "special needs" children are placed through adoption agencies. This is fortunate. The unique needs of these children almost preclude private adoption. These children need more careful screening and support systems than normal children. They also frequently need medical or psychological attention. The fact that most parents are not interested in adopting children in these categories means large numbers of parents need to be available in order to find the few who would be suitable for these children.

One of the major advantages with the agencies is their access to clearinghouse kinds of information on "special needs" children. The agencies share information about hard-to-place children and about parents seeking hard-to-place children. The Adoption Resource of North America (ARENA) (67 Irving Place, New York, New York 10003) facilitates the dissemination of information throughout the country on "special needs" children. Aid to Adoption of Special Kids (AASK) (3530 Grand Avenue, Oakland, California 94610) has a similar service. This agency is run by the DeBolts, who have done so much to publicize the adoption of "special" children. Another group, the North American Council on Adoptable Children, Inc. (3900 Market Street, Suite 247, Riverside, California 92501), provides "information, encouragement, and local contacts" for people interested in "special needs" children. These resources are rather like listing your house on a multiple listing; you significantly increase the exposure of your house by advertising and thereby multiplying the number of prospective buyers who know of its being for sale. Basically, that is what happens with these hard-to-place children. The adoption agencies advertise them to other agencies in the hope of finding a prospective parent for them. This listing has been a tremendous benefit in finding homes for "special needs" children.

In Chapter 5, I indicated that if you were unwilling to consider having a "special needs" child, you might not get very far in the application process with the adoption agencies. I believe it is beneficial for you not to eliminate any of these children immediately or the agency is likely to eliminate you. On the other hand, you should not take a child you do not want! The last thing these "special" children need is to be placed in a home that is unprepared or reluctant to have them. Be open about what children you would consider, but you can put the stops on at any tme you feel you have reached your limits. To go beyond what you would really feel comfortable with in a child is a disservice both to you and to the child.

Agencies do a great deal of screening of prospective parents of "special needs" children. They are seeking parents who sincerely want "special" children. They are trying to weed out those potential parents who are only settling for "specials" because they can't get what they really want. They don't want families to take a "special needs" child as a second choice or out of pity.[1] Ideally, I concur completely. However, many times these children are taken because no "normal" ones are available and they don't have much choice. If you don't have much choice, does that mean these children are not then second-choice children? Isn't adoption itself a second choice for most people? In actuality, many who adopt are taking these children somewhat out of pity. These are people who feel this would be a worthwhile thing to do, to take a child no one else wants. Others, labeled liberal or radical, take a hard-to-place child because they believe this will strengthen and improve our world.[2] These "do-gooders" can make good parents. Altruism has a place in parents too.

The primary intent in agency screening of potential adoptive parents should focus less on motivation for adoption of a "special needs" child and more on making certain that parents understand the potential problems as well as the potential joys of these children. Although it would be ideal for all parents of "special needs" children to be outstanding parents (this is true for all adopted children and children by birth as well), this is probably less critical than the people's willingness to be parents under these special circumstances. Certainly the same motivation is not always present in the parents who biologically produce a "special needs" child. Screening out is inappropriate but screening in is critical.

"Special needs" children need homes ... they need parents, they need families, they need houses, they need activities, they need stability and they need love. *They need to be adopted.* The potential is there for the children to be adopted. The potential is there for these children to have a chance to lead a more normal life. Every effort of the adoption agencies needs to be made to secure homes for these "special" kids.[3]

Handicapped Children as Adoptees

Usually when people think of "special needs" children, handicapped children—especially physically handicapped children—come to mind. Perhaps this is because we view children in a picture and a physical handicap is something we can most easily picture. We can imagine a child who is in a wheelchair or who is blind or who is in leg braces. Yet many kinds of handicaps are not handicaps we can see.

The decision to adopt a handicapped child needs to be seriously considered before beginning the adoption process. The variety of handicaps possible are far too vast for most people to grasp. In the past, the standard question of the adoption worker was would you consider taking a child with a correctable physical handicap? Adoptive parents had a choice, in fact, they had one of three choices as a way to answer the query:

1. No, I want a child who has no known physical problem.
2. Yes, I will take a child with a physical problem as long as it is correctable.
3. Yes, I will take a child with a minor physical problem.

The fourth choice that was not even mentioned to the adopting couple of the past was a child with a major problem that was not correctable. The only times these children were placed for adoption was when a couple *sought* a severely handicapped child. As you can imagine, this was not frequent. Children with handicaps, especially severe ones, were placed in foster home care indefinitely. Today, many of these children have a chance to be adopted.

Physically Handicapped Children What constitutes a physical handicap is not always clear. What appears to be severe to one person may not be considered a serious physical problem to someone else. Some couples would be overwhelmed to have a child who is epileptic; this same physical limitation in another home situation might be considered only as a minor inconvenience.

Before you begin to pursue adopting a child with a physical handicap, find out what kinds of physically handicapped children are available. Learn what these different handicaps might mean to your life. Most people have only heard of cerebral palsy; few people could describe what a child with cerebral palsy actually faces. Do you know? What about a child with spina bifada? What about a child who is deaf? What about a child without arms? The list could go on but you can get a general idea of the types of children who are in need of placement for adoption.

While you probably cannot know all of the physical handicaps a prospective adoptee might have, you can know some things in general about raising a physically handicapped child. Is it important to have a child who appears normal? Is it important to have a child who can be treated in a rural facility if your current home is not in the city? Is it important to have a child who can travel because travel is an important part of your life? Is it important to have a child who is not confined to a wheelchair because you have all of the bedrooms upstairs and no extra money to move or to change this? Is it important to have financial help if the child has significant medical bills which your family could not afford? Is it important that the child have the capabilities to live alone as an adult? You need to think about what kinds of physical handicaps could be integrated into your life without disrupting your life. Not every child with a handicap will fit with the same ease.

Fortunately you don't have to know exactly how every different handicap might affect you and the child. You will learn somewhat gradually from the adoption agency worker about different kinds of problems. The worker will not tell you to hastily pick up this specifically handicapped child without giving you a great deal of time to consider how the child would fit in your family. You will have plenty of time to consider, to read, and to assimilate how a specific physically handicapped child would fit into your home.

Adopting a child with a physical handicap is a major commitment that exceeds the commitment to raise a normal child. Not all people can do this. The DeBolt family most vividly demonstrates the commitment it takes to make adoption truly successful with a physically handicapped child.[4] Their story, depicted on television, probably did more to advertise the joy of having adopted a child with a physical handicap than any adoption agency promotion ever did. Their thirteen adopted children, many with severe physical handicaps, cause most of us to look on with sheer admiration for the life they have chosen.

The concept of adopting the child with a major correctable defect or a non-correctable problem runs absolutely counter to the idea of perfecting the physical health of the child in utero or aborting the defective child (See Chapter 4). This is how it should be. Life needn't be consistent. While some people would categorically reject the idea of knowingly having a defective child, others would feel that this was meant to be for them. The same is true in adoption. For some people, adopting a known-defective child would be wrong for them. For others contemplating adopting, they believe this might offer them a chance to provide a home for a child that otherwise might not be adopted. They willingly accept the commitment this entails. Neither group is right or wrong . . . their views are merely different. Surely we have room for differing view in our society on a subject this basic. The choices are open to all people so that their lives can be structured to fit these different possibilities.

One of the significant advances in recent years in helping parents adopt physically handicapped children has been the Model State Subsidized Adoption Act (See Appendix). This act allows people of moderate or low incomes, who would otherwise be unable to afford the expensive medical cost of caring for these children, to adopt children who are physically handicapped. It also opens the way for the foster parents who have cared for these children for long periods of time to adopt a child without losing the financial support that they have needed in order to maintain these children.

The situation with Kathy was a good example of subsidized adoption for physically handicapped children. Kathy was placed in a foster home when she was just two years of age. After another year of hesitancy, her divorced mother finally decided to relinquish her for adoption. She had been with her mother until her mother found she was unable to meet the demands of having a child with cerebral palsy. Kathy's foster parents had become very attached to her in the fifteen months they had her in their home. They had struggled with her as she learned to walk. Her limited use of both hands had prompted her foster parents to help her strive for independence rather than to overprotect her and cause her to become unnecessarily dependent. In all ways, these foster parents were ideal for Kathy. They had even considered adoption, but hesitated because they felt unable to meet her medical costs, which from time to time were very high. The need for surgery in her third year would have been completely impossible for them if she had been their own child. The adoption worker, recognizing their financial situation and the difficulty of placing Kathy in another home, approached her foster parents about adopting Kathy with a subsidy to help with the medical costs. The foster parents and Kathy were delighted with the prospect. The procedure in this case was relatively simple because it met everyone's needs. Kathy's special adoption was made possible by the financial assistance provided by a subsidized adoption. Without this help her adoption would not have been possible for these people.

In other cases, assistance for the high medical costs of raising a physically handicapped child is given by Crippled Children's Services. This was the case of Gary who had been crippled from birth with arthritis. His adoptive parents felt able to handle the problems Gary's handicap might present. He needed to have considerable attention given to his exercises to prevent extreme pain, but at the same time these exercises could also be somewhat painful. These time-consuming and emotionally draining activities presented no problem to the people who wanted to adopt Gary. As Gary grew older, the loving support of his adoptive parents helped him with the taunts and jeers he received from his not-too-understanding peers. His arthritis was not only painful, but it was also visible. At times, his medical bills were exceedingly high. While his normal medical costs could be handled by his adoptive family most of the time, at times they needed some extra help which they were able to get from Crippled Children's Services. This special help from time to time was all they needed to be able to adopt Gary. Knowing this was available to them at the time they adopted him opened up this opportunity for him and for them.

Adopting a child with a physical handicap should be carefully thought out by families or individuals who are considering this possibility. Undoubtedly, the assimilation of a child with these specific needs into the family is far more difficult than when a "normal" child is adopted. The reward, as with any child, can be tremendous if you are the right people.

Mentally Handicapped Children As with physically handicapped children, it is not always easy to define who is a mentally handicapped child. For couples who only want a quick-learning and bright child, a child of average ability could appear mentally handicapped. In general, when we speak of mentally handicapped children, we mean children whose level of intellectual functioning is below normal. These are children, who may need some special help to function in society because of the degree of impairment they experience. The severely mentally handicapped child may never be able to function independently in society.

The dilemma of choosing one of these children is similar to that of choosing a physically handicapped child. You need to fully understand what this means to you and to your life situation. If you enter this process with a clear understanding of what adopting a mentally handicapped child would be, you are likely to find the experience rewarding. If you enter this process unsure of what you are undertaking, you can end up feeling overwhelmed and disappointed.

Few people have a chance to experience the problems encountered by those who work with or raise children who are mentally limited. If you might consider adopting one of these children and have not had an opportunity to see what it is like to be with children who are mentally retarded, make the opportunity. Visit schools for mentally retarded youngsters. Learn the difference between a moderately retarded child, a slightly retarded child, or a severely retarded child. See if you have limits and see if you have specific choices. These schools can tell you about parent groups in your local area. Go to the group meetings and learn about the problems and the delights of raising a child who is first a child and secondly, a child with a unique special need.

Some advantages accrue to the family that adopts a child who is mentally handicapped that do not exist if the child is born to them. While our society believes a physically handicapped child can result through no fault of the parents, less understanding is given the family that produces the mentally or emotionally handicapped child. In some ways the family stigma of these handicaps is removed from the families where the child is adopted . . . the family does not have to bear the burden of guilt that they believe occurs with the birth of the child. This is true even though mental retardation knows no limits any more than physical handicaps do. Any family is at some risk of having a child who is mentally retarded.

Closely associated with the idea of fault in producing a mentally handicapped child is the role environment plays in changing this particular child's level of functioning. Most researchers would agree that environment plays a significant role. However, if a child is extremely limited in his level of mental functioning, the environment can improve this situation but it does not make a bright child out of a child who is considerably below average. Modifying, enhancing and influencing are all things the environment can do . . . even perhaps the concept of taking the child closer to his or her potential is possible with a stimulating, loving, attention-providing environment. The change seen in *Flowers for Algernon*,[5] where the mentally retarded man becomes a brilliant person, is simply not possible today. Adopting parents need to understand the limits of environment. The right environment offers tremendous opportunity for growth for any child, but no child can become completely changed even in a changed environment.

People planning to adopt a mentally retarded child need to be prepared for the response of others. Friends, relatives, neighbors, and even professionals frequently discourage adoption of these youngsters or other "special needs" youngsters.[3,6,7]

Elizabeth and Roger had spent a long time considering adoption to increase the size of their family. Their two boys were nine and eleven and Elizabeth felt she had the time, patience and energy to consider raising another child . . . a "special" one. Elizabeth and Roger wanted a girl. But they also wanted to adopt a child who might have difficulty finding a home. After spending many hours with their caseworker from the adoption agency, discussing different kinds of "special needs" children, they finally decided a girl who was mentally retarded was what they wanted most. As they sought to share their enthusiasm in this new venture, they found neither of the child's future grandparents very eager for this new family addition. In fact, both sets of parents repeatedly suggested they not do this "radical" thing. They told Elizabeth and Roger that a mentally retarded child would be a burden on them and would not fit into the family. Elizabeth and Roger were upset with their parents' response but they were determined to proceed. The social worker from the agency urged them to give the future grandparents time to digest the thought as both Elizabeth and Roger had. Eventually their parents came to accept the new baby granddaughter Elizabeth and Roger brought them, but their reluctance made the process much more difficult. Their sureness of what they were doing gave them the strength to pursue their goal despite the discouragement.

The primary difference in preparing yourself to adopt a child with a mental handicap as opposed to a physical handicap is that a mental handicap is more limited, more specific. You can focus your attention on one area and learn about it. With physically handicapped children you have great difficulty anticipating what physical problems your potential child might have. On the other hand, people are generally more accepting and less cruel to children and adults who have physical limitations than to those who have mental limitations. No matter which type of handicap your adopted child has, it is obvious that a loving, supportive home can best provide these youngsters with the stability they need to face a world which sometimes stares and frequently whispers about them.

Emotionally Handicapped Children Emotionally handicapped children are probably closer to mentally handicapped than physically handicapped children in the problems they experience. Again, the problems are less visible and harder to understand for many people than a physical handicap is. Emotionally handicapped children are probably less understood and, consequently, shunned even more than mentally handicapped children.

Emotionally handicapped children include children with a number of different kinds of problems. Children with compulsive personalities who need order to maintain their aggressive feelings when their behavior becomes extreme would fit into this category. Frequently children who have been shifted from home to home can develop mistrustful personalities; they become suspicious and paranoid. At times, children experiencing emotional problems become isolated, they retreat into fantasy life. Other children react to their life situation with emotional problems that they act out, they become aggressive and difficult.[8] These are only some of the kinds of emotional handicaps that can confront the adoptive parents who consider adopting an emotionally handicapped child. Without knowing what particular disorder your child might have, it is difficult to prepare yourself for the unique problems your child might bring with him or her. Your social worker from the adoption agency will explore with you the different kinds of children available who are exhibiting symptoms of emotional disturbance. However, in order for you to evaluate how a potential adoptee could fit into your life, you need to understand the specific problems that confront the specific child you might adopt.

The way to determine how impaired a child might be and how likely you might be to help a child with this problem is to find out as much as possible about the birthparents and child's history. You want to understand the potential genetic basis of the disorder this particular child has. Then, either consult someone who specializes in helping emotionally disturbed children or read about this particular kind of emotional disturbance so that you clearly understand what this specific child might mean in your life. These children are called high-risk adoptions. It is estimated that one in eight of these children is returned to an agency before the adoption is finalized.[9] Your chances of success in adopting a child with an emotional handicap is less than in other kinds of adoption involving normal children. The belief that love will conquer all of the problems leaves families in a weaker position to solve problems than if they had adequately prepared for them. Find out before you move ahead how you need to respond to help a specific child. Find out what the chances of success are in a given set of circumstances. Find out if this disorder is caused by the child's life situation or if it is a hereditary problem that you are unlikely to be able to solve.[10] Find out the information you need so that you can evaluate your fitness to handle the situation in the best possible way.

Rusty and Dana had met in college when they were both training to teach classes for handicapped children. Their obvious similar interests drew them together immediately and they married a year later. Soon thereafter, Dana had their first child. They had always wanted to adopt because they felt overpopulation was the most significant problem facing the world, so they decided that they would enlarge their family through adoption for their second child. They also decided they had special skills they could bring to parenting a "special needs" child because of their background. Dana especially wanted this opportunity because she had never had a chance to use her experience and training. An adoption agency in Chicago gave them their chance. After a lot of scrutiny about their motives, the social worker from the adoption agency began to speak with them about Tina. Tina was four and had recently been relinquished by her birthmother after a long legal battle. Tina's mother had routinely abused her. Perhaps her mother's divorce at the time of Tina's birth had caused the mother to focus all of her negative feelings on Tina. Perhaps it was because Tina was premature and had spent her first month in a hospital and the bonding process was not established as it should have been. No matter what the cause, Tina was a frightened, withdrawn child who had asthma, nightmares, and little trust for anyone. The adoption worker felt Tina might be just who Rusty and Dana wanted and Rusty and Dana might be just what Tina needed. The process of establishing trust with Tina was extremely slow. At times even now, after two years, the problems she had in her first four years re-emerge. Dana's patience has been critical. Her ability to reach out to Tina but to not overwhelm her have helped Tina in her struggle with her many fears. Both Rusty and Dana have learned a great deal about child abuse and the effects it has on the child. They are also trying to understand Tina's first mother in order to help Tina understand as she grows older what might have been happening in her early years. Obviously their college training has helped them understand "special" children, but even more important to their success has been their willingness to be open, to seek help when needed, to learn, to read and to listen.

Frequently children are emotionally handicapped because of the home situations in which they have been raised, as in the case of Tina. These children have many times been in other adoptive placements that have failed.[9] Emotionally handicapped children, because of the high-risk factor and the multiple home backgrounds they come from, frequently are the older children placed for adoption. These children have many strikes against them. Patience and understanding of the adoptive parents is a critical ingredient in the success of these adoptions. Most adoptions of emotionally disturbed children are very successful. Most people who have adopted a child with these kinds of problems strongly believe it has been worth all of the efforts involved in making the adoption work.

Older Children as Adoptees

No one buys a cat; they buy a kitten. No one wants to bring home a dog; they want to bring home a puppy. The same is true in adoption . . . everyone wants an infant; few people would choose an older child.

Everything we learn about child development says the child is formed in the very early stages. The impact we as parents make on the lives of our children is most significant before the age of five. Some child psychologists would say our most significant impact is by the age of three. Psychologists recognize the need for bonding between parent and child to begin as early as possible in the child's life in order for the child to achieve maximum emotional development. Other psychologists maintain that a person who has never been able to feel love as a child will have great difficulty forming loving relationships later in life.

Given the fact that all of this might very well be true, then what do we do with the older children who need homes . . . throw them away? We won't do the same things with children that we do with dogs and cats. Therefore, our usual technique is to shunt them aside, mostly into foster homes, and to try to forget about them. The older, hard-to-place children seem to share the fate of the elderly in our society . . . we simply don't know what we should do with them!

Older children are considered hard-to-place and also are "special needs" children because they are not as much in demand for adoption as infants. What constitutes "older" children is not always clear. It used to be that children over six months were considered older children. Then children over three were the new breaking point. Now, older children are those over six or maybe even over eight years of age.

The reasons these children are older at the time of placement varies. Some children are available for adoption late in life through a death or deaths of the only existing relatives they have. In other words, they only entered the system at a late age. Other children have only recently been released for adoption. Their parents may not have been willing to relinquish them, in the hope that maybe they could reestablish family stability and take the child back. These children may have been in and out of foster homes for several years. Other children are older at the time of their adoption placement because of compounding problems that have previously prevented their adoption such as emotional disturbance or medical problems or being part of a sibling placement. It is estimated that between 100,000 to 120,000 such children are currently waiting for families to adopt them.[11]

The amount of trauma the child has received as a result of the delay in adoption depends on the child's life history. It is possible to adopt an eight-year-old child who has been in only one home. The primary problem here would be to deal with the separation from the one known family. This child may have experienced in his eight years great stability and love. Another four year old may have been in seven or eight homes by the age of four. He may have lived with a parent, then relatives, back to parents, then into multiple foster homes. Age alone will not tell you the extent of the rejection the child has experienced. Hopefully, the history will. Be sure to get as many details on the child's history as possible from the adoption agency.

Renee and Jay were in their late thirties when they married. They knew Renee could not have children because she had a hysterectomy three years before they married. Adoption was the only way they were going to have a family. Renee wanted to raise a child but was not intent upon having an infant. When their adoption worker recognized this openness, she directed their home study toward considering an older child. Both Renee and Jay felt this would offer them many advantages. They began reading about the problems of adopting an older child and felt they could handle the situation. Their worker agreed and introduced them via pictures to a nine-year-old boy. Danny was a nice-looking, attention-seeking young man. He was being removed from his current foster home because his foster parents were divorcing. He had been in two previous foster homes. He was extremely reluctant to leave his current foster home because he had established strong ties with his foster sister and brother. Unfortunately, he had no choice. He met Renee and Jay on a picnic. They were okay but that didn't make him like the situation. He finally was willing to "give it a try" even though he was hardly overjoyed. He moved in but didn't want them to try to get him to change his name. Renee and Jay took their time. They anticipated some of the problems and had not planned on "instant love" so they were not disappointed. Knowing of Danny's background, his previous attachments and rejections helped them handle the situation with realistic epectations.

Adopting an older child, as in all adoptions of "special need" children has some unique problems. You are adopting a child who has a past. In order to have the adoption be successful you cannot "pretend" that the past does not exist. Rather, it is of utmost importance that you help the child become comfortable not just with who he is now, but also with who he has been before you adopted him. The use of photo albums from previous homes to help the child integrate his life have become a very common part of adoption of older children.

A newer use of this idea has been to have the potential adoptive parents prepare a photo album for the child they are considering adopting.[11] In this way, the older child gets to learn about the people in a more controlled and cautious way for him. The pictures show the child the people who are interested in adopting him, any other existing family members, the house, the kinds of things this family likes to do, the animals, the room the child would be in, and anything else that would help the child learn about this potential family. The child finds out quite a bit about the family through a medium that communicates fully with the child . . . pictures.

In order for the adoption of an older child to work successfully, the child is usually involved in approving the prospective parents. This is the reason that these adoptions are frequently referred to as being more of a marriage than an adoption.[12,13] These adoptions work because not only do the adoptive parents want it, but the older child also makes a conscious decision to accept these parents. Perhaps one of the reasons these adoptions work at all, despite all of the potential problems that might complicate them, is this very involvement of the older child who really wants to be adopted.

One of the ways to learn about adopting older children is to talk with others who have done so. You have to talk with them for a period of time because many times people just quickly tell you all of the good things and fail to mention the difficulties. Your social worker from the adoption agency can give you names of people or groups who work as support systems to people adopting older children. Read books on adopting the older child.[11,14,15,16,17] Also read books designed for older adopted children in order to understand their perspective.[18,19,20,21,22,23]

Since adopting older children usually involves both parents and child agreeing to the adoption, the process is handled somewhat differently than regular adoptions. You may have several meetings with the child before the child goes home with you. You may also take the child home for a temporary visit before the actual placement occurs. Older children placements for adoption are usually handled very slowly in order to assure the success of the placement.

It is becoming more common to have post-adoption group sessions for parents who adopt older children.[24] These kinds of support systems help people deal with the problems without just responding with fear. People who anticipate the stages of adjustment that the older child experiences in an adoptive home are prepared to handle them effectively.

As with other "special needs" children, sometimes the pesenting problem is more complex. Sometimes these children are older because they have other problems as well. Perhaps they have been in other adoptive placements, or even when they have been in several homes, the age factor becomes more prominent. It is never possible to completely piece together the history of an older child placed for adoption. As a result, current behavior or responses of the child are at times difficult to understand. Yet understanding is the critical ingredient in making these kinds of adoption work.

Adopting an older child is different than adopting an infant. It has its own special advantages and its own problems. It is not for everyone, but for those who do overcome the problems, they are delighted with the success. As with all adoptions, most of the adoptions of older children become great successes.

Siblings as Adoptees

The idea of instant family sounds good on television and in the movies. It is even a romantic concept when we think how cute twins or triplets are. Few people, however, really want to start families this way. Yet this is just what occurs in sibling adoptions. Because this idea sounds best from a distance, few ultimately choose to adopt more than one child at a time. For this reason, sibling adoptions become "special needs" adoptions.

Not only do sibling adoptions become hard-to-place adoptions due to the numbers of children involved, but also by the ages of the children. In all hard-to-place adoptions, the time lag works to the disadvantage of the children being placed. The longer they are not adopted, the more unadoptable they become.

The placement of siblings together should be a prime consideration in the adoption of these children. When these children have been together for years, they frequently become the only stable factor in each other's lives. Siblings, as any parent can attest, usually cling together when other factors are working against them. Brothers and sisters can present a strong defense when united. This response on the part of siblings being placed for adoption gives them an added sense of security in their new home. To lose parents through rejection is one thing or to lose foster parents through multiple moves is another, but to then lose the brother or sister who has been a source of united strength and stability is almost always too much of a hardship. Every possible effort should be made, and usually is made, to keep siblings together.

In the case of siblings, as in the case of all "special needs" children, the families willing to adopt these children have significantly increased since fewer infants are available for adoption. Families not finding their first choice open to them when they seek to adopt are more willing to consider the alternatives which are available to them. In each way that you expand your openness to adopt more than the white infant, you increase your chances of adopting.

For some people, adopting siblings can be an especially good solution to their childlessness. The older, childless couple who really want a family can get a quick solution to their problem and can provide a home for more than one child at a time. Meredith and Jeremy had been married three years in a marriage that was the second for each of them. Since they were forty and forty-two, the adoption agencies would not consider giving them an infant but would consider only an older child. That was fine with Meredith and Jeremy. Never, however, had they ever considered more than one child at a single time. Then they heard about two brothers from Mexico who needed a home. These brothers, four and six, had been without any family contacts for three years. They lived in a loosely run orphanage in a border town. No one had ever relinquished them. After consulting a Mexican attorney, Meredith and Jeremy found out how they could adopt these "abandoned" boys. The adoption itself went rather quickly as Mexican adoptions frequently do (See Chapter 8). The shock of the two additions to their family was handled with relative ease once the language problems began to dissolve. The company of each other in this rapid and radical life change cushioned the impact for each of the boys. Meredith and Jeremy didn't set out to adopt two children, they set out to begin a family. When confronted with the possibility, it sounded great to them. They strongly advocate adopting this way.

It is difficult to find many people who have adopted more than one child at a time. This is less common than most types of "special needs" adoptions. There are not the same parent groups to act as support systems that many "special needs" children have. You forge ahead on your own. However, it really is only a matter of multiplication of the problems of the parents who adopt a single child.

In the past, adopting anyone other than the white infant was viewed as altruistic behavior on the part of the adoptive parents . . . they were "do-gooders," and as such, were highly suspect. Their "save the world philosophy" did not fit the mold the agencies were looking for in their adoptive parents. Even the adoption agencies wondered about the motives of people who would seek children that were not like ordinary children. As a result, many times these children were not even offered for adoption. Siblings were seldom suggested because the agency *knew* people didn't want them. *Today, siblings are adoptable as a unit.* It is merely a matter of finding who wants this situation because certainly some people do.

Racially Mixed Children as Adoptees

No area of "special needs" children has received as much publicity, nor as much controversy, as adopting children from different racial backgrounds. The professional reaction from the National Association of Black Social Workers has been loud.[25] The legal reaction from the courts has been strongly felt. The emotional reaction from the minority groups and from the white neighbors of the adopting families has been mixed.[26] Very few remain quiet, except the adoption agencies who make many of these placements.

The primary cause of the controversy has been white parents adopting racially different children. Some of these children have been brought to the United States in the Vietnam baby airlifts or from other countries where poverty is significant. Usually these children are from Asian or Latin American backgrounds (See Chapter 8). The primary mixed racial adoption which has aroused controversy in this country has been the black child or the partially black child adopted by white parents. The adoption of Indian children has also caused alarm from the Indian community. The cry from the minority groups whose children are being adopted by white families is that the child loses his or her racial identity. Charges of racial genocide are hurled into the battle.

For years the white adoption agencies catered primarily to the white community. Little effort was made to recruit minority homes for the minority children who were relinquished for adoption. Many of these minority children spent the majority of their growing years in foster care. Now the trend has been reversed. At the same time that there is greater demand for children of different racial backgrounds, the social workers are reluctant to put these children in white homes.

Lou Ann and Jim knew it would not be easy to adopt a child from a mixed racial background. They wanted to adopt a second child and felt they would need to expand their views of what kind of child they would accept. After considerable thought they decided they wanted a child who was partly black. They told their social worker at the adoption agency and she was reluctant. They told their relatives they were going to adopt a black child and Lou Ann's mother was furious. They told their friends they were going to adopt a black child and they were surprised. They scrutinized birth announcements, their living situations, the potential schools and all areas that they felt might be affected by having this black child. They really prepared for this "special" child's hoped-for arrival. After an uphill battle, the agency worker agreed they would get their partly black child. Their four-month-old black child, whose birthfather was black and whose birthmother was white, arrived. He really didn't look very black but they assumed he would get blacker looking as time went on. He grew older but remained not very black. Their total preparation of their lives to accommodate a black child appeared to be in vain. The family conflict was unnecessary. In fact, their new son looked only slightly darker than his white adoptive father. A black child or a partially black child was sought by this couple. The black child is not as hard to place as he once was. For Lou Ann and Jim there almost existed a case of reverse discrimination.

If Lou Ann and Jim tried to adopt their son today rather than five years ago as they did, they would meet with much more difficulty with the adoption agency at the earliest stage of their request for a partly black child. The first approach most adoption agencies use today is to try to place black children in black homes. To do this, the agencies have become much more active in recruiting in the black community. Individual adoption agencies, in response to criticism of policies by black social workers, have attempted to recruit black social workers and administrators to their staffs and to their boards.[25] The story of black children being available for adoption has been stressed on radio and television. Pamphlets and lecturers have sought to inform the black community about adoption through adoption agencies. The black parents who wanted to adopt but who previously were eliminated because they did not fit the typical agency model of parenting are now being recruited.

One of the reasons many minority children were not adopted was the financial burden it placed on minority parents whose incomes were significantly lower than that of white parents. The blacks complained they could not outbid their white counterparts for the black infants who were available for adoption.[26] As subsidized adoption becomes available for lower-income families, especially foster care families, these families find themselves able to adopt a child previously not possible for financial reasons. As blacks have learned about the availability of children for adoption, as they have learned they will be accepted by the adoption agencies, and as they have learned about potential financial assistance which is available to them if it is needed, blacks have significantly increased their adoption of black children.[27]

Despite the increased recruiting of minority parents, the effort still lags behind demand. For that reason, many of the children who remain hard to place are minority children. They frequently are "special needs" children for reasons other than race alone. Because they are harder to place they frequently also become older children. Their lack of stable homes increases their emotional difficulties. Their problems compound because the system does not fit their needs.

Adoption agencies are only beginning to understand the parents who seek to adopt a child of a different race than their own. As a result, agency workers frequently are skeptical of those seeking "different" children. The outcry of the black social workers against placing blacks or partially black children in white homes has alarmed the adoption workers who enjoy the role of not being questioned on agency policies or decisions. As a result, agencies have significantly decreased the number of interracial adoptions, yet they deny any wrongdoing. Because the agencies remain in a position of tremendous power in the adoption scene, they seldom respond to criticism. They may change directions from time to time, but seldom is a direct response given to criticism of their positions on adoption.

The potential parents, seeking a child of another race, would do well to know of the support systems in their community. The Open Door Society, which exists throughout the United States, offers valuable information in their newsletters and in their meetings. The chapters vary from area to area but you can certainly find out about the one closest to you by getting in contact with any of these agencies.[1] These groups have meetings and you can learn about the problems and peculiarities involved in interracial adoptions. The individuals involved in these organizations are also a great source of information about the character and potential response you might receive from the local adoption agencies when you seek a child of a different race. Adoptive parents who have worked in the system can give you valuable information on how the system works.

Several books have been published on the subject of interracial adoptions.[25, 28, 29, 30] They are worth reading to get a perspective on the difficulties you are likely to encounter in the adoption process as well as the ways to minimize problems in raising a child of a different race. There are also some excellent books for children in mixed racial families that are worth reading to understand the child's perspective on his unusual family.[31, 32] Anyone considering the adoption of a child of another race should read the story of *Edgar Allan*[33] which vividly tells of an adoption that failed. Adopting a minority child is like any "special needs" child. It has some unique problems and some unique rewards. It is best entered into if you fully understand the process before you begin.

Summary

Children with "special needs" present problems for everyone. They simply don't fit into the mainstream of our picture of adoption. They seem to make people work harder to figure out where to put them and they seem to create more problems in making the fit between parent and child work.

Sometimes the placement of these "special" children does not work. The children are returned because the placement is too difficult for someone in the group. Sometimes a similar misfit also occurs between biological parents and their children. There is certainly no question that more of these "disruptions," as they are called in the adoption field, occur in this group than in "normal" adoptions. Yet the amazing thing is that the great majority work. Adoption of "special needs" children works, even though everything seems to be working against it. Agency social workers say the reason they work so well is because of the effective screening of the parents. Maybe. But then again maybe it is *despite* all the ways we interfere and separate these children from others. Perhaps our belief that these children are hard to place does in fact make them even harder to place. Our view that these are the last-chosen children may cause us to suggest them only as a last resort.

"Special needs" children have a great deal in common, partly because the specific groups which comprise the "special needs" children overlap and merge. The problems of one group intermingle with those of another. The demands on the families who adopt them, while different in specific ways, are common in many others. The happiness that these children bring to the families who share their lives with them is another characteristic they share.

So many of the demands, problems and joys these "special needs" children share is because they are children first and "special" second. They are grouped under "special needs" so that we can discuss them separately, but in reality their "specialness" is not primary in their lives. Their "specialness" is a label for our convenience in considering them. On a personal basis this label is not of value. You deal with Johnny or Suzie or Tim ... they are specific people with their own unique set of needs, desires, hopes and dreams. So while you cannot separate the child from the "special needs" he brings, that is not who he is ... he is much more ... he is really just like everyone ... he is a unique individual. Ultimately, no one has such a handle on life that in some way he or she could not be labeled a "special needs" person.

10
THE
SPECIAL MOMS
AND DADS

Children with "special needs" have difficulty being placed for adoption; parents with "special needs" who want to adopt have difficulty being accepted to adopt. The main problem both of these groups have is that they are different. Because they are different it is hard to accept their appropriateness for being part of our stereotyped American family. They do not fit our Walt Disney model of daddy coming home to mommy in the house with a white picket fence and the boy, the girl and the dog running out to greet them. The fact that the Disney-like model of the American family seldom exists any longer does not seem to improve the acceptance of "different" kinds of families.

The "special" moms and dads in our society include single parents, handicapped parents, parents with medical problems, parents of larger families, older parents, foster parents, and homosexual parents. Each of these groups of people runs into special problems when they seek to adopt a child; however, each group has demonstrated successful parenting skills when the children have been born to them. We do not try to take their children away from them because they are not completely fit to be parents. We only question their capacity to parent when they seek to adopt a child.

Single Parents as Adopters

Single people have adopted children ever since adoption has been a part of our society. At times these arrangements were informally made between the new parent and a friend or relative. Many times arrangements were made through private adoption. Not until 1965 did the adoption agencies put their official stamp of approval on large-scale, single-parent adoptions by their active entrance into this type of "special" adoption.[1] Then, just as this area of adoption began to open up, the baby shortage arrived. The babies were not available and the priority for the regular families pushed single-parent adoptions into the bottom drawer of the agency's files.

Single parenting is not a new idea. Many families with two parents, in reality, are examples of single parenting. The rise in divorce rates in recent years has made single parenting a common phenomenon. In many cases of divorced parents raising children or of single parents adopting, we are talking more about temporary singleness rather than single parenting. Most single parents are single only for a time.

Even children placed in adoptive homes with couples must contend with the possibility that they too will be raised by single parents for a period of time. Adopting a child is no marital guarantee. Divorce, or even death, is a possibility in homes that adopt children. The adoption agencies' emphasis on two-parent homes can be an exercise in futility.

Studies of single parents who adopt compared with couples who adopt find that the children from single-parent homes do very well. When other factors are controlled, such as the age of the child at placement, the researchers find that little difference exists between the children's adjustment to the single-parent adoptions and to the adjustment children make in couples' adoptions.[2, 3] The studies find differences in characteristics such as the age of adoptive parents, level of education, amount of income and other demographic details, but not on success of adoption or on adjustment of the child to adoption. Single adoptive parents seem to be doing a good job if they can get through the system to get a child. That isn't a very easy task.

Despite these realities, adoption agencies view single parents seeking to adopt as parents of last choice.[3, 4, 5] Viewing these applicants as last choices, the agencies only give them children as a last resort. The adoption agencies give the least desirable, hardest-to-raise children to the parents they view as least desirable and least equipped to be good parents.

Adoption agencies carefully scrutinize the motives of the single person seeking a child. Be prepared with the appropriate answers for their questions. They will also want to know of the support systems in your family. Single parents who have support from and strong relationships with friends and relatives are viewed much more favorably by the adoption agencies. Show the social worker that the child will have people of both sexes in his or her life. These areas, coupled with all of the ordinary traits adoption agencies hunt for in prospective parents, are essential in order to be considered. Yet, even when you clearly demonstrate that you meet all of their specific criteria, you still have a minimal chance against a couple who wants the same child. You, as a single parent, are in a difficult place to compete in the adoption game if you are going through an adoption agency to find a child.

In some special situations, agencies welcome the single parent. Alicia was thirty-two, single and black. Her singleness was not to her advantage when she went to adopt but her blackness was. The fact that she wanted a child who was at least five was also a distinct advantage to her. The adoption agency welcomed her with open arms. They had far more black children than they had black homes. If they could not place a black child with a couple, their second choice would certainly be a black single woman rather than incur the wrath of the black community. The last choice for the agency was to place this black child in a white home. Even though white couples actively seek black children, this is a last alternative for the adoption agencies. While most couples who are white would wait for a long period of time to have a child placed with them, Alicia was rapidly processed and approved. Within six months of her initial inquiry, the agency invited her to hear about Alexandra. Alexandra was six years old. She had been relinquished for adoption by her birthmother about ten months previously because the birthmother felt unable to care for her child. Before her relinquishment, Alexandra had a series of baby sitters who had been her primary caretakers. Alexandra seemed exceptionally mature in her ability to handle most situations but exceptionally immature in dealing with people. She carefully evaluated and tested people before allowing anyone to get close to her. She was used to temporary relationships and consequently believed all relationships to be the same. With this in mind, the adoption agency worker felt the home Alicia could provide would be a good one for Alexandra. Alexandra would not be as overwhelmed as she might be in a two-parent home. They cautiously met each other and slowly got to know each other, little by little. The placement of Alexandra did not occur until Alicia had a vacation from her job as a schoolteacher so that they could spend time together before school began. The first day of Christmas vacation, Alexandra and one small suitcase came to stay permanently in her new home. Even Alexandra is beginning to believe this is a permanent home for her now that her adoption has been finalized and now that she has been with Alicia for over a year. She had never been with any one person before for that long a period of time.

A few situations compel the adoption agencies to seek single-parent homes for children they place, as with Alicia. A child may have some specific problems that preclude his or her adjustment to two parents at the same time; this child would be better placed in a single-parent home. Another child may have been the recipient of sexual abuses in a previous home which may prevent his or her adjustment in a couple adoption; this child might be better placed in a single-parent home. Another child might simply not find an adoptive placement with a couple; most people would believe that a permanent placement with a single parent is far better than no placement at all.

As an adoptive parent applicant, help teach the agencies about the role single parents can have in remedying problems of certain "special" children. Convince the agency of your ability to help with the "special needs" child; however, as a single parent, your chance of convincing them that you are the better parent for the "normal" infant is almost **zero**.

Harriet was an exceptionally bright, independent woman who had completed medical school and was in private practice in a small community. She had never been married and did not consider this a possibility in the near future, but she did want to have a child. She felt she had a great deal to offer a child. She felt very strongly about the effect of early childhood experiences and therefore, she wanted an infant. She approached the adoption agency in a nearby city and told them what she wanted. Everyone at the agency who met her was impressed with her friendly, intelligent manner. Her financial independence was obviously in her favor also. She was thirty-one which was well within the age limits the agency sought for parents to be given infants. Yet her singleness was against her. At any other time when babies were more available, the adoption agency would probably have accepted an applicant of Harriet's caliber. But in today's adoption scene, Harriet's application was denied. The adoption agency would not consider giving her an infant. The social worker from the agency talked with her about older children or children with other "special needs" but Harriet really felt she wanted an infant and felt she was not ready to compromise on what she wanted. She left the agency with little encouragement. Alone, she simply could not compete with a couple in the adoption agency's view of what was needed to be a good parent.

Jake was twenty-nine and single. He had been active in Big Brothers for five years and decided he wanted to do even more with children. He decided he wanted a son to share his life. He knew he had little chance with an adoption agency. He knew it was even harder for a single male to be accepted than for a single female. He had almost given up hope when he met Jason. Jason was five and one of eight children. Jason's parents both worked and the children were pretty much left on their own. Jason spent more and more time with his neighbor and new friend, Jake. Every day Jason came to Jake's house, or to the fire station where Jake worked, so that he could spend time with Jake. Because of Jake's work schedule, he was able to spend a lot of time with Jason. Jason and Jake traveled together during summer vacation. Jake had Jason over for dinner most nights of the week. It wasn't long until Jason was hardly ever at his "real" home. Jason was outspoken about wanting to come to live with Jake. He asked Jake if he could stay permanently. Jake agreed that he too, would like this but he didn't know how Jason's parents would accept the idea. Finally, Jake made arrangements to meet with Jason's mother and father about Jason. The parents felt Jason was happier with Jake than when he was home and they felt unable to make things any better for him, so they agreed to have Jake legally adopt Jason. This situation was a rare way for anyone to find a son, but it worked. It's possible that Jake's strong desire for a son helped him to get into a situation that found him one. Jason still has contact with his birthparents and his brothers and sisters, but he calls Jake, his dad.

Given the difficulty of changing the adoption agencies' bias against single parents, the easiest way for single people to get a baby is to find a child privately. This is probably the *only* way a single person will get a normal infant. If you, as a single parent, expect to get a child through an adoption agency, be prepared for a long, arduous process. Be prepared to prove your parenting skills and motives. Be prepared to be put far down on the waiting list for a child to adopt. At the same time, the singles who are most likely to get a child are those who really go after one. The person who is not content with waiting to hear from an adoption agency goes out to find a child. Pursue all of the agencies, but also pursue a child privately. If you really want a child, go after one . . . even if you are single.

Find out about the problems of both getting a child and also of raising a child as a single person. All of the literature on single parenting is equally appropriate to adoptive parents as it is to other single parents. Write to the Committee for Single Adoptive Parents (Post Office Box 4074, Washington, D.C. 20015) to get additional information. Attend parent meetings of groups who have "special needs" children because if you can adopt a child through an adoption agency, that is probably the kind of child you will have placed with you.

Adopting a child as a single parent is an uphill struggle. People will question your motives and react with disbelief that a single person would willingly choose to raise a child alone. As with any highly motivated person, the more work, the more effort and the more approaches you pursue, the greater the likelihood of your finding a child.

Physically Handicapped Adopters

The possibility of physically handicapped people adopting through an adoption agency is very limited. The agencies seldom publicize this because they would have lawsuits immediately charging discrimination. However, the chance of having a child placed with a parent who has a major physical handicap is slight except in unusual circumstances. The discrimination is not on the books but rather it is in the attitude toward the physically handicapped applicant.

If there were many babies and few adoptive applicants, physically handicapped people would have less difficulty adopting through an adoption agency. Since just the reverse is true, physically handicapped people are placed in an extremely difficult position. They simply are too far down the list of acceptable applicants to have a chance for a child.

In certain situations, the adoption agencies believe that a child with a physical handicap might be best placed in a home where one of the parents has a physical handicap. The "special needs" of a child permanently confined to a wheelchair mandate that the home be able to accommodate the wheelchair. To find a physically handicapped parent with a similar handicap may provide a home already equipped for the child. To convert a home to accommodate a wheelchair can be quite costly. At other times, the child's adjustment to his or her handicap may not be going well. The emotional support of a parent who also has a handicap might help the child to better adjust to his or her own situation.

Lauren was a case of a child who did not adjust well to her handicap. She was twelve years old and had cerebral palsy. She had spent most of her life in a wheelchair because of her medical problems. Unfortunately, she was withdrawn and depressed. She had made two suicide attempts which ultimately caused her to be made a ward of the court because her mother felt unable to cope with her depression and her rages. As greater publicity caused the children in long-term foster care to be given closer scrutiny, Lauren's social worker approached her mother about relinquishing Lauren for adoption rather than to have her remain in her current foster home. Lauren's mother felt that any possibility would be worth it if Lauren would be happier. Lauren had been in psychotherapy for several years; her therapist felt her depression was related to seeing herself as different from everyone else and recommended that, if possible, she be placed with a person who had a similar handicap. The adoption agency's psychological evaluation found similar evidence that Lauren would be best placed in a home with someone who had a problem like that of Lauren's. These recommendations gave Ted and Marie the only chance they had to adopt a child. Marie had been confined to a wheelchair since she was paralyzed in an automobile accident at the age of nine. Since that time, she had learned to be relatively self-sufficient. She could drive a car which was specially equipped for her wheelchair. Ted and she had made all the necessary changes in their house to accommodate her wheelchair. The halls were wider than usual, there was a ramp to the front door, the shower was specially designed, and the doors were all extra-wide. Ted's help and understanding and Marie's fortitude and perseverance had enabled Marie to function rather independently. The adoption agency felt Marie's example and Ted's help could be extremely beneficial to Lauren. Lauren met Ted and Marie. She told her social worker she didn't like them. The social worker encouraged Lauren to give it some time. Lauren stayed overnight with them and began to watch Marie as she maneuvered about the house so expertly in her wheelchair. Lauren could see Marie doing things Lauren had never considered doing for herself. Each new visit brought Lauren closer to Marie and Ted. She finally admitted to the social worker that she wanted to stay. Lauren's change has been dramatic in her new home; it doesn't usually happen that quickly. But Lauren has found a new way of life because she found some "special" parents who wanted to adopt a child.

These circumstances mentioned above are rare. Most handicapped people would not be willing to wait for these occasional occurrences. As a result, these "special" parents generally seek a child elsewhere. Fortunately, most handicapped people are able to have children biologically without anyone's permission. Many times, if the wife is able to have children but the husband is unable to impregnate her, their problem of childlessness may be helped through artificial insemination. Others, who want to parent and who have not succeeded, probably seek a child privately rather than through an adoption agency. Generally, these "special" people would prefer to adopt through an adoption agency, but they recognize that choice is seldom available to them.

Handicapped people are not very well understood in our society. We look at them from afar and generally our response is pity for them and gratitude that we are not in their place. We debate philosophically at what point we would no longer want to survive as a disabled person. This is easy to debate when it isn't reality. Few people understand the richness and the value of living that is open to the handicapped person. Unless you have personal knowledge of someone who is handicapped, it is difficult to comprehend their life. Very few of these handicapped people would evaluate their lives as worthless or unproductive. They anticipate and enjoy life in many ways that are similar to "normal," and in some ways that are not open to "normals."[6,7]

In the past, handicapped people were not expected to live long or productive lives. With technical and medical advances, the life span and the capabilities of people who are the most seriously handicapped have been significantly improved. Emotionally, our responses to them are still antiquated. Our primary concessions to the physically handicapped population are parking places and special restroom facilities. We are not yet able to view them as people with similar needs and dreams. We are not able to view them as meeting our criteria for becoming adequate parents.

The physically handicapped, "special" parents have a hard battle to fight to get children from adoption agencies. They have to overcome the ignorance of society in terms of their limitations and capacities. At the same time they fight society's prejudices they must also confront the biases of the adoption agency's social worker. They have to prove themselves for an endeavor which is basic to most people ... to be a parent.

Older Parents as Adopters

People who are older than most parents fall into the category of "special" parents. They do not fit into the fixed categories that adoption agencies have set as the normal ages for parenting. Therefore, when older couples approach adoption agencies, the only children the adoption agencies will consider giving them are "special" children. Usually these are handicapped or older children.

Nature has set a biological limit on women who want to have children. Once the woman has reached menopause, she cannot conceive any longer. Women in their late forties are usually no longer able to have children. In our society, women generally have children in their twenties, but this age is increasing because many women are delaying their first pregnancy.

The adoption agencies are looking for parents of what they would consider "normal" child-bearing age. In general, this means someone who is between twenty-two and thirty years older than the child they wish to adopt. Therefore, when women of forty seek an infant, the agency places their application at the bottom of the list. The forty-year-old woman's choice to have an infant is denied since the agency deems her choice not within the normal range.

The greater the number of children available, the greater the age range considered appropriate for an infant to be placed for adoption. So, in this time of scarcity, the older parents become "specials" who must be willing to accept "special" children or they will not be considered for adoption by most adoption agencies.

Millie and Lester had led an interesting life since their marriage twelve years earlier. They had both served in the Peace Corps in their early twenties and had met at the time of their training. They both loved to travel and so when they met again years later, they married and set off to see the world. They collaborated on articles that supported their expenses as they lived in one country after another. When they finally decided they were ready to settle down in one place and raise a family, Millie was thirty-nine and Lester was forty-two. They found no reason that would explain their infertility but they also did not get pregnant. After trying for a year, they approached the local adoption agency. They wanted a baby. The social worker spoke with them about the scarcity of babies and about older children who would be available sooner. But Millie and Lester felt they wanted to experience a baby first, so the adoption agency turned them down. Fortunately, Lester and Millie in their world travels had met many people in different foreign countries. These connections eventually led them to an infant born in Colombia. They flew to Colombia, filled out the necessary papers, got their baby and came home. Their adventure in baby hunting not only gave them a darling baby daughter, Lina, but also an article that they subsequently sold.

Obviously, Millie and Lester don't fit into the regular categories of parenting. At the same time, it certainly seems that the interesting backgrounds of their lives would be a great addition to the life of any child they would adopt. From the adoption agency's standpoint, they could have enriched an older child's life just as much. But it's hardly as if Millie or Lester were ready for a geriatric ghetto at their ages. Many parents have successfully raised children they have had late in life.

Sandy and Al wanted a child even though they were in their early forties. When they approached the adoption agencies, they were told of the situation. As they heard about adopting an older child, this concept seemed extremely appealing to them. They wanted a child, a baby wasn't the issue for them. They were able to work within the adoption agency system because it fit into their ideas just fine. This doesn't make them any better parents than Millie or Lester who couldn't fit into the adoption agency system.

Older parents definitely fit into the category of "special" moms and dads. If these "special" parents want "special" children, they may be able to get one through an adoption agency. The quality of parenting from older parents is not the issue because there is no reason to believe older people make better or worse parents than others. The issue is more that older parents aren't "normal" and the adoption agency system is currently designed primarily for "normal" moms and dads.

Parents with Medical Problems as Adopters
People who have medical problems but who wish to adopt children through adoption agencies are in an extremely difficult position. Adoption agencies routinely seek a medical checkup before they will consider placing a child with a couple. If this checkup indicates there are any serious medical problems, the adoption agency will undoubtedly place this home on the ineligible list for obtaining a child.

Although people who are not in the best of health get pregnant and people who have children may discover at any point that they have a serious medical problem, this same "luxury" is denied the infertile couple. Excellent health is a prerequisite for parenting ... at least if you are adopting.

John and Marianne sought to adopt a child through an adoption agency ten years ago and were turned down. John is a diabetic who must use insulin to control his diabetes. The adoption agency denied their application because of his medical problem. They felt they had no other choice but to adopt independently. They have two children, a boy nine and a girl seven. They were forced to go outside of the agency or to be childless because they had a medical problem.

Sarah and Allan wanted to adopt a child through an adoption agency. Sarah had a heart problem and the adoption agency would not consider their application. Sarah and Allan know that she may not live to an old age, but they do believe she is likely to be able to live at least until a child reaches adulthood. No matter how unable they are to foresee their future, they know they want a child in it. They are searching now to find a child to adopt independently.

Margo and Brian had been married for four years and had been unable to have a child. The doctors finally decided Margo will be very unlikely to ever have a child because of severely scarred tubes. Margo and Brian went to the local adoption agency but felt they received a very cold response. Their application for a child was never accepted. No one told them why they were rejected but they both believe it was because of Margo's weight. Margo weighs two-hundred-twenty-five pounds. She does not believe her weight affects her ability to adequately mother a child. The fact they have subsequently adopted two children who are happy and healthy verifies her belief in herself as a mother. It would have been easier for Margo and Brian to adopt through the adoption agency. The question for them was not *will* we adopt but *how* will we adopt.

All of these couples wanted a child and their first choice would have been to go through the adoption agencies. But agencies, seeking the "best" parents, have set standards none of these couples can meet. This is certainly an understandable problem in today's adoption scene but it does not make it fair to the many applicants that it eliminates. Surely there are ways the adoption agency system can accommodate these people, too . . . especially since these people want and ultimately can get children for adoption anyhow.

Parents of Large Families as Adopters

Couples wishing to adopt a child but who already have two or more children have very little chance of adopting through an agency. This may be because of the lack of adoptable children but the other cause could be that, once again, these adopters fit into the category of "different."

Most adoption social workers have difficulty thinking of a large family as the best available home for adoptive children. The adoption agencies' belief that a large family system could not meet the special needs of an adopted child, especially one who may have some difficulties, prevents the placement of children in homes with large numbers of children. While the successes of large adoptive families such as the DeBolts with their thirteen adopted children are well known, it is clear that they cannot get their children through the regular adoption agencies. Probably most agencies would reject the DeBolts before they adopted any children on the basis that they already had children. Large families, through lack of understanding, are not considered appropriate.

For some adopted children, however, a large family situation would be the most ideal home. A large family, rather than being detrimental or a family of second choice, to some children would be the best home available. Margaret Ward, a Canadian writer,[8] speaks of the kinds of children who might be better placed in a large family adoptive home rather than a smaller one:

1. Children who cannot relate easily to adults or parental figures.
2. Children who are emotionally detached, who need to move slowly in forming new relationships.
3. Children who become stifled by the demands of adoptive parents for intense parent-child relationships.
4. Children who need to experience social contact in a small, close situation before being able to handle the demands of society for social contact.
5. Children who are withdrawn, who may need stimulation.
6. Children who have language problems because they have not learned to verbalize adequately.
7. Children who need structure, but structure with flexibility.
8. Children at high risk.
9. Children in need of nurturing.
10. Children lacking a firm sense of identity.

The involvement of not only adoptive parents but multiple siblings provides diverse role models and sources of contact. At the same time, the contacts are not as concentrated or as intense. Large families are generally verbal which enhances communication. Siblings take on more important roles in large families that may be especially beneficial to certain adopted children. Having many members in a family gives many sources of love and affection and offers a miniature society in which children can experiment with different behavior. Large families, while generally imposing structure and demands on each of the family members in order to function, seldom are rigid. They simply don't have the time to be rigid. This allows the flexibility that certain children need.

Molly and Tim were both from large families. Molly came from a family of nine children, Tim from a family of five children. When they married, they knew they would like to have a large family. They had three children by birth and then, unexpectedly, Molly had to have a hysterectomy to correct a medical problem. Undaunted, they went to the local adoption agency intent upon enlarging their family in a different way. They were good parents, acceptable to the adoption agency in every way except that they had three children. Despite all of their pleas, they were told their application would not be accepted because there were simply not enough children to go around to all of the people who wanted them. Molly and Tim didn't know where else to go. Two months after their rejection, the social worker from the adoption agency called them back and asked them to come in for an interview again. They learned that a birthmother insisted her child be placed in a home with at least three or four children. The adoption agency now wanted Molly and Tim to complete their home study so that this child could be placed with them if things worked out. They had a fourth child in their family within two months.

Molly and Tim are not a good example of a family whose child's needs would best be met in a large family, but they are a good example of the adoption agency bending rules to meet people's needs. They are also a good example of the control the birthmother can have in the placement of her child through an adoption agency if she insists on certain requirements. The need exists for greater pressure on adoption agencies to modify their procedures. Adoption agencies routinely turn down requests from parents with large existing families. Parents who wish to adopt and who are in this position need to take more aggressive roles in educating the adoption agencies about the quality of life in large families.

The concept of the large family as a desirable choice for some children being placed for adoption has not been studied thoroughly. It is difficult to study something that happens so rarely in adoption. Before categorically eliminating this choice, perhaps it should be proved inappropriate first. The obvious and usual successes of large families by birth would point to the appropriateness of children being placed in this type of family situation. Adoption agencies, however, do not have to defend their choices. But, remember, they are not the only game in town!

Large families offer a special milieu that may be beneficial to some children. The adoption agencies need to consider these homes individually rather than categorically denying their applications. Many large families will continue to adopt children, but most will do this through independent adoption . . . they have no other choice.

Foster Parents as Adopters

Foster parents are not like any other kinds of parents. They have children but they don't really. They are supposed to love them and commit to them but also to easily give them up when the "temporary" placement is ended. They are supposed to be available to but not demanding of the social workers with whom they work. They are supposed to be knowledgeable about raising children but they are not involved with the decisions about the child's welfare. If children in foster care are called "children in limbo," many foster parents could well be called "parents in limbo."

Many children are currently in foster homes. Estimates range as high as 500,000.[9] Basically, children who are in foster homes are children whose birthparents for some reason do not choose to care for them or who are unable to care for them. Parents who are unable to cope with their children, for one reason or another, find someone to become a substitute parent. People who have little money have their children put in foster homes. People who have enough money to hire a substitute parent hire baby sitters, boarding schools, nannies, or relatives to help. If we add the large numbers of children who are being raised by people other than birthparents but who are not actually in foster care, the figures become alarmingly high.

Children in foster homes fall into one of several categories. The first group are children waiting for adoption. These are children who have been relinquished and for whom no home has yet been found. Most of these children will have no difficulty being placed for adoption.

The second group of children are those whose birthparents are committed to them but due to temporary problems are unable to care for them. These are children who have contacts with their families but live in temporary foster homes.

The third group, and currently the group being given considerable publicity, are children who remain in long-term foster care homes. These are children who have not been released for adoption but whose families do not remain committed to them. Nothing is being done to change the circumstances for the child, nor is anything being done to change the circumstances of the parents. These children stay and stay and stay in foster homes.

The foster parents of these different groups of children have different feelings about their parenting. The first two groups see their role as temporary, as indeed it usually is. The third group of parents find themselves providing homes for these children on a more permanent basis. In these more permanent foster home situations, the foster parents at times want to adopt the child for whom they have become primary parents. The permanency of the situation has created strong family ties in these foster homes. Previously, adoption agency workers who saw this closeness developing between foster parents and foster children immediately removed the child.[10] These parents were approved to be foster parents not adoptive parents. The rules for becoming adoptive parents were more stringent than for becoming foster parents. Since many times the most difficult-to-raise children are kept in foster homes, it would seem that the foster parent is the parent who should be most carefully screened.

Foster parents, seeing the contradictions of their role and the unfairness in past practices regarding their eligibility to adopt these children, have become more organized. Groups like the National Foster Parent Association (NFPA) (Post Office Box 16523, Clayton, Missouri 63105) and the Organization of Foster Families for Equality and Reform (OFFER) (Post Office Box 110, East Meadows, New York 11554) have been organized and offer help to foster parents in gaining greater control over the children they raise. These groups also provide information to foster parents who want to adopt the children they have been raising. These groups also disseminate information to foster parents on subsidized adoption programs that are available.

Foster parents are seeking greater control in several areas of their involvement with their foster children. They are slowly gaining greater control in decisions involving the children who are in their care. At times, their opinions are solicited before adoption proceedings are formalized or adoption placements are made. They are seeking greater control over the length of time a child will stay with them and why the child will be removed. Most importantly, they are receiving consideration as adoptive parents for the children who have been in their care for long periods of time. Foster parenthood used to prevent people from being chosen as adoptive parents. Although not frequently, the reverse now can be true. At times, foster parenting is a way to become an adoptive parent.

Arlene and Howard had been foster parents ever since their biological children entered school. It was a means to earn a little money for Arlene while she stayed home, but her primary motivation was her real love for children. They had two foster children when Jody came to live with them. Jody was two when she first came. It was supposed to be a temporary placement but the birthmother repeatedly hesitated to sign the relinquishment papers that would have allowed Jody to be adopted. Even though her visits became shorter and less frequent, nothing could be done to persuade the birthmother to move ahead more rapidly. Arlene and Howard became Mommy and Daddy to Jody, who heard her foster brother and sister call them by these terms. Jody had one additional problem . . . she had only one arm. Arlene and Howard helped her in her adjustment to her handicap, enjoyed her, loved her, and saw her through two additional years of her life. This was the first child they had for a long period of time and they understandably became very attached to her and she to them. When they learned that Jody's birthmother had finally signed the relinquishment papers, they asked the social worker for consideration as Jody's adoptive parents. The social worker was hesitant. Even though Jody was considered a "special needs" child, she would be easier to place than many others because she was still under five and she was a girl. Arlene and Howard persisted in their requests. After a lot of investigation, they were finally approved as a potential adoptive home. They had to go through the same process as people who were completely unknown to the system. Finally, Arlene and Howard were approved and Jody was put in their home for a probationary period until the adoption was finalized. Six months later, Jody became their legal daughter.

Arlene and Howard were fortunate that they had nothing against them. Anything that could possibly have been used to deny their petition to adopt Jody would have been. Foster parents are not first-choice adoptive applicants. The term "psychological parent" that entered the adoption scene with the publishing of the book, *Beyond the Best Interests of the Child* [11] did more to change the status of foster parents than any other single factor. This same book has also made a tremendous impact on the overall view of long-term foster care in general. The amount of time considered tolerable for a child to be apart from his or her parents before the child experiences feelings of abandonment has been reconsidered. Psychological abandonment varies on the basis of the child's age. The authors of this book would maintain that the younger the child the sooner this takes place. As a result, long-term foster care is being given careful consideration. At times, a more active and aggressive stance is being taken by agencies to have foster children declared legally abandoned so they can be placed in a permanent adoptive home.

The biggest difficulty for children who have been caught in the foster care system is not being able to establish a feeling of permanence or rootedness. [12, 13] Children who come to feel all homes are temporary learn to withhold love. When these children are finally released for adoption, the task for the adoptive parents is a difficult one. This is the reason that the current push toward shortening the stay of children in foster homes has occurred and it is also the reason that, in some cases, adoption of children by their foster parents is now being allowed. At least the beginning stage of establishing roots has been started in the foster home.

A different approach to foster parenting is being used by some adoption agencies. In order to facilitate the early placement of children into more permanent homes, children are sometimes being placed in the home which will adopt them prior to the birthmother's relinquishment. This riskier approach is being used to help the child develop a sense of permanence as early as possible. It is also extremely beneficial for the adoptive parents who need to begin as early as possible to develop a relationship with the new child.

As the role of the foster parent changes, foster parenting is being seen for the first time as an avenue toward adoption. Some of the recommendations of agencies are that this role should be used regularly in cases involving "special needs" children. While foster parents are now being accepted as adoptive parents, this does not mean that this is currently a good way to adopt a child. Foster parents are merely considered appropriate in some circumstances to adopt the child they have been raising. Foster parents are not adoptive parents of first choice but they are "special" moms and dads who are finally being *at least* considered in adoption cases.

Homosexuals as Adopters

The emotional response to the entire issue of homosexuality is evident in many areas of our lives. The avowed homosexual has only recently felt any degree of confidence in proclaiming his or her sexual preference. With the proclamations have come condemnation. Homosexuals have been fired, harassed and ridiculed. Homosexuality has won many legal battles under the banner of discrimination but it has only begun to win slight approval or tolerance in our society. One area where this is most certainly evident is in the adoption of children.

Homosexual parents are like just about any parents. They are as good or as bad as any other group of parents one could evaluate. There has been nothing that would substantiate fears that children raised by homosexuals become homosexuals.

Despite the data that indicate homosexuals are like any other parents, adoption agencies do not knowingly place children for adoption in homes of homosexuals.[4] Their position is understandable because of the potential criticism from non-gays who are seeking a child. The negative publicity this issue would generate would run counter to adoption agencies' studiously maintained low profile. At the same time, the adoption agencies maintain no written policy about placing children with homosexuals because to do so would be overt discrimination.

Discrimination is not a new concept for adoption agencies. But when any group discriminates against another, they usually do it against small groups who are not vocal. When the adoption agencies discriminated against blacks, it worked well until the blacks gained more power and became vocal. Then the outcry of the blacks forced changes by the adoption agencies. This situation has the same potential with gays as with blacks.

Lori and Sally knew of discrimination against lesbians. They had lived together in a lesbian relationship for over six years. They were happy, productive and living in many respects a normal life. Lori went to work daily as a social worker. Sally reluctantly worked as a grocery store clerk, but her real desire was to have a child. She approached a physician to do artificial insemination but it did not work for her. After six months of trying, she gave up on the idea of becoming pregnant. Lori's experience as a social worker with the Department of Welfare was enough to keep her abreast of the field of social work and for her to recognize that they were not going to get a child from an adoption agency. Sally nevertheless tried an adoption agency in an attempt to adopt as a single mother, but they told her there were no children available for single women. Then Lori heard of a woman on welfare who was unhappily pregnant and too far along for an abortion. Lori talked to her about giving the child to her and Sally. She was open about the relationship she had with Sally. She emphasized the stability of the relationship and how loving a person Sally was. The pregnant woman met Sally and liked her. She already liked Lori so she decided she would give them her child when it was born. Sally adopted the child legally as a single mother. The agency investigating the home never learned about her relationship with Lori. Sally and Lori were lucky . . . the odds were really against them ever getting a child to adopt. Most homosexual couples would not have these contacts or this good fortune.

In order to effectively prove that homosexuals are unfit for parenting, some studies will have to substantiate this claim. So far none has. In fact, the subject is seldom studied at all. One recent study reported in the *Lesbian Tide*[14] found children of lesbians are different from children raised by non-lesbians. The researcher found that the sons of lesbians were more gentle and concerned with other people's feelings than were other boys. She also found the daughters of lesbians had stronger qualities of leadership and outgoingness than other girls. These findings may or may not be substantiated in other studies in these areas where unfitness to parent is claimed.

At the same time, some recent changes in this area have occurred. A case in Denver, Colorado was won by a lesbian woman who was the lover of a woman who had died, leaving her custody of a seven-year-old daughter. The lesbian woman sought and won custody of the child Page despite the objections of the deceased woman's family.[5] Recently several other states have sought gay foster parents for gay teenagers with behavioral problems.[15] These are substantial gains into previously excluded areas for people who are openly gay.

The homosexual person seeking a child through an adoption agency is fighting a losing battle at this point. That does not mean the battle should not be fought . . . in fact, someone always has to pave the way for change to occur. On the other hand, the greatest chance for homosexuals to have children is to have them biologically (as most do) or to get pregnant by artificial insemination or to adopt independently.

Am I advocating placing children with avowed homosexuals? I would advocate placing children with anyone who wants them unless it can be shown that it would be harmful to the child. If it can be proven that there would be harm in placing a child with a homosexual, then a child should not be placed in a homosexual home. If it cannot be proven, then why not place children in homosexual homes?

Summary

For some "specials" the current picture of adoption is a blessing and for others it is a curse. The "special" child has a better chance of being adopted now than ever before, but the "special" parents have less chance of finding a child to adopt than ever before.

At the same time, the "specials" in our population, when closely examined, become less "special." About one of every ten children is labeled handicapped and one out of every five adults is labeled handicapped; this constitutes a significant number in our society who are mentally retarded, emotionally disturbed or crippled, have learning disabilities or impairments of speech, vision or hearing.[16] Despite these large numbers of people labeled handicapped, adoption remains a difficult, and at times, impossible process for the one labeled handicapped or "special" who wants to adopt a child.

"Special" moms and dads are in trouble. It is hard enough in the United States today for anyone to adopt, but for "special" parents, adoption through the normal adoption agency channels is nearly impossible. The few who will succeed are those who really push to prove their parenting ability and those who are just plain lucky. No matter what your chances, fight the system if you want a child but be prepared to lose. Get on the adoption agencies' waiting lists but be prepared to wait indefinitely. But for you who are "special" and want to be a parent, look around . . . look everywhere. Your options are more limited so you must be even more creative and diligent in your approach than most people who want to find a child to adopt.

11
DEEP
DARK
SECRETS

Secrets are powerful. They are powerful producers of curiosity, action, guilt, rumor and panic. They cause people to feel worthless. They demean and shame people. They haunt people and they obsess people. The impact of secrets is jolting and far-reaching.

Despite this tremendous power, mostly negative, that secrets hold, no single institution is as riddled with secrecy as adoption. Adoption secrecy supersedes the amount of secrecy which surrounds mental health. It ranks above the secrecy that shrouds physical illness. It surpasses the secrecy of issues such as cheating, abortion, drugs, pre-marital sexual activity, or illicit affairs. Secrecy exudes from the adoption scene from the moment that adoptive parents learn of their infertility, from the discovery of the pregnancy by the birthmother, from the careful choosing of words to describe in non-identifying ways the "other" parents, from the surreptitious transfer of the child from one home to another, from the fearful sealing of the records on adoption and from the reluctance of the adoption agencies to support needed change.

Why, in our society today, is this secrecy in adoption necessary? What are we supposed to be trying to protect? Is it healthy for the people involved in adoption to have this much to hide? Are the reasons for the secrecy as valid today as they were a generation ago? What's wrong with being open about adoption?

The primary area of secrecy currently coming under attack is the sealed record. This single issue has caught the imagination of the media and the attention of legislators. The sealed record issue has also caused the adoption agencies to cringe and protect, the adoptive parents to shout and fear, the adoptees to unite and fight, and birthparents to fantasize and anticipate.

The sealed birth record is not the only secret part of adoption, it is merely the issue of today. The changes in this area will predict the potential opening of other secret areas in adoption. It is impossible to tamper with one area of adoption without causing reverberations throughout the whole system.[1,2] No matter whether we are opening Pandora's box with the issue of unsealing the sealed birth record or not, the militants (who must exist for any significant change to occur) say they will not rest. Opening the sealed record in adoption is a hot topic that does not seem to be dying out with time.

Current Laws on Adoptee's Birth Record
The laws giving adoptees access to their original birth certificate vary from state to state. Few laws are specific, and therefore, are open to the individual judge's interpretation. Even if the birth records are opened, exactly what information will be disclosed to the adoptee is not clear. Unless the laws are clarified, the end result is likely to be many individual and frequently contradictory rulings.

The laws from state to state vary from year to year also. Since 1976, Minnesota, Connecticut and North Dakota have opened birth records for controlled access by adoptees. Ohio mandated the disclosure to future adoptees of non-identifying medical and social histories, but Virginia and Louisiana have passed measures to curtail access to their records.[3] Many bills introduced but dropped in recent legislative sessions will undoubtedly be reconsidered.

The current Minnesota law is being given the most attention and is frequently referred to as the model legislation for other proposed laws. This law provides that adoptees over twenty-one can have their original birth certificates unsealed as long as the birthparents consent. This consent can be given at any time. If an adoptee seeks the opening of these records, the Department of Public Welfare has six months to contact the birthparents. If either parent listed on the original birth certificate refuses, is no longer living, or cannot be located, the birth certificate can only be unsealed by obtaining a court order.

Other states have great variety in their specific laws that say the adoptee must be eighteen, not twenty-one, some have review boards if the adoptee does not like the decision, others give out information but not identities.[3] In order to know what is happening in each specific state, you need to check with that state at the time you want to have access to the records.

Definition of Terms

The terms used in discussing the sealed birth records are not always clear. In order to discuss this topic with clarity, it is important that the terms used are familiar.

Sealed Birth Record refers to the birth certificate that is amended at the time the child is legally adopted. The old birth certificate with the name of at least the birthmother is then sealed and may not be opened unless the specific requirements of the state are met.

Adoption records refer to the records kept by the adoption agency about the individual adoption. While names of birthparents are found in these records, much additional information is also there. Medical information and background information on birthparents, adoptive parents and the adopted child are found in these records.

Good cause is a legal term used in cases where a determination is being made if the birth records will be opened to the adoptee. An example of good cause would be suspicion of genetic life-threatening medical history that might be verified by contacting the birthparent. Good cause is interpreted differently from state to state and from court to court.

Searchers are adoptees who seek information on their birth history. They may want general information, they may want specific indentifying data and/or they may want to have contact with the birthparents. Most people agree that before anyone would be willing to help people in their birth search the adoptee should be an adult.

Reunions are the personal contacts of the adoptee with the birthparent.

Changes in Adoption

In the beginning of adoption, the needs of the child were considered far less important than they are today. The adopting parents were the primary clients being served and this was done on a rather informal basis. The adopting parents were the focal point in early adoption; they were the ones who had saved this orphan from a terrible fate. At times, the motivation for adoption was more to provide help to the adopting parents than to find a home for an unwanted child. As time went by, the procedures and motivations for adoption changed. Children became slightly more valued. Bloodlines were at least intellectually considered less important in the United States, where it was believed that everyone could be successful if they tried. In the early 1930s, formal adoption emerged; it was a white institution founded to place white infants in white families. Concurrently, the field of social welfare developed. Adoption became a formal process handled by the formal institution called the adoption agency. Emphasis was on screening children to find the right child for the couple. The child was not the central ingredient but instead, the adopting parents were.

As adoptive parents formalized this process legally, they also sought privacy to build their future around this new family that they wanted to be "normal." In order to maintain privacy, the birth records were officially sealed. In other words, no one could find out who the birthparents of an adopted child were without going through the courts. The adoptee, or anyone else, could only have access to the amended birth certificate which identified the child only with his or her adoptive parents. The only way the birth certificate was identified as that of an adopted child was the fact that it said amended on it.

The next change in the adoption scene was the development of the "in the best interest of the child" concept. The new emphasis on the child came about as babies, especially white ones, were more in demand. There were more people who wanted babies than there were babies. So now we began to put the emphasis on what would be best for the child. In reality, this is a relatively new concept in adoption.

Clamor for More Change

Until fairly recently, no one seemed upset about the fact that birth records were sealed. This should be no surprise. In the first place, despite the fact that there are at least five million adoptees in the United States,[4] they constitute a small minority. Not only is this a minority group but it is a minority group made up of minority groups. In other words, it is a minority group fragmented into other special groups such as white adoptees, black adoptees, and older adoptees. It is hard to get diverse segments to identify strongly enough with each other to have their impact felt.

The second factor in the recent emphasis on opening the sealed record is the age of the adoptees. Since birth records were not sealed until around the 1940s, it is a fairly recent demand to open these records. Many of the adoptees affected by sealed records are only currently reaching the age of majority.

The third fact which has underscored the sealed record controversy has been the advent of militancy as a means of causing changes in our society. The sixties showed the United States the impact of vocal minorities when they shouted in unison. Groups, previously quiet, rose up as they saw other minority groups succeed by making continued, loud demands.

The fourth factor influencing the demands to unseal the birth records of adoptees was the emphasis on genealogical and historical heritage. The popularity of Alex Haley's *Roots*[5] strongly emphasized people's heritage and links with the past. We are part of a long chain of history that needs to be understood if we are to understand ourselves. The adult adoptee feels part of this chain of identity is missing.

The fifth factor emphasizing the need to open the birth records of adoptees was the cry of discrimination. Discrimination in most forms is viewed negatively in our society. There is no doubt that in adoption discrimination is rampant.

The clamor for change was not voiced by all of the people involved in adoption. In fact, the clamor came primarily from one group. Perhaps the advent of the concept of adoption being in "the best interest of the child" made adoptees feel they had a central place in adoption and they sensed the power this gave them. Now they wanted to exercise their power. They sought to have the laws changed. They wanted their birth records opened. Others in the adoption scene were not too sure about the adoptees' demands and some totally opposed these demands.

The other people in adoption, the adoptive parents, the birthparents and the adoption agencies responded differently to the demands of adoptees that the birth records be opened. All involved, however, including some of the adoptees, have responded defensively.

The Emotional Issue of Opening the Birth Record

Adoption itself, as we have discussed, is an emotional issue. Since the opening of the sealed record is the argument at hand, it seems to be symbolic of the entire adoption issue, encompassing all the emotionality that adoption engenders. The pain for each of the participants is real, yet none of the antagonists seems to understand the opponent's pain. The pain seems shared but different . . . separate but equal . . . to all of the people involved in adoption.

Each of the participants must deal with the stigma of shame and guilt attached to adoption and currently embodied in the issue of opening the sealed record. The adoptive couple must once again confront their feelings of failure in not conceiving. The artificiality of adoption brings this home for them as they recognize that their children are not their children. Our society believes that adoption is a secondary means of achieving parenthood and so do most adoptive parents. The potential opening of the sealed birth record of their adopted child further enforces in their minds that these are different children and they are different parents. If they had not failed to conceive in the first place, they would not be experiencing this problem. They feel guilty and ashamed that they are not *real* parents.

The adoptee must deal with the likely stigma of his or her past. The specter of illegitimacy is not as large today as in previous years but it still exists. If the birth record is opened, the adoptee would no longer be shielded from knowledge of potential inherited weaknesses. Yet, the unknown stigma for the adoptee may seem worse than the reality of the known, no matter how bad. The stigma of rejection is never fully erased for the adoptee even with the continual reassurance of "being chosen." The adoptee feels guilt for his rejection.

The stigma of guilt and shame fall also on the birthparents at a time like this when the entire foundation of adoption is being scrutinized. The birthmother especially must look again at the issue that involved great pain for her at another time in her life. Her problem may be further compounded by how she has incorporated the relinquished child into her new life. A hidden secret, the relinquished child, may cause her feelings of guilt and shame to be exacerbated. Her unresolved feelings about having "given away her child" may cause her guilt to reemerge with great intensity.

The stigma of guilt and shame is also raised by the role of the adoption agencies. Beliefs of the past are no longer held as truth. The agencies, viewing their past roles in convincing the pregnant woman what was best for her, are now not quite as sure of that role at this time. The secrets of the past now may be opened and the role of the adoption agencies may not look quite so humanitarian under careful scrutiny. The adoption agencies are being asked to account for their roles in past practices in which they no longer believe and in which they may even regret their participation.

Along with all this guilt and shame, fear emerges. The adult adoptee fears he won't like what he finds out about himself or he fears the second rejection from the birthparent. The birthparents fear the blame their son or daughter will have for them for what they have done. The adoptive parents fear the loss of their child to another set of parents. The adoption agencies fear criticism for what they have done and for what they have tried not to do.

The fear, the stigma, the defensiveness all come with each of the participants as they seek to solve the sealed record problem. No one listens, everyone seeks to prove his or her point. Research studies, seldom conclusive, are quoted that support the side each person chooses to defend. Everyone shifts the blame to someone else. Communication becomes non-existent. The wheels of compromise and understanding grind to a halt.

A Suggested Approach

So what is the answer to the problems posed by opening the sealed records of adoptees? How do we overcome the issues each side presents? Where do we find the meeting ground of compromise?

Of all the chapters in this book that I have found more complex to report, this is by far the hardest. As with everyone else involved, the issues are personal for me, too. It is so easy to take a stand to support my role as an adoptive mother. Yet, that is too frequently the case for all of us who are so close to the issues being debated. It is time to stop taking stands and approach the problem differently.

As I read and speak with the people on all sides of the issue, I am struck by several things.

> Each person I speak with or read about really believes in what he or she is saying about opening the sealed adoption records.
> I essentially believe what each person tells me . . . they convince me of the rightness of their stand.
> If everyone is right, then this must be an individual issue.
> Individual issues must be handled individually, even in adoption.

The reason I am struck by these points is because of the philosophical point I begin with as I examine this emotional issue. The only way to solve the problem of the conflicting views on opening the sealed records must be to have a philosophical stand on the issue. My philosophical stand on opening the sealed birth records for adoptees is based on being a birthmother, an adoptive mother, a wife, a daughter, a psychologist and a teacher.

I believe in the individual adult's ability to decide for himself or herself. For me to tell another what is best for them is to tell them that *they* do not know what is best for them, to imply that *they* are not competent to run their own life. For me to decide the direction of another person's life is to be arrogant and pompous. For me to prevent people from making mistakes says mistakes are wrong, but they aren't. I can help people see other ways of approaching an issue but I cannot make decisions for anyone's life but my own. If I allow people to make only the decisions with which I agree, it means I have not really believed in people at all.

This is a time to seek to understand the views of others, not to find fault with their views. To seek to assess blame is futile and divisive. Right or wrong is not necessary to establish in order to find direction. One person is not made right by another's wrongness. On personal issues, right is a personal matter.

The most critical ingredient in solving problems is open communication. If we try to communicate our specific view and our opponents try to communicate their specific view, this is not communication. Communication is possible only with listening. Talking isn't the key . . . *listening* is. You already know where you are on this issue; now *really* seek to hear where the other people are. Try to figure out what possible reasons they have for taking the position they do, rather than looking for the fallacies of their argument. It is time to hear what all the sides are saying instead of only seeking to tell them your side.

The ability to be open to change is an essential ingredient in life today because we live in a changing world. The absolutes of yesterday are the outdated concepts of today. New situations demand new solutions. New needs of people demand different policies. If there is no room to change or modify our positions, there is no need to try to communicate.

In order to evaluate the importance of any disagreement, you must evaluate the potential loss if the other side wins. What is the worst thing that can happen if you lose this battle? If winning the battle becomes the most important goal, then the issues are no longer of importance. We are then arguing simply out of pride. Seeking vindication prevents seeking solutions. Ultimately, even if a "wrong" solution is imposed, people will survive. The resiliency of children that people involved with adoption have seen demonstrated time after time exists in adults also.

Different Views on Opening the Sealed Record

In order to better understand the issues involved in opening the birth record of the adoptee, it is essential to look at some of the ways each person is or might be affected by this change. What is the stand of adoptees and why? What does opening the sealed record mean to adoptive parents? What happens to the birthparents in this process? What is the role of the adoption agencies and what could this role be? There is no way to consider this issue without trying to look at it from the perspective of each of the people involved.

The Adoptee and the Sealed Record When the sealed record issue is brought up, it is the adoptee who is first considered. They are the ones who want information on their history. Some want information and others want specific facts and names. Virtually all the adoptees believe the information given out about the birthparents and the adoptee's history should be provided only to the adoptee who is an adult.

The studies of adoptees so far are limited. We do know generally some things about adoptees who search for additional information and reunions with their birthparents. We know several things, for example, from the research done by Sorosky, Baran, and Pannor which they reported in *The Adoption Triangle*.[6]

1. Most adoptees who search are female.
2. More reunions seem to be sought by adoptees who are told fairly late in life of their adoptions.
3. Most adoptees were satisfied with their reunions.
4. About half of the adoptees developed a meaningful relationship with the birthparents.
5. Searches for birthparents usually seem to be triggered by some significant event like the birth of a child or the death of the adoptive parent.
6. The adoptive family relationship was rarely permanently damaged as a result of the reunion.

Their research is not a truly random sample of adoptee and birthparent reunions because the subjects voluntarily came forward to be studied. However, it is the best research reported so far.

We don't know how many adoptees would really search if the records were in actuality opened. In Scotland where birth records of adoptees are open, approximately one percent of the adoptees seek this information.[7] One adoption agency in Texas reported less than one percent of the 14,000 adoptees they have placed have initiated attempts to locate or identify their birthparents.[8] It is difficult to predict from these figures how many adoptees would indeed search. The dilemma now is that even if the adoptee wants to search, he or she cannot in most states in this country.

We only have sketchy background material on this subject, because studies are necessarily new and quite limited. Therefore, it is important to read primarily personal views on this subject. That's great . . . those are the best kinds. Remember, this is a personal issue. We are trying to understand all of the views of each of the people involved in the adoption picture and personal accounts can tell us their stories in a context within which we can identify. It is not that each of the adoptees represent all adoptees but more that they represent a view that is part of the adoption picture. No one person represents adoptees or birthparents or adopting parents or even adoption agency social workers.

The Search for Anna Fisher is one woman's account of the trauma of her search.[9] It was one of the beginning points in the quest of adoptees to have their birth records opened. Florence Fisher, who wrote the book, has been an outspoken voice for opening the birth records of adoptees. Her story is a moving, emotional appeal to open the birth record for any adoptee who wants this information.

An even earlier voice was that of Jean Patton from a group called Orphan Voyage. Her work in this area has been a steady plea for change. Reading the literature from her group is a helpful way to seek to understand the needs of adoptees.[10]

The single book most representative of the research being done is *The Adoption Triangle* mentioned earlier.[6] This book, written by a team from Vista Del Mar, a former adoption agency, is must reading by all who choose to debate the subject of opening the sealed birth record. Other books and articles have been written by adoptees telling their side of this issue.[11, 12, 13] Just about any of these will help people understand the specific point of view of each of these individual authors.

Another source of help in understanding the adoptees' point of view is to attend meetings of some of their organizations. These support groups, whose members help other adoptees in their searches, are a valuable source of understanding. They usually welcome people from other sides. Groups such as the Adoptees' Liberation Movement Association (ALMA) (Post Office Box 154, Washington Bridge Station, New York, New York 10033), Orphan Voyage (2141 Road 2300 Cedaredge, Colorado 81413), or Adoptees in Search (Post Office Box 41016,

Bethesda, Maryland 20014) are all adoptee organizations. Remember, these groups are as varied as adoption agencies. Some will seem extremely harsh in their approach. Others will seem more moderate. The approach of each group changes as its membership changes.

Carey found the help of one group in California extremely important in her search. Carey was twenty-five and had just gotten divorced when she read in a local newspaper about the possibility of adoptees finding their birthparents and the impacts of the reunions. The more she thought about this concept, the more it appealed to her. It wasn't because she was unhappy with her adoptive parents; she wasn't. In fact, as she told them of her thoughts, they told her they would be glad to help her. She sought information about her birthparents from the private adoption agency in Texas from which she was adopted, but she was turned down immediately. A letter from her adoptive parents indicating their support in her search didn't help. Prior to Carey's divorce, she had learned she was having difficulty getting pregnant. Her physician asked for information about her mother and her birth history. Carey realized she had none of the requested information. Because of the medical need for seeking information, because of her adoptive parents' support in her search and because of the help from a group of adoptees who told her what to do at each step, she contacted a lawyer in Texas who indicated his willingness to legally seek to have her records opened. The judge in the case was in complete agreement with the cause which Carey had shown for opening her record. And, with this judgment in her favor, she received the name of her birthmother. But then what? Again, the adoptee support group told her of ways to seek her birthmother now that she had a name ... their ways were ways that had worked for other adoptees who searched for their birthparents. She was able to find out that her mother had lived in a small town near the agency when she had relinquished Carey. Relatives in the town, after hearing of an old friend who was hunting for her, gave Carey the information that would allow her to make contact with her birthmother. Even with this information, Carey was not sure how to proceed. At this point, she even went into limited psychotherapy to examine her motives for searching. Fortunately, her therapist encouraged her to go on in her search. The therapist also urged her to be mindful of the others involved because Carey's birthmother had remarried. Finally, a friend of Carey's contacted Carey's birthmother on the phone. The friend asked if this was a good time to talk because she had information about the woman's daughter whom she had placed for adoption twenty-five years ago. The woman said the caller was wrong but she didn't hang up. The friend asked if there would be a better time to talk and Carey's birthmother said yes. They arranged to talk the next day. Carey, listening to the call, was elated, fearful, anxious and apprehensive. She called the next day and identified herself to her birthmother. Her birthmother acknowledged to Carey that she was her mother but that was over now ... she had a new family who knew nothing about Carey. Carey's birthmother said her husband had just had heart surgery and he could not learn about this now. She knew that somehow, she would meet her birthmother and her half-brothers and half-sister. But for now, she was willing to wait. Carey talked to her birthmother three times that year. They exchanged pictures and some information. Carey is content for now. She is hoping to ease her birthmother into the relationship, but she says, adamantly, she will not wait forever. She knows that at some point she will show up on the doorstep and announce her arrival, with or without an invitation.

Carey says she is not seeking a new family; she is seeking a missing link. This attitude is frequently conveyed by those adoptees who search. Reunions or sometimes simply just additional information given to the adoptee will complete this missing link. Without it, the adoptee's identity is not complete.

Some argue that searchers will not like what they find. There are histories of incest, child abuse and mental disease. The adoptees respond that truth is better than fantasy. Truth helps the adoptee know what he or she is up against even if the reality is harsh.

Jill was my first introduction to an adoptee's fantasies and search. I was in my first year of teaching in high school and she was a member of my ninth-grade English class. I was twenty-four and she was fifteen. She began to send me anonymous letters saying she thought I was her mother. Then she began to call me and I told her we should talk about this in person. She finally agreed and came forward, identifying herself as the one who had been calling and sending the letters. We talked for a long time about her adoption. She felt her parents knew of her birthparents but wouldn't tell her. She had searched through everything in the house trying to find out the identities of her birthparents. She had no reason to think I was her birthmother but she wanted one so much that she fantasized that women she liked were her "real" mother.

It is hard for anyone who is not adopted to fully understand what being adopted means. The closest that other people come is probably the sense of isolation that losing both birthparents brings. At times, the militancy of the searchers catches others off guard. Their anger seems so out of proportion. They feel an intense sense of frustration in their attempts to piece together their genetic medical history or even just their social history. Not all adoptees will experience this intense need to search for their birthparents. For those who do search, however, the barriers they encounter seem to them to be senseless walls dividing them from themselves . . . they seem like roadblocks to wholeness.

The Adoptive Parents and the Sealed Record Adoptive parents look at the current upheaval in adoption and feel their own fate is once again out of their hands. To be dependent on others through their infertility struggle and through their efforts to adopt a child had been bad enough. But now the threat of having their children taken from them again by another set of parents gives them a lack of control over the destiny of their own lives. Many adoptive parents are alarmed. Their illusions of their "normal" family are shattered.

Not all adoptive parents are responding in this way. In fact, with searches being such a personal matter, it is hard for many adoptive parents to even understand what precipitates an adoptee's search. Dana and Jim had given little thought to searches by adoptees except to be curious about the current articles they were seeing about unsealing the birth records. But that was not really relevant to them because their adopted children, Mark and Amy, were only thirteen and ten. Perhaps they would cross that bridge sometime but they hoped not. Amy had many more questions about her birthmother than Mark, but they felt that they had handled her questions without much trouble. So when Mark stated one evening that he needed to find out about his birth-parents, Dana and Jim were shocked. Mark knew the hospital in California where he was born. He further and quite accurately reasoned, "There could not be that many baby boys born at 7:08 in the morning in that hospital on that day." He wanted to call right then and get his birthmother's name. Dana and Jim felt awful. All the thoughts of failure rushed through their minds. Trying to remain calm, Dana told Mark she didn't think the hospital would give him this information although he was welcome to try, but why did he want to know? Mark responded with great seriousness, "I really want to find out if I'm related to George Washington." Searches are very personal.

Adoptive parents who learn more about searchers become less threatened by the prospect. Knowledge, especially personal knowledge, seems to make searches or reunions seem less potentially harmful to the adoptive relationship. The amount of literature from the adoptive parents' perspective on the issue of the sealed birth record is limited. However, as accounts of reunions and searches are read, adoptive parents learn how others have responded. [6,14,15]

The support groups that adoptive parents have established have been a helpful system for them. These groups have been one of the primary reasons why much of the legislation on opening the sealed records has been stopped. With the tide continuing to flow toward opening the records anyhow, reunions and searches become more common to the members of these groups. Adoptive parents will know better how to react when this threat is posed to them.

Accepting the differences of adoption as a method of parenting is difficult for some adoptive parents. No matter how hard you wish, you cannot wish away the existence of another set of parents for your child. Your love for the child is a commitment to raise the child, not to cut the child off from anyone in his or her life. In fact, the child may need your love and commitment even more if he chooses to search for his birthparents. People who argue that searches bring grief or pain do not consider the potential help of the adoptive parents who are supportive of the child they have raised to adulthood. The marriage of a child does not lessen the bond of those people who have raised him; it is simply a different kind of relationship . . . a non-competitive relationship because there is no need to compete. Adoptive parents have already done that which they sought to do . . . to raise a child. This is the same case in reunions. These are just different people but they do not compete with what adoptive parents have done because, again, they have already done it.

One of the reasons birthparents are threatening to adoptive parents is a fantasy. Adoptive parents, frequently older than birthparents, have difficulty viewing birthparents as growing older . . . just like they, the adoptive parents, have. Because of the secrecy in adoption, we seem to freeze these people as beautiful, youthful people . . . they aren't. Annie was adopted independently when she was six days old. Her adoptive parents, Sue and Rod, met the birthparents. They maintained contact through the years by letter but it wasn't until Annie was eight that the birthfather asked to see her. The meeting was arranged to be held at a park where the birthfather could watch Annie play but not have direct contact with her. Sue took Annie. The meeting at the park may have helped the birthfather but nothing like it helped Sue. Sue's last contact with him had been eight years before. The father was young and handsome. She and Rod were ten years older than either of the birthparents. To now see the birthfather eight years older was a revelation to Sue. The concrete image of the birthfather helped her to dispel the fantasy she had established about Annie's birthparents. As with adoptees, the fantasy we have may create more problems than the reality we might experience.

While understanding that adoption is a different way of parenting, there are many ways that it is like any other kind of parenting. We are all seeking to make our children happy, self-sufficient human beings. We are trying to meet their needs without forgetting that we, too, have needs. But it is possible that both can be met in similar ways. One adoptive mother whose background in raising special children speaks poignantly of good parenting:

> *On first reflection, there is something threatening to a parent about a child wanting to go off and find his or her 'real parents.' It feels like rejection, as if the adoptive parents were not all they should have been or did not do their job well. But when examined from the perspective of the child's needs, it is apparent that good parenting involves encouraging or even becoming a partner in the search. In a sense, the true function of parents is to make themselves obsolete; that is, to prepare their children for the time when they will no longer be dependent on the parent.* [14]

Allow your children to grow and to become. No one can take them from you because you do not own them. For a significant part of their lives, you were a significant person. After you have been that in another person's life, it can never be taken away. If searching is an important thing to your children, then help them to search. There is nothing you can save them from, nor anything you can do for them. Your help and support, and maybe your permission, is what they want and need from you. If pain is the result of their search, help them with their pain. If joy is a part of their search, then experience this joy with them by your participation in and permission for their endeavor.

The Birthparent and the Sealed Record   Birthparents have been the primary sufferers in adoption, the ones who may have felt only the pain and anguish. For some, the pain has lingered ever since the relinquishment of the child, despite the reassurances of, "You are doing the right thing" or, "You will put this behind you and build a new life." Like everyone else in adoption, each birthparent has responded to the opening of the birth records in a very personal way.

Some of the birthparents have welcomed the controversy over the sealed records as a possible second chance to tell their story to the child they gave away. Others wait in dread for the phone call or knock on the door which may bring back their past. Some birthparents search for their children placed for adoption and some hide for fear they will be found. Most birthparents seem to feel positively about the potential contact they might have with the children they placed for adoption.[6]

Previously, birthparents have sat quietly at the sidelines as others in the adoption scene wrestled over what to call them. "Biological parents" was the chosen term for a time, despite the mechanical ring. "Natural parents" was found objectionable to adoptive parents who already felt unnatural enough. "Real parents" met the same objection. Other choices that have been used from time to time have been "genetic parents," "original parents" or "first parents." Birthparents seems to be the term of choice for today.

Perhaps our choice of terms to describe women who have placed their children for adoption is somewhat based on our acceptance of them. The changing view about pregnancies of unmarried women and their greater acceptance today, undoubtedly help the birthparents of the majority of children now placed for adoption. As birthparents have become more vocal, we better understand their position in adoption. Books such as *Birthmark*[16] help us to understand the plight of the woman who chooses to place her child for adoption. The story of her hopes to do otherwise and her continual involvement with her daughter help others in the adoption scene to more realistically view the birthparent.

Organizations of birthparents like Concerned United Birthparents, Inc. (CUB) (Post Office Box 573, Milford, Massachusetts 01757) help the birthparent find support which further encourages them to come out of hiding. These organizations help birthparents feel less stigma than previously. They also help the birthparents who seek reunions with their adopted children to know how to search for them.

The role of the birthparents in the opening of the birth record is a controversial one. The question exists as to what rights the birthmother has in this area. If she placed a child for adoption in the belief that the record was forever sealed, what now happens to this implied contract? Some of the more militant proponents for opening the birth record say she has no rights . . . she abdicated her rights at the time of her relinquishment. Others say that her rights must be protected because she was told that her secret would never be revealed. Still others would say that most birthmothers want to meet or know of their child. And the remainder say, "Let's ask her first." Let's set up the means to update information and also to update feelings about the necessity of confidentiality. Today is not the same as yesterday.

In *The Adoption Triangle*,[6] subjects, including birthparents, voluntarily came forward to discuss their adoption experience. While this sample is necessarily biased, it is the only study of people who placed children for adoption. Of the group of thirty-eight birthparents, half of them continued to feel the loss and pain of the relinquishment; this was despite the fact that they had relinquished their children between ten to thirty-three years before the interviews. Of the group, 82 percent said they would be interested in a reunion but eight percent said they did not want reunions because of their present families. A small percentage of birthparents were actively searching for their children. Not wanting to hurt or upset the adoptive parents was mentioned by the great majority of the birthparents who were interviewed. While these figures are helpful, the personal letters quoted by the authors show with more impact the views of the birthparents.

Birthparents' abilities to incorporate their past child into their lives vary. Eleanor just turned fifty-three. She has been married for thirty-five years to a man who, until this past year, did not know she had a child when she was eighteen. In fact, neither did Eleanor's son nor any of her other relatives know of her daughter's birth. Eleanor's secret was always safe because so few people knew. Then the publicity started coming out on adoptees searching for their birthparents and Eleanor read the stories with mixed feelings. On one hand she felt it would be wonderful to hear from her daughter, to know what she looked like and how she was doing in life. On the other hand, she felt fearful of how others in her life would respond to the news of a daughter. The day for which Eleanor could never be quite prepared came when her daughter called. A reunion was set up which allowed time for Eleanor to break the news to Frank, her husband. The reunion was strained but satisfactory. The life of Eleanor's daughter had gone in a completely different direction than that of Eleanor and they found they had little in common except a birth history. They exchanged short letters after their meeting but little other contact was ever made. That seems to be satisfactory to each of them. At the same time, each of them discusses the reunion with positive feelings. It met a need for each of them and they are happy they met.

The role of the birthfather is more obscure than even that of the birthmother. Some reunions are between adoptees and their birthfathers. In the case of Alex, he wanted to meet both of his birthparents. The meeting with his birthfather was even more critical after he found his birthmother was mentally retarded and in an institution. Fortunately, his birthmother's relatives were able to provide him with the information he needed to find his father. He made contact with his birthfather and found they had phenomenal areas of similarity. They both were avid fishermen, they both liked wildly colored shirts, and they both had jobs in similar fields of work. Alex found his birthfather and continues to maintain contact with him on a regular basis. He even introduced his birthfather to his adoptive parents who supported his desire to search for his birthparents.

Birthparents are frequently viewed as they were at the time of relinquishing the child. The adoptive parents of the child often view them as young and beautiful but mixed up. The adoption agencies continue to view them as young people who were immature, sexually permissive and confused. Our image of the birthparents is frozen because they are finished with the adoption process after they fulfill their function of providing a child. There is no continuing contact with the birthparents and so we know very little about them. The birthparent is not allowed to mature, to grow older, to get straightened out, or to change his or her mind.

In order to understand the position of birthparents in adoption, we must speak with them and listen to them. We must try to understand their place today because viewing them from an outdated, twenty- or thirty-year-old perspective distorts who they are and prevents us from understanding their place in adoption today.

The Adoption Agencies and the Sealed Record The adoption agencies approach the sealed record from a slightly different perspective than the other people we have talked about . . . the adoptee, the adoptive parent, or the birthparent. However, as with each of these other groups, the adoption agencies also approach the sealed record issue from a personal perspective. Adoption agencies have policies, but social workers in the adoption agencies respond personally. It is the worker who personally experiences the joy, the rejection, the fear, or the hurt . . . not the adoption agency.

The adoption agencies have rules about how the social workers who staff the agencies are to respond to requests for birth information. Each agency has its own general framework and each worker interprets the rules of the agency somewhat differently. While each worker feels some obligation to support the system within which he works, many workers are actively seeking changes within the system. Other social workers are incensed with the potential opening of the birth records to adoptees and are actively seeking to maintain the system as they have known it in the past.

The adoption agencies and their workers feel trapped by the cries for change in opening the records. They find themselves the scapegoats for everyone's anger. At times, the criticisms are justified, and at times, the criticisms are unfair. Birthmothers who look back on their time of relinquishment feel that they were unduly influenced by the social workers who told them that relinquishment was the best thing. They forget their confusion and desperation when they came to the agency for help. Adoptive parents are angered with the adoption agencies who guaranteed them they would be the permanent parents for their adopted child. They also now feel they were not given accurate and complete information on their child's background. They too, forget their feelings of expectation and gratitude toward the agency as they received their greatly desired child. The adoptees, feeling like pawns in the system, vent hostility on the agencies who have the information they want about who they are. They too, forget that the adoption agencies were acting in the way the times dictated. Times have changed rapidly and agencies aren't always able to change with equal speed.

In the past, the adoption agencies have been very much in control in adoption. Laws that have been passed seem to put adoption agencies more and more in the position of being in control of adoptions. While minor setbacks have occurred in the increasing power of the adoption agencies—such as when they were mandated to provide accurate, truthful and complete information to adoptive parents on the child's medical and social history—the power of the adoption agencies has been increased over the years. The greatest threat the adoption agencies have ever experienced is opening the sealed birth record. Some agencies believe opening the birth record will signal the end of adoption as we know it in the United States. Other agencies are already accommodating to the proposed changes by modifying their current practices accordingly.

The approach of some agencies is to do nothing ... to wait until the courts mandate an opening of the records. This approach says that to set up the current system so that records could be updated would take too many people and would be contrary to the temporary role adoption agencies have traditionally maintained.[7] Many agencies, feeling pressure, are advising all of the principals involved in adoption of the potential changes occurring in the law. Some agencies will go no further than that. Others are far more creative and forward looking.

Already, some agencies when contacted by the birthparents, the adoptee, or the adoptive parents, are seeking to do what these people request. One private adoption agency was contacted by a birthparent who wanted to know about the child she had placed twelve years ago. She wanted to know if the adoptive parents would be willing to give her some additional information about the child. The adoption agency contacted the adoptive parents, who willingly consented, and asked that the birthmother also update her medical file with the adoption agency. The same agency is actively passing information back and forth between people involved in adoption. Sometimes this merely consists of information but not identities. At other times, identities may be given. This adoption agency does not feel it is their choice to decide how much information will be passed on. They believe that the people involved are the ones who should decide.

Obviously, approaching adoption in this way is time consuming but it is also a humane way to serve the people the adoption agencies say they want to help. This humanitarian approach to adoption is exemplified by Linda Burgess, an adoption agency social worker who maintains that to force an adoptee to show "good cause" for opening his or her own birth record perpetuates the dependency the adoptee has on the judgment of others. She maintains the changes needed to bring about the opening of the birth records will cause concern for some of the people in adoption in order for other people in adoption to grow.

> *The agencies, the courts, the doctors, and the adoptive parents, faced with the eventuality that facts formerly hidden will be revealed, will have to substitute candor for concealment and honesty for distortion. The effects will ripple backwards to free adoptees still in childhood from adult pretense. Adoptive parents will more readily face the fact that their adopted children are not their possessions, that they are born in one heritage, raised in another and will emerge as adults into the larger world which belongs equally to everyone.* [17]

Adoption agencies are approaching the opening of the sealed records in widely divergent ways. Perhaps this is a necessary time so that many alternative ways to opening the records can be considered. It is not necessary to find the *one* way to do this but to perhaps find many ways. One of the reasons adoption has failed to meet the current needs of many people in our society is because adoption has been approached from a single, rigid format. Maybe we can profit from previous mistakes and provide multiple ways to meet people's varied needs.

Preparing for Opening the Birth Record
Adoption agencies need to prepare themselves and their clients for the

potential opening of the birth record. So too, do the individuals involved in adoption need to prepare themselves. Birth records are likely to be opened on a gradual basis and everyone has a part.

Agencies need to keep letters from people who are seeking contact. Even though birth records may not be opened now, when they are, current statements from people stating their wishes will be important. Agencies should encourage their past clients to make their wishes known. At times the auxiliary groups of some of the adoption agencies are very active. Suggesting through these auxiliary groups and their publications that adoptive parents communicate their wishes to the agencies might help agencies be more timely in their arguments. The use of the news media to help agencies encourage the updating of addresses and information would be a helpful preparatory approach. Even if the birth records were never opened, it would enable people to have medical updating of the records that might be extremely helpful.

Each of the adoption participants should inform the adoption agency of how they feel about the possible opening of the sealed birth record of adoptees and make certain their file is updated. Adoptive parents who believe it would be fine for their children to have additional information and/or to have reunions with their birthparents could inform the adoption agency. Just updating information on the child you have adopted may help the birthparent who wants information about the child she has relinquished. As an adoptive parent you may inadvertently prevent the agency from releasing records that may be of help to your child if the agency feels it needs your permission before they will even give out general information to your child. Your permission may be needed in a formal way or it may be the formal permission that gives the adopted child the psychological permission to search.

The birthparent could make contact with the adoption agency also. The birthparent certainly should keep their file updated with significant medical information. At the same time a birthparent could update the file with personal information and file his or her wishes about contact with the adoptee. The adopted child who is having some problems with his or her adoption may be satisfied just to know a bit more about the birthparent as he or she is now. This may be especially helpful if the birthparent chooses not to have contact with the child but is willing to provide information about himself or herself. While more information and reunions involve birthmothers than birthfathers, it is helpful to have accurate and timely information on both birthparents. If either birthparent is willing to have contact with the adoptee when the child becomes an adult, this is important information for the adoption agency to have.

The adoptees, of course, need to take responsibility to let the adoption agencies know of their feelings about opening the sealed record. Before an adoptee seeks legal recourse to obtain the birth record, he or she should first see what the attitude of the adoption agency is that handled the specific adoption. The adoption agency may be able and willing to provide all the help the adoptee needs. It certainly is the place to start. When adoption agencies testify about the limited numbers of adoptees who want records opened, it might be because adoptees have not first tried asking the adoption agencies. If the adoptee would like to have contact with the birthparent, the adoptee should be certain that the adoption agency knows this.

Adoption agencies are supposed to be experts in adoption. They are supposed to know what everyone wants in respect to the opening of the sealed record. Their views are sought by lawmakers who scrutinize pending legislation. Currently, adoption agencies are not in a position to represent any of the parts of the adoption triangle with any degree of accuracy. The only way the views of all of the adoption participants will be known to adoption agencies is if many people tell them. It is not a matter of depending on the adoption agencies for our welfare as in the past . . . it is a matter of educating the adoption agencies about where we are on this important issue.

While it is important for the adoption agency to know each individual's desires about opening the birth record, it is also important that these personal thoughts be conveyed to legislators. Legislators look to the adoption agencies to be experts and to represent all of the parties in adoption. That may be inappropriate. It may also be that adoption agency bias prevents them from representing all of the individuals involved in adoption. In order to be certain your views are conveyed to the lawmakers, contact individual legislators and tell them how you feel about the opening of the adoptee's birth record. No one else represents you as well as you do.

Summary

Previously, the potential that an adoptee would try to make contact with the birthparents was frightening. The stigma attached to having a child out of wedlock was too great. Our society had too strong an emotional response to sex outside of marriage and to illegitimate children. Everyone needed to be protected from finding out about the "sinful" details that surrounded adoption.

Despite phenomenal changes in our attitudes toward sexual behavior, including sex outside of marriage, illegitimate pregnancy and single parents, these changes are slow to be felt in the adoption scene. Adoption is still viewed in a maternalistic manner . . . everyone needs to be protected. The adoption agencies believe they know what is right for the child, for the adoptive parents and for the birthparents. Even when all the parties involved would like to try new, innovative approaches, the adoption agencies frequently resist this force into the present. Traditional adoption is maintained with great resistance to change.

The same secrecy which safeguards the identity of each person in agency adoptions is maintained in the court system by the sealing of the birth certificate of the adopted child. Perseverance, luck, and occasional help by an individual adoption agency or court may unlock these records for the adult adoptee. But for many adult adoptees who search for information on their past, they will be denied access to the information that primarily concerns them.

Adoption agencies have an opportunity with the potential opening of the birth records to review previous policies and practices. Perhaps the changes brought about by opening these records will provide the impetus to review the whole secrecy issue that has pervaded adoption in the past. When adoption can shed its dependence on secrecy, it has the potential to become a healthy, viable alternative method of parenting.

12
LETTING
IN SOME
LIGHT

Secrecy implies shame. There is neither need nor justification for the amount of secrecy that currently exists in adoption. The sealed birth record discussed in the last chapter is only the tip of the secrecy iceberg in adoption. The adoption process can survive and thrive with openness and honesty. It is time to let in some light on adoption.

Some of the ways to become more open and honest about adoption are quite simple. They involve changes that can easily be adapted into the adoption scene now. Other changes involve changing more basic ways in which adoptions operate. Some changes involve individuals and some changes involve the institution. The question is not whether there is a need for change in adoption; the question is only which things should be changed first.

Individual Honesty in Adoption

Such a simple statement . . . put honesty in adoption . . . and yet it is so complex. The "differentness" of adopting causes new problems for families and compounds the regular problems. To say we should be honest in order to avoid additional conflicts is readily agreed upon by most people. To put this agreed upon concept into practice is the real test.

David Kirk, an adoptive parent, speaks to the need of incorporating empathy and understanding in adoptive families. The mutualism of their shared adoptive situation is the very ingredient which helps each child accept his or her adoption.

> *Sentiments of belongingness are strengthened when members are engaged in mutual aid arising from mutual needs. The condition of mutual needs in the adoptive parent-child relationship is the condition of mutual need of all parent-child relations, enlarged and emphasized by the discrepancies and losses both parents and children have suffered. As a method of integrating the child into the family, mutualism always begins with the parents. They must institute it and make it work. It is for them to set up the channels within which they can identify themselves with the child's situation, so that he, in his turn, can reach out to them and recognize them as the people to whom he unqualifiedly belongs. To be able to do this, the parents must have come to accept naturally, with comfort, their position in family and society.*[1]

The adoptive parents must be honest with themselves about their infertility and their substitute method of parenting. Without this personal honesty that precedes sureness and confidence, the adoptive parents cannot empathize with or understand fully their adopted child and his or her pain. Love is a critical ingredient in all families but the adoptive family needs another essential component. The adoptive family needs understanding and empathy.

The adoptive family is built on pain. We gloss over this as we talk of "chosen babies" and "How lucky we are to have found you" and how "Your first mother gave you away because she loved you." But in truth, that is not what happened. That pretends that pain was not there . . . that pretends specialness by omission.

Adopted families are special, I have no doubt about it. The specialness comes out mostly with honesty not with omissions, illusions, fantasies and pretenses. These give a false foundation to all of the participants. There is no substitute for honesty in adoption.

Honesty begins first with the parents, the adoptive parents. Early in this book, the importance of coming to grips with your infertility was discussed. If you have pretended that it was *not* important that you failed to get pregnant and it *was* important, this stays with you for a long time . . . forever. If, rather than pretend, you can tell your spouse or someone else significant to you how truly important this was, you are laying the foundation of honesty with yourself. In order to be honest with your child you must learn to first be honest with yourself.

Another means of pretending to yourself is making believe your adopted family is like a "regular" family. It isn't. It is different. If you try to live with the illusions, then comments about "other" parents or "real" parents become especially painful. These comments plunge you back into reality. You leave yourself open to hurt when you fool yourself about yourself. If you know your family is different, you don't have to have your defenses up when someone tells you your family is different. You have a foundation that is based on reality.

If you are clear in your own mind about adoption and how you fit in society, the questions from your child about his or her adoption are easy to answer at any time. Feeling secure yourself about adoption lets your child feel secure also. If you hide things about adoption then something must be bad about adoption to make it necessary to hide.

When your three-year-old adopted daughter asks about her birth, tell her the truth . . . never lie to her. You are beginning a long process that tests your trustworthiness and your self-confidence. Even if it is easier to handle the three year old's questions with fibs or fabrications, the three year old will soon be a thirteen year old.

The messages and questions of the child who is older are more subtle. The eight-year-old adopted boy whose friend's parents have divorced and each remarried can talk about how hard it is for his friend to have two sets of parents. What is he really saying? Is he talking about himself? Why not ask? Why not draw the unspoken parallel for him? Why not use this as an opportunity for openness and honesty about his adoption?

The same problems you confronted with insensitive people about your childlessness now confront your child about his or her adoption. The seven-year-old girl whose friends ask her lots of questions about her adoption force her to deal with her differentness. She is just not like her friends at a time when she wants to be *just like* her friends. If you have set the foundation of honesty and openness with her as a child, she can afford to bring her concerns to you. If you have implied you are uncomfortable with the topic of adoption, or if you seemed threatened by her previous questions, she learns early that these questions are too painful to bring to you. If you present adoption as only beautiful and rosy, she feels there must be something wrong with her when she feels hurt and different about being adopted.

The later problems and questions the adolescent has about his or her adoption are a whole different matter. This is a time for coasting if you have been honest and open in the past. You have already answered the difficult questions. If the foundation was never built, it's tough to do it now. The possibility of this age-level child giving you another opportunity to be open and honest again about adoption is slight. No matter what the odds are against you, however, try it anyhow.

Adolescence is a time where most of the concerns and questions about adoption are answered by peers. Your primary task is to make certain that the child has learned to be strong enough as a toddler and as a preadolescent to ask questions.

As the child grows older, the adoptive parents need to convey to him or her that questions about birthparents are not threatening . . . questions are okay to have and to ask. Many times adolescents are very concerned that they not hurt their adoptive parents. The fearful adolescent, or the adolescent with no apparent questions, can be encouraged by the parents to bring up questions. When Melinda was twelve, her best friend Jessie began to mature physically much faster than Melinda. Melinda's astute adoptive mother used the developing difference between them to help Melinda talk about her feelings about being adopted. Her mother brought up that she imagined that Jessie's mother had matured early physically also and probably Melinda's birthmother hadn't. This gave them a chance to talk about ways that adopted children can't look to their adoptive parents to get clues as to how they are likely to develop. It was a chance to say many children don't look like or develop like their birthparents but it is a bit easier when you know what birthparents looked like. Mainly this was a time to open up the subject with Melinda.

There are many times like this. If the child has an eye problem and no one else in the family has one or the seventeen-year-old boy begins to show signs he may bald early or the adolescent has a strong interest in something no one else in his adoptive family is interested in . . . all of these situations are opportunities to deal openly about adoption. You are helping the adopted child feel comfortable with his birthparents, which ultimately helps him accept himself.

Movies, books, television and newspapers are another source of conversation openers. General questions are usually more readily answered than questions such as, "How do you feel about being adopted?" If you read an article on illegitimacy increasing in teenagers, ask your child if she read it and what she thinks about it. If you have a book that relates to adoption, ask your son if he has read it. Some excellent movies have appeared on television about teenagers relinquishing their child for adoption . . . these are usually easy to discuss with young people. Ask what each character should have done or who had the hardest time. Give your opinions also. You certainly don't want this to sound like an inquisition. Maybe after a while you will have each opened up enough to say, "What would you do under these circumstances?" Make opportunities for openness.

One school of thought on adoption says not to tell the child he or she is adopted or to wait until the child is of school age. The psychological issues that are involved here are clear. In all theories of child development, the importance of a trusting relationship with parents is stressed. The child uses the parent as a sounding board to the larger world. The child who feels betrayed because his parents lied to him has great difficulty developing the ability to trust others. The child thinks that, "if these people who love me lie to me, then, of course, other people who don't love me will lie to me, too." The need to lie about adoption is simply not there.

To tell a child his first mommy gave him away because she loved him tells him that if he is loved he may be given away. Instead tell the truth in a way that is appropriate to the child's age, the previous questions he has asked, his level of maturity and on the basis of what he has already learned from others. Even a young child can be told that his mother was very young and in school when she got pregnant. She had no money and felt the child would be better with people who were married and who could give him a home and love, too. To say "I don't know" when you don't know is appropriate. To say "I'll tell you about that when you are older" is also appropriate if you will tell later. Whatever your approach, however, let it be based upon being honest.

Does this mean that when your adopted six-year-old son asks you to tell him about his birthmother that you tell him everything you know? Not at all. You wouldn't say, "Your birthmother was a drug pusher who slept with every guy in town" even if she was and did. You might say, "Your birthmother was a young woman who was having a great deal of difficulty in her life and who couldn't keep you because of the problems she was having." Answer questions honestly but appropriately.

If you have learned to be honest with yourself and honest with your children about adoption, you can also be honest with relatives and friends. You would think that, after you had fielded all the questions about why you couldn't have children, you would be an expert on callous, unthinking questions about adoption. The experience helps but it doesn't prevent this whole new group of questions from being asked.

When your relatives ask about your adopted child's background, it is important to be honest with them. You have no necessity to reveal all to them if you don't want to, but whatever you do choose to tell them should be true. Your stories to these people will ultimately be stories to your adopted children. You want the stories they hear from auntie and grandma to be the same ones they hear from you.

Honesty carries over to areas that you don't like . . . for example, how relatives respond to your child's adoption. One adopted child's grandmother consistently introduced her grandson as her adopted grandson. She was proud of him . . . she even liked this specialness because of his adoption. The adoptive mother finally said to her mother that she didn't like her son being introduced this way. They discussed together that this was not intended to be negative and that the grandmother was indeed proud of this little boy and loved him deeply. The discussion held openly and honestly enabled them each to deal with their feelings about adoption and how being special sometimes doesn't feel good. It hurt a little bit because most people don't like to be criticized. It helped a lot because it openly solved a problem and it was truthful.

Sometimes it is okay to hurt when you are being honest also. A newly adoptive mother had a neighbor who continually pried into the background of their new child. It started out fairly innocuously . . . how old was the mother, was she from this area? Then the questions became too specific. The adoptive mother finally said to the woman, "I am uncomfortable with your questions about Tim's background. We feel this is a very personal thing and we don't want to talk about it." The neighbor was indignant. She said she didn't want to pry. A rift developed between the neighbor and this family. That's sad. It didn't need to be that way but the neighbor chose to handle it in that manner. Being honest isn't always pleasant but neither were the prying questions from this nosy woman.

The adoptive parent has an additional chore in this process in order to fully help the child resolve his or her own feelings about the adoption. The adoptive parent is the primary provider of information and of understanding of the birthparent's side of adoption. The adoptive parent who wants to help his or her child feel positive about being adopted must seek to feel positively about the birthparents who relinquished the child. Only the adoptive parents who can identify with the birthparents' pain can present these people lovingly to the adopted child. Sometimes adoptive parents who have not adequately resolved their feelings about the birthparents pass their unsettled and perhaps competitive feelings about them on to their adopted child. Adoptive parents who know or who have met the birthparents generally have the easiest time conveying positive feelings about the birthparents to the adopted child.

These are individual ways to be honest and open about adoption. It's hard to do this if you are not sure of yourself and your views about adoption. It is also hard to do this when the whole system of adoption you have been involved with has encouraged secretiveness and pretends everything is "normal."

Honesty and Openness in the Adoption System

Many simple ways exist within the current adoption agency system which would allow for increasing the openness and the honesty in adoption. Making every effort to be honest and open in adoption encourages the people who use adoption to view the process more positively. In a system that deals with people who have experienced so much hurt and pain, it is essential that the process that resolves this pain be built on positive, not negative, solutions.

The adoption agency system today is designed to be in the best interest of the child. In the initial stages of adoption proceedings, except in some "special needs" adoptions, the child is the one who has the least pain over the process. In some ways we need to be less concerned about the child and more concerned with all of the other adoption participants who are in greater need of help.

The three other groups of people the adoption agencies work with at this stage of adoption are the birthparents, the adoptive parents and the foster parents. Each of these groups could be dealt with differently than they now are and significantly improve the mental health of the people involved.

Many of the changes in openness and honesty in adoption could be easily incorporated into the adoption agency system that now exists. I believe that the adoption agency system needs a basic philosophical overhaul, but I am also a realist. Since many of the adoption agencies will never go as far as I suggest in the next section on open adoptions, it seems important to suggest interim means of changing to a less secretive and consequently healthier approach to adoption than now exists.

Adoption Agencies and Birthparents People are naturally far more perceptive than we think. You frequently know how people view you without anyone saying a word to you. You also know when you dislike someone and you convey this to them. The same is true when you like them. Adoption agency workers are likely to show in some way their feelings toward the clients they serve. The negative view that adoption workers at times have of birthparents is difficult, if not impossible, to hide.

The attitude of adoption workers toward the birthparents comes out in many ways. The small group meeting in one class on adoption brought this point out vividly. The woman head of an adoption agency who had worked with pregnant women giving up their babies for adoption for twenty years spoke with fervor. She was discussing, not adoption, but sex. She felt premarital sex was *absolutely immoral*. There were no circumstances that she could think of that would condone this type of behavior. All sex outside of marriage indicated promiscuous behavior. It would have been impossible for this woman not to convey her feelings to the hundreds of birthmothers and, at times, birthfathers, with whom she had been working for over twenty years. It would be difficult for these birthparents to gain positive feelings about themselves in this stressful time when their own social worker felt so negatively toward them.

If the social worker from the adoption agency is shocked by the behavior of the birthparents, this negative view is likely to be conveyed. If the social worker does not like the birthparent, she will probably show this in some subtle way. If the worker is disapproving of the woman because she sees her as sexually permissive or loose, these feelings will be difficult to hide from the birthmother. The social worker who wants to be effective with her birthparent client must be able to genuinely care for this person. To try to provide help for someone you do not respect, like, or approve of, is impossible and dishonest.

It seems reasonable to suggest that social workers should have some degree of respect and genuine concern for the people they say they are counseling and helping. In order to sell someone a car, concern and caring aren't necessary. In order to provide information to someone, this type of therapeutic relationship isn't necessary. But to counsel someone, to help them therapeutically, is impossible if the counselor disapproves, dislikes, or distrusts them.

Does this mean social workers have to like every client? *Yes*. If they want to help the client, it's imperative. When workers find that they do not have positive regard for the client they are working with in a therapeutic relationship, they should be honest with themselves and with the clients and turn the cases over to other social workers. Either the clients are sent to workers who can like them and feel positively toward them or they should be told that they will be given information only. When a social worker feels the client is so incompetent that he or she cannot make decisions, there should be no pretense that the client is being counseled. The client may be told what to do, but he or she should not be manipulated under the guise of counseling.

The client who is truly being helped will be given thorough consideration of where he or she is in this adoption. The social worker should find out what the best way is for the individual client to relinquish the child and should work to make the relinquishment as healthy and growth producing as possible for the client. To do this may entail modifying agency procedures. If this is impossible within an adoption agency, the adoption agency is wrong. If adoption agencies are not really providing counseling to the people they say they serve, then they are merely providing babies. It is just another form of selling babies.

Birthparents at times resist adoption agencies because they don't want their child placed in a foster home first. Fine. An adoption agency should be able to accommodate these women with no problem by having direct placement with adoptive homes for the babies of these women.

Birthparents at times resist adoption agencies because they want to know how their child is doing from time to time. This too, should present no problems to an adaptable adoption agency. As long as adoptive parents know this is to be part of the adoption, what is the problem with periodic updates for the birthparents?

Birthparents at times resist adoption agencies because they want to know the adoptive parents. These cases should not be too difficult to comply with and many adoptive parents would readily agree. It doesn't mean the identities are necessarily exchanged, it just means people meet and talk together. If the parties involved aren't against this idea, why should the adoption agency prevent this small degree of openness to the people who wish it?

Birthparents at times resist adoption agencies because they receive little or no financial support while they are producing the baby. This should be an issue addressed by each adoption agency. Financial help does not mean a baby is being sold. Financial help allows a woman to maintain her dignity despite the fact that the child she is carrying will be placed for adoption.

In serving any client therapeutically, the social worker must first find out where that person is and what are his or her wishes for the relationship. *The role of a social worker in an adoption agency is not to provide solutions for people, but rather to help people find the best solutions for themselves.* The social worker is a facilitator in the clients' growth, not the leader. The social worker is a helper toward their goal, not the decider of their fate.

A great need exists to counsel people who are considering relinquishment of their children for adoption. This is one of the main reasons for going to an adoption agency in the first place. When adoption agencies begin to view the needs of all the people who come to them in adoption as equally important, then counseling, real counseling, will be provided.

Adoption Agencies and Adoptive Parents The fact that adoption agencies are threatening to most people who apply with them for a child should be viewed by the adoption agencies as a failure on their part. Certainly it gives the adoption agencies a position of power in adoption, but the goal for adoption agencies should not be power but service.

If the adoption agencies viewed potential adoptive parents as clients to be served, how much more effective and honest everyone could be with each other. If you as an adoptive parent felt the agency worker were there to help you rather than there to eliminate you, how much more beneficial this time would be for you. The emphasis in adoption studies should be on preparing people for parenting.

Adoption agencies are not currently (although maybe more than they should be) preventing their parent rejects from adopting babies. The agency has said you are not good enough for us but that doesn't stop you from going elsewhere to get a baby. Recognizing this, it seems that the agencies should examine why they feel a couple is not ready for a child and help them get ready, rather than to merely eliminate them from the system or to force them to find a child somewhere else. This is the only place in our entire society where people are screened for parenting. Why not use this vehicle as a place to improve parenting skills rather than simply say no to them?

The adoption agencies, of course, reply that because there are too many parents and not enough children to adopt, they must eliminate people. Why? Why instead don't they seek to improve their services to all of the people involved? Maybe then adoption could be more positive and appealing to more women and the scarcity of infants could be alleviated.

The adoption agencies tell their prospective parents to be honest with the agency. The reward for their honesty many times is elimination from the adoption agency system. *The winners of babies are selectively truthful.* They know that to be totally honest is likely to cause their elimination. They have learned how critical it is to be secretive in adoption.

The time the potential parents spend with the social worker from the adoption agency should be real counseling time. All of their feelings of deficiency and inadequacy about infertility should come out here. Their fears about adopting a child should be discussed here. Their disappointments about this kind of parenting should be dealt with here. These are not insurmountable problems ... these are not problems that indicate a couple *should not* adopt a child. This is the place where counseling of this nature should occur. This is the place where adoption agencies say that it does occur. But how can it occur when the adoption agency is trying to judge your fitness to parent? Judging and counseling are not compatible goals. Counseling can occur with adoptive parents only if the adoption agency system's goal is to help the adoptive parents become the best parents possible to their newly adopted child. Some people may become better parents than others, that is not the question. The goal of the adoption agency needs to be changed from the judging of to the helping of people who want to adopt children.

Adoption Agencies and Foster Parents The role that adoption agencies take with foster parents fails to utilize the foster parents to the best advantage. Foster homes become a place to tuck away children while the social worker at the adoption agency decides the child's fate. As a result, isolation of the foster parents has resulted and the foster parents become little involved with either the child's past or future.

As adoption is currently set up, the child who is adopted by some chosen couple is placed with foster parents until that placement is determined. In actuality, the foster placement in most adoptions should be eliminated. When it is necessary, the stay in the foster homes should be as brief as possible. When there are complications with the child or with the birthparents, the child's stay may be longer. It seldom needs to be as long as most foster home placements are. While I strongly believe these stays should be as brief as possible, I also believe that this foster home needs to be more integrated into the adoption process. The increased involvement of foster parents as important participants in the adoption scene can improve the process for the child, the birthparent, the adoptive parents and the foster parents.

The foster parents who believe their opinion is valued could become more involved with the child in their care. Someone, the adoption agency, should want to know their opinion. The adoption agency should want to know how they evaluate this particular child. What things does this child respond to? Is this a demanding child? Is the child socially responsive? The foster parents can make a valuable contribution to the evaluation of a child because they know the child; therefore, they should be involved in the future placement of the child. Especially in long-term foster care, who knows more about the child than the foster parents? Even in short-term foster care of one or two months with the new infant, there is seldom anyone else who knows as much about the child or who has spent as long a period of time with the child as the foster parents have. As you increase the importance of the position of the foster parents in adoption, you are also likely to attract more and more qualified people to this position.

When foster parents see their role as being important, they are also most likely to do a good job. Foster parents who view themselves as only temporarily useful, but never very important, have less involvement with the child than those who see their role as more critical to the child's future placement.

The birthparent who turns the child over to an agency should also turn the child over to the foster parents. What information the birthmother has about her child will be most valuable to the next people who will be caring for the child. This makes the transition healthier for all of these people. The birthmother should be an active participant in the transfer of her child to the next home. She has a chance to view herself as caring enough about the child that she wants this transition to be smooth for the child. If she has spent any time at all with the child, she should have a chance to discuss the child with the next people who will care for him. It makes the birthmother's role more important and it makes the transition of the child easier.

The foster parents should also be involved in the transition of the child from their home to the new adoptive home. There should be an opportunity for these two sets of parents to talk about the child's habits and behavior patterns. Depending on how long this child has been in a foster home, the role of these people takes on increasing significance. To have the foster parents merely write down the child's schedule and a few items about him or her minimizes the role the foster parents have had with the child. Meeting the foster parents, like meeting the birthparents, makes them more real to the adoptive parents. The adoptive parents can see how the child has been cared for . . . how the diapers are put on, how the bottle is held, how the bath is given. The child, even as an infant, is a creature of habit. Changes in his or her routine are not easily tolerated. The fewer changes to be made during major transitions, the better for the child.

The role of the foster parents in adoption is varied. The part the foster parents might have as potentially adopting parents is discussed elsewhere in this book (See Chapter 10). The primary area of discussion at this point is the need for foster parents *not* to become invisible parents in this transition period of the child's life. The importance of the role of the foster parents should be increased. Opening of contacts between each of these sets of parents should strengthen the continuity the child feels in this difficult period. The child who is experiencing this upheaval in his or her primary parenting figures needs as much consistency as possible in the move. Eliminating the separateness between each of his or her homes should help in giving greater consistency and increasing a sense of stability.

Many of the things adoption agencies can do to increase honesty and openness in adoption are simple. The changes don't necessitate the system being shaken to the core. The changes do require adoption agencies' commitment to the elimination of secrecy and separation and to the addition of honesty and openness in their place.

Open Adoption
Open adoption has been a concept studiously avoided by adoption agencies. Their entire being is based upon being an intermediary . . . the adoption agency is the go-between, the decision maker, the chooser, the eliminator, the secret keeper. They keep people apart . . . open adoption brings people together.

Open adoption is a difficult concept to define, mostly because it is multifaceted. Open adoption is basically where there is some degree of contact between the principals involved. The amount of contact is variable. All private adoptions are to some extent open adoptions. The adoption agencies, with rare exceptions, notoriously have avoided contact between birthparents and adoptive parents.

Different Kinds of Open Adoption
To illustrate the tremendous variety of openness that can be possible in open adoption, it seems worthwhile to show some examples of different degrees of contact in open adoption. Minimal, moderate and maximum contact in adoptions are used to describe the varying degrees possible. As a means of hanging material together, even though it seldom fits this neatly, I have chosen to define minimal openness as contact only at the birth of the child and then no more. Moderate openness in adoption is used to describe adoptions where there is some continuing contact between birthparents and adoptive parents but no personal contact. The maximum degree of openness would be in adoptions where visitations continue between the birthparents and the adoptive parents while the adopted child lives with the adoptive parents.

Minimal Contact in Open Adoption Probably most private adoptions would fit into this category of open adoptions. At a minimum, names of birthparents and adoptive parents are exchanged. At times, a contact is made in the hospital when the adopting couple comes to pick up the baby.

Many times this minimal contact between birthparent and adoptive parents is a feared part of private adoptions. In open adoptions it would be an accepted part of the process. It would be viewed as a planning and exchange session between two sets of caring parents.

Hank and Teresa had a chance to participate in an open adoption even though it occurred twenty years ago. They didn't realize how far ahead of their time they were. Hank and Teresa could not make babies, even though they had tried every fertility specialist around their area. They were planning to apply for adoption with an agency when they heard from a neighbor about her sixteen-year-old niece, Mary Beth, who was pregnant and wanted to place the child for adoption. The neighbor arranged for Hank and Teresa to meet Mary Beth. It just seemed that it was the right thing to do at the time. The three people agreed that Hank and Teresa would get Mary Beth's baby when it was born. Hank and Teresa paid Mary Beth's prenatal care. Just before the baby was born, Mary Beth's parents wanted to meet Hank and Teresa also. This time the five of them sat down together and talked about the baby. This would be the first grandchild for Mary Beth's parents and they were concerned about the welfare of the child. The meeting lasted three hours and included a friendly dinner together. Everyone wanted what was best for the child, but they also wanted to feel good about their role in the adoption. As Mary Beth and her parents talked to Hank and Teresa, they found out a great deal about the home in which this child would be raised. In turn, they felt they had a chance to let Hank and Teresa know about each of them and their beliefs and interests. When the meeting was over, everyone left with an extremely positive feeling. Three weeks later a baby girl was born to Mary Beth. Hank and Teresa visited Mary Beth in the hospital. They wanted to pick up their new daughter but it was also important to them to see Mary Beth who had become a very special person to them. Mary Beth said she didn't want to maintain contact with them. She said the contact would be too painful for her and would prevent her from moving ahead with her life. She also told them she didn't need to have contact because she knew how Hank and Teresa would raise her baby. Mary Beth never made contact again with Hank and Teresa. However, Hank and Teresa felt they could always talk positively to their daughter about the caring, involved people who were part of her life before they got her.

This example of a minimum contact went especially well for all of the people involved. There certainly is no reason why this same type of contact could not have been used in an adoption agency setting. It is just that it is not . . . the limitations are the agencies' limitations. These people didn't see anything particularly unusual in their open adoption. What they did seemed natural to them and they saw no reason to put on any limitations.

Moderate Contact in Open Adoptions Moderate contact in open adoptions involves longer contact between the people involved but not personal contact. It is easy to identify with the examples that involve no hesitation between the people involved, but sometimes there are problems.

The case involving Gloria and Don's adoption of a baby boy was filled with problems. Gloria and Don heard about a baby boy who had been left with a neighbor by a young woman, Julie. The neighbor knew Julie's sister. Julie had been involved in drugs and sex since she was twelve. She was a high school dropout at the age of fourteen. Her parents had no control over her. She was slightly retarded from an injury at birth which had also caused her to develop epilepsy. She had been in and out of foster homes and juvenile hall. At eighteen, she had gotten pregnant by a man she barely knew. His past history of violent behavior and a short term in jail for armed robbery didn't deter Julie at all. After she delivered the baby, the man said he didn't want it but she could come with him if she left the baby. Julie left the baby with Gloria and Don's neighbor and took off. The baby boy was obviously not well cared for before she left him with the neighbor. When Don and Gloria heard about the child, they were very interested in adopting him. They wanted to know more about him. They contacted the physician who delivered him but he very blatantly said to them that this child was a "mess." He warned them about the mother's lack of prenatal care and the potential for long-term physical and mental damage to the child as a result of the mother's neglect. He advised them to pass this one up.

They met the grandmother of the boy. It was reassuring to see that she seemed normal and there was no evidence of mental retardation.

Then the father of the boy heard that Don and Gloria were interested in the baby. He talked to them on the phone and they became alarmed. He sounded so rough and coarse. They became concerned that he would try to get money for the child because of threats to them and threats to take the child away. They became fearful and said they didn't want the child.

They were willing to pass on any information to anyone else who was interested in adopting the baby.

The next couple, Susan and Joel learned all of the details from Don and Gloria. Susan and Joel made some additional contacts with the family members, had some testing done on the boy who was now seven weeks old, and consulted a lawyer. Everything seemed acceptable to them . . . not good, but acceptable. Their lawyer said he would handle the case as long as the couple did not go along with any of the birthfather's demands. They agreed.

The other provision the family stipulated as a condition for Susan and Joel adopting the boy was that they maintain contact with the child's biological grandparents. Joel and Susan felt this was a reasonable request. They agreed to write to the grandparents regularly and to send pictures of the boy as he grew.

Joel and Susan hoped to get the birthmother and the birthfather to sign relinquishment papers if they could be found. Since their whereabouts were unknown to anyone, this possibility was uncertain. If they were not found, the plan was to begin abandonment procedures. The biological family of the boy completely supported Joel and Susan's adoption of the child. They knew that if this boy, with all of the negative factors in his background, got into the adoption agency system, he would be viewed as a "special" child. His adoption could be delayed by months, maybe years. They knew they needed to find an open couple who would be able to handle the negative as well as the positive information about this boy. They did.

The exceptional part of this story is that nothing was hidden. Everything was out in the open and the adoptive parents felt the information could be handled. All adoptions are not without negative input, but the desire to adopt a child is strong enough to handle a lot of negative information. Adults, like children, are resilient. The protective screening of negative information implies people are not able to handle it. This simply is not the case. You merely need to find the right people to handle it.

Maximum Contact in Open Adoption The third type of open adoption entails the greatest amount of contact between the birthparents and the adoptive parents. Because adoption agencies do not encourage contact between any of the groups involved in adoption, the example must once again come from private adoption.

Kent and Adrianne never considered adoption. They had two children and were quite content with their family. They were shocked when their very good friend, Tricia, called in a state of panic to tell them she was pregnant. Adrianne encouraged her to come over and talk with her about the situation.

Adrianne and Tricia had been friends for six years. In fact, they had been roommates before Adrianne had married Kent five years ago. Tricia had never married but she remained a close friend to Adrianne and Kent and their children.

Tricia was extremely agitated as she told Adrianne about her pregnancy. She had never dreamed she was pregnant. She had been sexually involved with a man whom she had broken up with two months ago. When her periods seemed a bit unusual, she thought little about it until this last month when she didn't have one at all. Thinking it was related to stress over being out of work, she did nothing. As she didn't feel quite like herself, she decided to go to her doctor for a checkup. She was amazed to learn that she was pregnant and very pregnant at that . . . she was over three months along. There was no way Tricia, who was Roman Catholic, would consider having an abortion . . . especially being this far along in her pregnancy.

As Tricia talked more and more about the situation with Adrianne, she calmed down considerably. She discussed adoption and how hard it would be to just give her baby away to strangers. She discussed keeping the child but she felt that was impossible in her circumstances. She kept coming back to adoption but felt it would simply be too much for her to handle. Then she surprised Adrianne by suggesting that Adrianne and Kent adopt her baby. Adrianne didn't know what to say.

Adrianne and Kent discussed the situation together. They finally decided that if certain areas could be agreed upon with Tricia they would seriously consider the possibility. The three of them talked about the situation numerous times in the next five months. They all agreed that Kent and Adrianne would be the parents . . . totally. Tricia could not interfere in the way they chose to raise the baby. Tricia completely agreed. They felt it was difficult enough for two people to agree on raising children without geometrically increasing the problem by adding a third point of view. Tricia was also very approving of Kent and Adrianne's approach to their one year old and three year old . . . her knowledge of how they were as parents made her confident about how they would raise her child. They all agreed that they would not tell the child that Tricia was his or her mother unless the child ever asked if she was. They were determined to be honest with the child. They felt that if the child discovered Tricia was his or her mother that would not destroy Kent and Adrianne's relationship with the child. At the same time, they all agreed it was easiest for the child to relate to Kent and Adrianne in the growing-up years as his or her only parents.

These arrangements took place six years ago. Adrianne and Kent are delighted with their three children. Their youngest daughter, Carrie, is a joy. Tricia is a regular visitor to the home and enjoys seeing Carrie and their other children grow. She would never dream of interfering. She is grateful to Kent and Adrianne who agreed to this unusual open adoption. Kent and Adrianne are also grateful.

This type of adoption would not appeal to everyone; but as of now, few people ever get a chance to consider it as a possibility. The world is full of many types of people . . . there should be room for many types of adoptions.

Adoption Agencies and Open Adoption

Few adoption agencies advocate a need for open adoptions. Most adoption agencies seem more interested in controlling all adoptions than in enlarging the scope of the way adoptions are being done. There are, however, some noticeable cracks in the usual unified front of adoption agencies.

One of the first voices to be heard to break rank with the traditional adoption agency stance of no contact between adoptive parents and birthparents came from the adoption agency that began the research on opening the sealed birth record, Vista Del Mar, in California. This group maintains that there is a need for a new, different approach to adoption that would appeal to the pregnant woman who is uncomfortable with traditional adoption approaches.

> *The young, single mothers who have an emotional attachment—whether positive or negative—to their children desperately need a new kind of adoptive placement in which they can actively participate. They want the security of knowing they have helped provide their children with a loving, secure existence and yet have not denied themselves the possibility of knowing them in the future.*[2]

These glimmers of new creative approaches to adoption within the adoption agency system hold out hope for seeing the changes necessary to make adoption a healthy, positive alternative to be considered by the unhappily pregnant woman.

A second, more recent shift comes from an adoption agency across the nation. The Peirce-Warwick Adoption Service in Washington, D.C. and The Adoptive Research Council in Maryland will give both sets of parents the option to exchange names, visitation rights and personal histories. They require all of the people to at least keep the adoption agency up to date so that the birthparents can know about the child they have placed for adoption.[3]

The reason this is being done is that one of the social workers, Linda Burgess, believes that open adoptions will make "more children available for adoption while making adoption healthier for the child and all other parties involved."[3] Burgess, who has written about adoption in other progressive ways,[4] believes that more mothers would willingly give up their children if adoption were approached differently, with new options as to how the adoption was handled. She feels traditional adoption being considered as an option has difficulty competing with abortion and keeping the baby. She advocates that this option in adoption will decrease the adopted child's sense of rejection. Being able to tell the child of the birthparents who wanted to be involved in the child's future will ease the feelings of being rejected. The meeting between the birthparents and the adoptive parents will help lessen the birthparents' sense of guilt over leaving the child. A chance to sit down and talk together should benefit both sets of parents and ultimately the child, too.

As part of this new approach from this group, the adoption records will be opened to the child when she or he becomes an adult. Burgess maintains that this is the "real beginning in this country for sane, healthy adoptions."[3]

Obviously this agency's approach to open adoption will be closely watched by other adoption agencies. The courage to be different in this field deserves applause and support.

Open Adoption Historically

Open adoption has probably played a more significant part in adoption in our society in earlier times. Especially in rural areas where adoption agency services were less expansive, the informal contact between adoptive parents and birthparents was more common in the 1920s and 1930s.[2] As the adoption agency system expanded and became more powerful, these open adoptions decreased. But in this area, as in many other areas of our lives, some of the lessons from the past have valuable application to today.

The experience of people who have been adopted in open adoptions is valuable to us. At times, contacts that have been maintained have even included the full knowledge of the adopted child that this other woman is his or her birthmother. Open adoptions have even included temporary visits with the birthmother which appear to have been beneficial to each of the people involved. There is no evidence to prove any damage has resulted in these open adoptions.

In the Hawaiian culture and the Eskimo culture, forms of open adoption have been successfully practiced for years. [2,3] The problems in these cultures seem to arise not with the openness of adoption but more when the modern American form of secret adoption is imposed on these people.

Risks in Open Adoptions

As with any procedure there are risks involved. There are risks to you if you are active or inactive. There is no way people can guarantee protection in their lives. Living is risk taking.

Of course there are risks in open adoption. Traditional adoption is not without risks either. The ultimate risk in open adoption is "Can I lose my adopted child?" Yes, you can. But, you can lose any child. Remember, no one owns their children, adopted or biological. The risk of losing a child to the birthparent in an open adoption is not greater than the risk of losing your child in a traditional adoption. The risk is more apparent because you know and can identify the threat . . . the other parent. This is true in divorce cases also. In divorce cases, however, there is generally more competition for the child. In open adoption, the basic underlying agreement is that there will be no competition for the child. It seems you have far less risk of losing your child in an open adoption than you might have of losing your child in a divorce.

In many ways it is far easier in any kind of competition to know who your competition is. To compete with a child's fantasy of his or her birthparent is probably much more difficult than to have this clearly out in the open.

Summary

A significant number of women are rejecting adoption as an alternative to their unwanted pregnancy. Adoption is not an appealing prospect to them. Adoption has failed for them to meet whatever need they had. We need to understand this failure and to make the necessary changes within the adoption agency system to make adoption appeal to more of these women. Adoption must change.

In our individualistic society it is important to be adaptable. Many kinds of women get pregnant. The healthiest way to deal with each woman's pregnancy is with a custom-made solution. There is room in our society for many kinds of people, many kinds of pregnancy solutions and many kinds of adoptions.

It is difficult to sell things that are hidden. Adoption is facing a public relations problem. It simply does not appeal to as many people as it needs to . . . that's why we have a shortage of babies available for adoption. One of the best ways to remedy this problem is to develop a new image . . . an image based on openness.

Changes in adoption involve not just changes in the attitudes of adoption agencies but also in the attitudes of individuals. Honesty is ultimately an individual issue. If you believe strongly enough in it, your influence will eventually be felt by the institutions who serve you and others in adoption. If enough people who go to the adoption agencies are open to new approaches, more open approaches, adoption will change. In order to help the most people toward a more healthy outcome from adoption we need these changes toward open, honest adoptions, and we need them now.

13
CLEANING
UP THE GAME

No book has all the final answers on adoption. Adoption needs to fluctuate and change with the changes in our society. Constant shifting requires an underlying attitude of adaptability. I, too, want that adaptability. The questions, answers and recommendations I have put forth in this book are not the only ones for adoption. As adoption changes, newer and better approaches should be suggested and tried. There are no final answers.

Certain factors could radically alter adoption as we know it today. New advances in curing infertility could drastically change the numbers of people who need to adopt children. Changes in society's attitude toward abortion could end the scarcity of babies available for adoption. The adoption field should be designed to accommodate changes rather than to perpetuate past practices.

It is apparent that adoption agencies have not accepted the challenge to change. When an institution fails to keep in touch with the people they serve, they lose their perspective. The institution of adoption has not remained vital . . . it has lost touch with the people it needs in order to justify its existence. The adoption agencies are *not* responsive to the needs of the clients.

Lawmakers, looking to the adoption agencies for information about adoption, pass laws that reflect the adoption agencies' view. As a consequence, the laws governing adoptions are not any more responsive to the need for change than are the adoption agencies. The most adaptable people in adoption seem to be the ones who seek to fight the adoption system. The birthparents and the adoptive parents who find their own ways to make adoption work show creativity and hope in an exemplary way to all people who want to improve adoption.

Because of this need to revitalize adoption, I have made numerous suggestions I think would significantly improve what is being done in adoption today. These suggestions are not the only possible solutions but I believe they would improve adoption for all of the people involved. Both adoption agencies and adoption laws should be based upon a flexible system which is adaptable to the changing needs of society. My first two sets of recommendations are specifically directed to the adoption agencies and the state legislators.

Finally I have recommendations for you people who want to adopt a child. The recommendations for you as potential adoptive parents are somewhat different. They are based not on a need for change but rather on the ingredients you need for a successful baby search. After all, helping you to succeed in your search for a child is what this book is all about.

Adoption Agency Recommendations
Although this book is intended primarily to help people find the child they want, the need to communicate with the adoption agencies is also apparent. Adoption agencies need to carefully scrutinize their procedures, rules and goals. The recommendations that follow are suggestions for changes which are urgently needed within the adoption agency system. While they suggest areas of needed change for the agencies, they also demonstrate to the adoptive applicants the obstacles which confront them in working with the adoption agencies.

RECOMMENDATION 1 ... ADOPTION AGENCIES SHOULD BECOME ACTIVELY INVOLVED IN RECRUITING BABIES FOR ADOPTION.

Adoption agencies have stayed in their sequestered agency settings long enough. The time has come for these groups to go out into the community and promote adoption as an alternative to unwanted pregnancies. More than a million women a year are obtaining abortions. Few of these women even know about or consider adoption as an alternative to their unwanted pregnancy. The adoption agencies need to present the adoption alternative to these women. It's not enough for adoption agencies to wait for women to show up on their doorstep between nine and five, Monday through Friday. Pregnancy decisions can't wait for the convenience of the adoption agency. The adoption agency needs to reach out to the women who are pregnant when the women need the help.

"Pregnancy counseling" is being done by lay counselors in the local communities. Few of the groups doing this "counseling" understand the current state of adoption and the scarcity of babies for adoption. Few of the groups doing this "counseling" know the techniques of counseling which are necessary to help a woman make the best pregnancy decision for her. To rely on these "pregnancy counselors" to present adoption as a good alternative to an unwanted pregnancy is naive and obviously not working.

The adoption agencies should become activists in promoting adoption in the pregnancy counseling clinics where pregnant women go to make their decisions. If the scarcity of adoptable infants is to be alleviated, the adoption agencies must talk to the woman before she decides what to do about her unwanted pregnancy. As the current system operates, the only women who go to the adoption agencies are those who have been unable to find a better way out of their dilemma. Adoption should be designed to be viewed as a good alternative to their pregnancy problem.

Adoption can be a healthy alternative to abortion or to keeping an unwanted child. Adoption agencies need to believe this enough to convince many of the women who chose abortion or who chose to keep a child they aren't certain they want. Whatever stops women from considering adoption as an alternative to an unwanted pregnancy should be carefully examined to see if it can be changed; adoption needs to be able to be made into a desirable pregnancy alternative.

Adoption agencies need to hire professional public relations firms in order to effectively "sell" adoption. They should use television, radio, newspapers and magazines. Free public service advertisements should regularly be used by adoption agencies to promote adoption as an alternative to an unwanted pregnancy. Booths should be established at local shopping centers and public events to tell about adoption. Schools should have presentations to tell about adoption today and the large demand for babies by enthusiastic, young social workers who can readily appeal to young women. Newspapers are always seeking interesting stories and adoption has interesting stories. Counterculture newspapers especially should be used. The attempt should be made to move out into the community to appeal to the pregnant women instead of sitting back and *hoping* they will come to the established adoption agencies. Many women would elect to place children for adoption if adoption were effectively sold to the public. Promote adoption ... it can be a good, healthy alternative to an unwanted pregnancy.

Adoption agencies need to be advocates for adoption. If adoption agencies aren't, who will be? Who is now an advocate for adoption?

RECOMMENDATION 2 ... ADOPTION AGENCIES SHOULD SERVE ALL THE PARTIES IN ADOPTION EQUALLY.

In order for all of the people involved in adoption to receive maximum benefits, the adoption agencies should be dedicated to serving each of them equally. There is no logical reason to believe that only one primary client's interests need to be served. Adoption agencies should be committed to meeting the needs and serving the interests *equally* of all of the people involved in adoption ... the child, the birthparents and the adoptive parents.

This philosophical change from serving only the interests of the child to equally serving the interests of all of the people will be a radical change for adoption agencies. This change alone should modify and improve the approach the adoption agencies take with the birthparents and with the adoptive parents. It also will change the approach the adoption agencies take with the adult adoptees.

One of the primary differences a change of this nature makes is that the clients being served are adults as well as children. When adults are served by the adoption agencies, their thoughts and their wishes must be given a high priority. Adoption agencies cannot speak for them as they have been able to for the young child. The implications are clear. The change would mean that adoption agencies would work with their clients to help them. Adoption should be a shared venture with the agencies and their clients working toward a common goal. The agencies should commit themselves to helping each and every person who comes for help. No one should be sent away as a reject. The adoption agencies need to commit to a new mission ... equality in adoption for every man, woman and child.

RECOMMENDATION 3 ... ADOPTION AGENCIES SHOULD MAKE ADOPTION THROUGH ADOPTION AGENCIES MORE APPEALING TO THE BIRTHMOTHER.

A pregnant woman who is considering adoption should be able to go through her pregnancy with dignity and self-respect. This is not easy to do with the adoption agency system operating the way it currently is. Because of this, the adoption agencies need to change to make adoption through them more attractive to the pregnant woman.

If a woman is pregnant she can obtain an abortion for a small cost. If she chooses to carry this child to term and place the child for adoption privately, some eager couple will gladly pay her expenses. If she chooses to carry the child to term and place it for adoption with an adoption agency, the pregnancy expenses must be borne by her. She may be forced to go on welfare, borrow money from family or friends, or barely subsist, but no financial help is given her if she plans on placing her child with an adoption agency. This is wrong. There is no reason adoption agencies could not change policies or even laws which prevent them from providing the woman with the financial help she needs. A woman should receive financial help with her medical and personal expenses when she plans on giving up the child for adoption.

In order for the pregnant woman to end up in a better place after this experience she needs to feel good about herself during her pregnancy. A regular financial allowance to help her with expenses even beyond medical expenses is just and reasonable. The adoption agencies have the ability to change the laws related to the expenses a birthmother can have paid to her. This allowance should not be enough to entice women to become pregnant for pay (although this perhaps should also be considered) but certainly enough to make her not feel demeaned or punished by her decision to place her child for adoption.

The costs of the medical and non-medical payments could be passed on to the adopting couple in most cases. If the same couple adopts privately, they will incur some expenses for the birthmother. If they get involved in black market adoptions they will assuredly pay far more. If the additional financial assistance would help more women to place children for adoption, it certainly should be considered.

The pregnant woman should have the right in an adoption agency to be involved in when and where the child is placed for adoption. The adoption agencies should promote this to women as an incentive for them to use an agency. Pregnant women should be able to have a say about the type of family the child will be placed with, the amount of contact or specific information she wants to have with the adoptive parents, and the potential of an immediate placement of the child in a new home. The decisions about the adoption should be made by birthmothers and the adoption agencies as *equal* partners.

RECOMMENDATION 4 . . . ADOPTION AGENCIES SHOULD MAKE ACCEPTANCE FOR ADOPTION EASIER.

Every effort needs to be made by adoption agencies to accept the people who apply to' them to adopt a child. Only in the most extreme cases should people be turned away. With proper help and support, most people's parenting skills can improve. The effort of the adoption agency should be to improve the parenting skills of potential adoptive parents, not to send them someplace else to get a baby.

Adoption agencies that become more flexible in meeting the wishes of birthparents also can become more flexible in accepting different kinds of people as adoptive parents. The adoption agency should ultimately decrease its power to accept and reject applicants and allow the birthmother to become more active in the decision about who will be the adoptive parent of her child.

RECOMMENDATION 5 . . . ADOPTION AGENCIES SHOULD PROVIDE COUNSELING TO THEIR CLIENTS.

The counseling services of the adoption agencies should be set up to really offer counseling to the birthparents, the adoptive parents and the adoptee. At a very minimum, a pregnant woman who elects to relinquish her child to an adoption agency should be assured she will receive adequate counseling. Certainly, an adoptive couple should be assured they will receive counseling on how to find a child and the potential areas of difficulty they might have with adopting when they go to an adoption agency. The adoptee having difficulty with his or her adoption should be able to receive counseling from the adoption agency.

Most adoption agencies are not providing counseling services to their clients. To truly counsel means to accept the client and be non-judgmental. Counseling means to believe there are choices; the person who needs to make the choices is the client.

The pregnant woman should be accorded greater respect from adoption agencies. Only social workers who genuinely like and respect the woman should counsel her. Anyone who disapproves of what the birthmother has done will pass their disapproval on and do more harm than good in the name of counseling her. The relationship between client and counselor should be based on mutual positive regard.

Counseling should be ongoing if the client wishes. The staff of the adoption agency should be open to contacts anytime after a placement is made, even when the adopted child becomes an adult.

Counseling feels good if it is done correctly. Counseling, when it is non-judgmental and accepting, is very appealing to most people ... a chance to talk about themselves with an objective person who helps the person view things from many sides. The agencies are an ideal place for counseling all of their clients to benefit them and society.

RECOMMENDATION 6 ... ADOPTION AGENCIES SHOULD ENCOURAGE OPENNESS AND HONESTY IN ADOPTION.

Adoption is ready to come out of the closet. The secrets in adoption are no longer necessary. The hiding and the separateness should be forced out of the adoption agency system and be replaced by openness and honesty.

Adoption's entire image needs to personify openness and honesty. The setting should be part of this changed image. Visiting the typical adoption agency is like visiting a medical clinic. The receptionist acts as a guard of all of the closed doors that line the long, dim corridors. Each cubicle exudes hidden secrets. Amazingly, children are rarely seen at the adoption agency. The surroundings are professionally foreboding at best. The setting needs to be opened, the people need to be opened and adoption needs to be opened.

One means of achieving this physical representation of openness is to go out more into the community. The agencies should become part of the community by having small centers that are open to talk about adoption in shopping areas. The free clinics and the pregnancy counseling agencies need to have friendly, equal interaction with the adoption agency social workers. Adoption agencies need to have their social workers on staff at the community agencies and their literature on site. Both staff and literature should be carefully chosen to appeal to young women. Visits to the schools can be done outside of the ordinary adoption agency setting. Take the message about adoption to the community in an open, outgoing manner.

Use the people who have adopted or who are adopted to openly sell adoption. Have art displays from adopted children. Have open houses where people involved with adoption can tell the public how rewarding it is.

Encourage the sharing of information in adoption from one person to the next. Instead of hiding one person from another, go the opposite direction. Let some social life into the social agency. Encourage the free sharing of information which brings people together rather than separates them.

Conditions that make it impossible for one person to adopt a certain child can be completely acceptable to another person. As adoption agencies accept many different kinds of adoptive applicants, it will be easier to adopt with openness and honesty. There is nothing to hide in adoption. The absolute worst imaginable things in adoption are acceptable to someone.

Openness and honesty can also mean to become actively involved in helping bring about reunions between birthparents and adult adoptees when requested. Reunions can be held in many different forms. The adoption agencies have a beautiful opportunity to help with reunions in the way the involved people wish. Reunions can be held with or without identities. Information can be relayed which meet some people's needs without going any further. Reunions can be made to order; let people have reunions in their own way. This is their game.

RECOMMENDATION 7 ... ADOPTION AGENCIES SHOULD FACILITATE AND ENCOURAGE IMMEDIATE ADOPTIVE PLACEMENTS WITH NO TEMPORARY FOSTER HOME CARE.

Foster homes are an inadequate substitute for permanent adoptive home placements. The child who is being shifted from one mother to the next should have as few switches as possible. In most infant placements, the child should be placed in the adoptive home immediately after the birthmother surrenders the child. Foster care between the two homes, while it provides absolute security and certainty about the birthmother's position, is detrimental to the child and to the adoptive parents.

Bonding is necessary in order for the child and the parents to feel secure in the new relationship. The earlier this is done, the better. The positive benefits of early bonding far outweigh the risks that the recommendation for immediate placement might entail.

There will be errors with this change. Some birthmothers may change their minds after the placement, but before the legal relinquishment is made. Those will be difficult cases. The adoptive parents need to understand the potential for this happening. Most adoptive parents will still choose this alternative over the security of having a foster mother raise their child for the first month or more.

RECOMMENDATION 8 . . . ADOPTION AGENCIES SHOULD BECOME INFORMATION CENTERS ON ADOPTION.

Adoption agencies should become the creative, dynamic hub of a healthy, vital adoption system. They should be the places to find out about all forms of adoption. They should be the place to which all information on adoption is channeled. Rather than trying to choke off all other ways to adopt, the adoption agencies should become centers to help all kinds of people find babies from everywhere.

The person trying to adopt a child today needs to search for huge amounts of information before he begins the process. The pregnant woman needs to know the right place to go before she seeks help in making her pregnancy decision. No single source of help and information is available to people to help them find the best direction. Adoption agencies could be this expansive, helping source.

Adoption agencies should know which lawyers in town are best qualified to assist in the adoption of a child from a foreign country. They should know which doctors are best for low-income women to obtain abortions from. They should know which parent groups provide support systems for private adoption in Mexico. They should know which physicians in town provide the most creative help to increase fertility. Adoption agencies that accept the alternative forms of adoption and all of the different kinds of people can afford to be creative and expansive.

Legal Recommendations

Some of the areas in need of change in adoption are neither the responsibility of the adoption agencies nor of the adoptive parents. Changes involving the institution of adoption, at times, primarily concern the legal framework which has developed around adoption. Laws, customs and precedence determine how adoption operates. The following recommendations are based on the belief that some of the laws in adoption need to be changed.

RECOMMENDATION 1 . . . ALL ADOPTIVE PARENTS, WHETHER WAITING FOR PRIVATE PLACEMENTS, INTERNATIONAL PLACEMENTS, OR PLACEMENTS THROUGH AN ADOPTION AGENCY, SHOULD BE EASILY LICENSED BEFORE THE PLACEMENT.

In effect, this recommendation means that adoptive parents receive a license to be a parent. This license should be good anywhere in the United States. It would mean you have met the requirements necessary to adopt a child.

The standards for receiving your license should be the minimal standards deemed necessary to be a parent. It should be like a driver's license . . . not so difficult that most people can't pass, but not so easy that if you are unfit you will be allowed to drive. If there are deficiencies that are apparent in your parenting skills, remedies should be sought that will correct the problem and allow you to be licensed to receive a child for adoption at a later point.

There are several reasons for this recommendation. First, there is no evidence that being eliminated by an adoption agency stops people from adopting children. Secondly, adoption placements, with all of their careful screening techniques, show no better results than in private adoptions where little screening takes place. The third reason for this recommendation is that if there are any obvious problems, this would allow people to remedy them. The fourth reason is that if people are licensed ahead of time, any child that becomes available for placement could then be placed more quickly with anyone who is already licensed.

Licensing should be acceptable in all agencies. Adoptive parenting licensure should have provisions for periodic updating.

RECOMMENDATION 2 . . . THE POST-PLACEMENT WAITING PERIOD IN ADOPTION SHOULD BE REDUCED OR ELIMINATED ENTIRELY.

The post-placement waiting period before adoptions are legalized are an unnecessary intrusion in adoptive families' lives. This time period should be significantly reduced or eliminated. It does little good and great harm.

If home studies prior to placement can't identify significant problems, why would additional home studies after the couple has the child be any more effective. In a very few cases a family incompatibility might be detected. The same incompatibilities are found at times in biological homes.

This unnecessary and repetitive study of the adopting home prevents bonding from occurring between the adopted child and the adopting parents. For this period of time, the adoptive parents are merely foster parents because the agency can remove the child from the home at any time. The child and the parents must fully feel the permanency of the relationship if the necessary parent-child bond is to be firmly established. This is a time for total, not partial, commitment.

RECOMMENDATION 3 ... FOSTER CARE SHOULD BE FORCED TO BE TEMPORARY.

Foster care becomes a way for people to avoid making decisions about the child. It prevents birthparents from deciding to keep or to relinquish a child. It prevents adoption agencies from moving ahead rapidly in placing children for adoption. It prevents birthparents from making the necessary changes they need to make in their lives in order to reclaim the child they have placed in foster care.

Except in rare circumstances, every child is adoptable. There is no reason a child needs to remain in foster care for lack of an adoptive home. When agencies find no home for a specific child it means they have not gone far enough, been open enough, or creative enough in their approach.

Foster care serves a useful temporary care approach for families having difficulty coping with day-to-day living problems. If the situation is not remedied in a brief period of time, the child deserves to have a permanent solution anyhow. Either the family is helped to reinvolve the child in their lives or the child should be given another chance with another family.

Foster care is expensive in terms of the child's mental health and in terms of the taxpayer's money. To allow children to remain permanently in temporary foster care is a disservice that can be remedied by mandating the length of time any child can be left in this state of limbo.

RECOMMENDATION 4 ... PREGNANCY COUNSELING AGENCIES SHOULD BE INVESTIGATED.

To advertise that a pregnant woman will receive counseling about her pregnancy is a very serious commitment. Counselors in most states are licensed by the state to make certain that they are qualified to perform the services they advertise. Yet, in the area of "pregnancy counseling" the same standards are not upheld. Anyone is allowed to counsel the pregnant woman.

Whenever pregnancy counseling is offered, the counselors should be qualified. The pregnant woman who seeks help with the decision about her unborn child believes the "counselor" she speaks with has the necessary qualifications and skills to help her. The pregnant woman should be assured that counselors are qualified.

In some agencies that do pregnancy counseling, their livelihood is based on which decision the woman chooses for the resolution of her pregnancy. Kickbacks, whether for sending the woman for an abortion or sending her to someone who deals in selling babies, prevent objective counseling.

Obviously pregnancy counseling clinics are meeting a need or they would not exist. In fact, many of their reasons for success should be lessons to the usual, traditional health care systems. It is time now to improve the operation of the pregnancy counseling groups. At the very least, the groups should be called pregnancy information centers not pregnancy counseling centers. Then the woman will know she received *information* about her pregnancy, *not counseling*. However, each agency should have some trained counselors to help women who are trying to decide what to do about their pregnancy. These trained counselors should fully understand the implications of each of the alternatives to an unplanned pregnancy.

The pregnancy counseling a woman receives can significantly affect her long-term mental health. It is unfair for women to receive counseling that may create problems for them in years to come. Having had an abortion is not a necessary requirement to being a "pregnancy counselor." Women need an opportunity to make well-thought-out decisions for themselves on how to handle their unwanted pregnancy. As in most areas of counseling, the choice must be theirs; their manner of making the choice can be greatly aided with the help of a trained counselor.

RECOMMENDATION 5 ... LEGAL PROVISIONS SHOULD BE MADE TO CHANGE THE ADVERSARY ROLE IN ADOPTION.

The legal fee for most normal adoption proceedings is significant. The fee includes a minimum amount of work by an attorney and a brief visit to court the day the adoption is legalized.

In most routine adoptions the work of the attorney can be done by a secretary or by the parties involved in the adoption; the routine court appearance is a procedure with little value. Adoption in most cases should be a routine civil procedure that needs neither an attorney nor an appearance in court.

This possibility should be considered as a means to reduce costs to the adoptive parents. Certainly there should be room for many kinds of adoption proceedings just as the public has insisted on making the same provision in divorce proceedings. Some divorces are such that the couple is able to do the legal work without the help of a lawyer; others are far more complex and necessitate extensive legal help. Adoption is ready for a similar distinction.

RECOMMENDATION 6 . . . LEGAL PROVISIONS SHOULD BE MADE TO OPEN BIRTH RECORDS OF ADOPTEES.

The legal provisions to open birth records of adult adoptees should be enacted. Rather than have the issue forced, the records should be opened in an orderly fashion. Preparation should now be made for this ultimate eventuality. All current adoptions should include preparation for the opening of the birth records when the child becomes an adult. Adoption agencies should become involved with updating past adoption cases.

RECOMMENDATION 7 . . . MANY DIFFERENT KINDS OF ADOPTION SHOULD BE ENCOURAGED.

In this time of scarcity of adoptable children, many kinds of adoption should be encouraged. Now is the time to be creative in attempting to make adoption an appealing alternative to unhappily pregnant women. With the many kinds of people there is ample room for many kinds of adoption. Open adoption is appropriate for some people; traditional agency adoption is appropriate for others. Some people's needs will be best met in private adoptions, others in agency adoptions. There is room for many kinds of adoption.

Adoption monopolies must be vigorously resisted before adoption agencies gain absolute control over all adoptions. No one group, no matter how well meaning, should be allowed to dominate adoption or to set rules and regulations for everyone. To meet the problem of the lack of adoptable children by giving all the power and control to the adoption agencies, is merely to develop a monopoly and is not a solution. No one group has all the answers for all the people in adoption. The law should reflect this.

Recommendations for Adoptive Parents
Many suggestions for finding your child have been given throughout this book. In all the suggestions given there is a great deal of overlap. Ultimately, searches for a child are based upon a philosophical approach to adoption. Specific suggestions fall into a general feeling about

searching for a child. The following recommendations are basically the philosophy of a search for a child.

RECOMMENDATION 1 ... BE THOROUGHLY INFORMED ABOUT EACH STEP YOU TAKE.

Throughout this book, the theme—knowledge of what you are doing—has been repeated. It is a critical ingredient in achieving success in pursuing a child or in getting the most out of many areas of life. You can save yourself time and frustration by knowing what you are doing ahead of time. The knowledge you have enables you to ask the right questions and to give the correct answers.

You need to be knowledgeable in pursuing your infertility. Know the doctors to go to, read the right books, ask the important questions. Know how far you need to go, for you.

You need to be knowledgeable in your visits with the adoption agency. Learn about the agency you are going to, read about adopting through an agency, find out what they are looking for in adoption applicants. Know how these fit you.

You need to be knowledgeable about private adoption as well as agency adoption. Know the differences, the similarities, the risks and the advantages. Figure out what sounds best to you but don't eliminate other options.

Knowledge can be gained from many sources—individuals, parent groups, adoption agencies, lawyers, physicians and books. Hear all sides because one source won't inform you of all options.

The knowledge with which you pursue adoption will help you assess where to go, when to stop, where to go next, and how best to proceed. Knowing yourself and the adoption system gives you the ability to most effectively move toward your goal.

RECOMMENDATION 2 ... BE ASSERTIVE AND A LITTLE BIT MORE.

The people who really want to find a baby are willing to push the issue. They actively pursue their goal rather than passively waiting for something to happen for them. They are able to be assertive in their baby search.

At times, it is necessary to take an approach that is a little bit more than assertive. This is not necessarily a combative approach, but it is more than just taking no for an answer. If the adoption agency turns you down, go back and seek the reasons why. Don't just take no and leave. After all, what do you have to lose? Find out if you can remedy your potential parenting "faults," whatever they are. What recourse do you have available to you to get them to change their minds?

There are times when additional letters of reference may prove your fitness. Evaluation of your mental health by a psychologist or psychiatrist may prove to the adoption agency your serious intent to pursue the attainment of a child to the limits. Let the adoption agency know you intend to find a child.

Sometimes a letter from an attorney discussing discrimination might be in order. At times, the reasons for a person's rejection are discriminatory.

Take control and go after what you want. In many ways your willingness to seek your goal vigorously is the most overt sign of the strength of your desire to have a child. Fight the system if you can; certainly fight the system if it might get you your baby.

RECOMMENDATION 3 . . . BE ADAPTABLE.

Adoption is a time of testing . . . testing your limits, testing your openness and flexibility, testing your patience and perseverance. Pursuing a child will cause you to stretch your limits in all of the areas. Stretching your limits requires adaptability. Be open to the many different ways to find a child. Be flexible in what kind of child you might consider adopting. Be creative in how you approach adoption with the child you ultimately find. Basically, be adaptable to today.

Think carefully before you say "no" to any of the suggestions that might be put before you. Is there a way for your "no" to possibly be a "yes"?

Your openness to different ways to look for a child, things to read, places to go, people to meet, all significantly increase your chances of getting a child. It is easy to sit at home and think about how it would be best to just get pregnant or how it would be great to have the agency hand you a darling new baby. The daydreams are nice but you have to deal realistically with the world as it is. Determine what the critical ingredients in your dreams are. See if many situations might meet your criteria and if other parts of your dreams aren't quite as critical as you thought. Adapt your dreams to the reality of adoption today.

RECOMMENDATION 4 . . . PURSUE FINDING A CHILD FROM MANY APPROACHES SIMULTANEOUSLY.

Adoption should be pursued from more than one direction at a time. Before you can be sure you need to adopt, you may need to be certain you are infertile. At times this final diagnosis is difficult to make. However, you may want to begin to look for a child even before you are absolutely positive you cannot get pregnant.

If time is ticking by each time you proceed on one course to find a child you must use your time wisely. If you wait until you are certain that this course will not give you a child before you go on to a subsequent course, you might be too old to pursue all of the many possibilities open to you. Pursue alternatives concurrently. After it seems you are unlikely to get pregnant, begin to pursue adoption even before you have a definite answer about your fertility. Pursue a child privately at the same time you are trying to adopt through the adoption agency.

If your goal is a child, go after it in several ways at the same time. You will increase your chances of success significantly. If all of a sudden you simultaneously find yourself accepted by the adoption agency, pregnant, and a lawyer is calling to say he has a baby for you—that's great! There are plenty of people around who want the children you are not able to accommodate . . . no one will be left out. The dilemma this poses is certainly better than pursuing one alternative at a time. Just knowing that you have some other possibilities makes failure at any juncture easier to handle.

RECOMMENDATION 5 . . . TRY TO BECOME COMFORTABLE WITH FAILURE.

Failure is the primary result you will have as you search for a child. All you need is one success, so expect some failures before your one success. You may fail in your fertility attempts, you may be rejected when you apply to adopt, you may find most people unable to help you find a baby. It is important to view the search for a child as a series of failures in your search for one success . . . a baby.

I always like the lesson I learned from one of my students years ago. He tried to explain how he had failed at his task. He said he didn't really fail, it was actually a "near success." Perhaps adoption searches are not filled with many failures but merely a lot of "near successes."

RECOMMENDATION 6 . . .ONCE YOU HAVE YOUR CHILD, ENJOY HIM FULLY WHILE YOU HAVE A CHANCE TO PARTICIPATE IN HIS LIFE.

Hopefully your journey to find a child has taught you to be risk taking, flexible, persevering, open, assertive, and eager to participate in raising your child. The adoption search will probably have improved your parenting ability, so the search itself has not been a waste of time.

Some studies have indicated that adoptive families seek psychological help for problems in greater numbers than non-adoptive families. Researchers imply that this is because the people who have worked with adoption agencies come to rely on agencies to solve their problems. Hopefully, the new adopting parents will have learned far more than their adoptive parent predecessors.

Let the lessons you have learned carry over into your concepts of parenting. Enjoy your child so that he can learn to enjoy life. Be honest with him about life and about his origins so he can learn that honesty is not only tolerable, but also desirable. Teach him to pursue the things in life that are valuable to him, as you have done. Help him view the problems he confronts from many directions so that he sees many solutions to life's dilemmas. Encourage him to become comfortable with his failures, not so that he becomes defeated by them, but so that instead he becomes resilient and ready to try new approaches. Show him the value of new ideas that open up new choices for him when he feels the rest of the alternatives have been exhausted. Let him experience the rewards of being in charge of his life rather than being buffeted by others.

Adoption searches have value beyond the goal that is pursued. The quest for a child teaches us many of life's lessons. Share your learning with your child in order that he, too, may gain from your finding him.

And Finally . . .

The adoption game isn't an easy game to play, but it can be an exciting one. Illogical rules and undocumented, unspecified criteria for success make the game suitable only for the most skillful players. Still, it is no wonder that people willingly participate . . . the winners get such a fantastic prize.

There is a strong need to change the adoption game . . . in fact, to eliminate adoption from being viewed as a game at all. But, the unnecessary barriers and the artificial roadblocks in adoption create a gamelike quality to the adoption process. Adoption will no longer be a game when it becomes a healthy system designed to thoroughly serve all of the people who participate.

While adoption remains a game, it is incumbent on you, who seek to use the adoption system, to make it as good an experience as possible. Hopefully, the experience you have in the adoption game will cause you to become motivated to change the system to a healthier, more vital means of finding a child to raise. Your adoption involvement does not end with getting a child . . . that is merely a point along the way. In one way or another, adoption holds you forever once you begin.

Adoption can be a negative or a positive in your life. Infertility can be viewed as a deficiency and a punishment, or it can be viewed as an exciting opportunity to pursue a different kind of family. Your search for a child can be viewed as an opportunity for growth and new experiences. Your ultimate success in finding a child can be viewed as a culmination of your search to have a family like everyone else or it can be viewed as a beautiful chance to borrow a child to enrich both your life and the life of the child. While feelings of rejection, deficiency and isolation will undoubtedly be a part of your baby search, do all that you can to feel positively about the time of your life you are experiencing. You *can* make a positive out of a negative.

Believe you will get a child and you are most likely to find one. While you maintain hope you have a chance . . . a good chance . . . to find a child. When you get discouraged, talk about it, think about it, find out why you are discouraged and then you can begin again. Discouragement means not defeat, but rather, that it is time to approach the search in a different way.

The problem is not whether there is a child for you, but how do you get to your child. If you truly believe there is a child out there for you somewhere, your goal is to be creative, adaptable and innovative in how you reach that point. Believing in yourself makes miracles . . . miracles like children.

FOOTNOTES

CHAPTER 2. WHERE HAVE ALL THE BABIES GONE?

1. "Children Now Running Behind Automobiles as a 'Consumer Preference,'" *Behavior Today*, June 4, 1979.
2. C. Bird, *The Two-Paycheck Marriage: How Women at Work Are Changing Life in America* (New York: Rawson, Wade Publishers, Inc., 1979).
3. *Statistical Abstracts of the United States, 1978*, U.S. Department of Commerce, Bureau of the Census (Washington, D.C.: U.S. Government Printing Office, 1978).
4. "Number of Children in Divorces Triples," *Los Angeles Times*, July 2, 1979.
5. B.D. Colen, "Use of Pill in Sharp Decline," *Los Angeles Times*, November 18, 1979.
6. "Almost 3 in 10 Pregnancies Found to End in Abortion," *Los Angeles Times*, January 6, 1980.
7. L.A. Krames, *Contraception? Facts on Birth Control* (Los Angeles: Price/Stern/Sloan Publishers, Inc., 1979).
8. "New Contraceptives for Both Sexes Seen," *Los Angeles Times*, October 24, 1978.

9. B. Varro, "Don't Expect Perfection in Birth Control," *Los Angeles Times*, March 24, 1980.

10. C. D. Martin, "Psychological Problems of Abortion for the Unwed Teenage Girl," *Genetic Psychology Monographs*, Vol. 88 (1973), pp. 23–110.

CHAPTER 3.   FACING INFERTILITY

1. B. Varro, "Help for the Heartbreak of Infertility," *Los Angeles Times*, August 23, 1979.

2. H.A. Katchadorian and D. T. Lunde, *Fundamentals of Human Sexuality* (New York: Holt, Rinehart and Winston, Inc., 1972).

3. B. Liddick, "The Agony of Infertility—One Woman's Story," *Los Angeles Times*, September 18, 1977.

4. B. Varro, "Scientific Advances in Fertility," *Los Angeles Times*, August 28, 1979.

5. M. Blais, *They Say You Can't Have a Baby: The Dilemma of Infertility* (New York: W.W. Norton and Company, 1979).

6. A. Decker and S. Loebl, *Why Can't We Have A Baby?* (New York: Warner Books, 1978).

7. J.T. Howard and D. Schultz, *We Want to Have a Baby: The Couple's Complete Guide to Overcoming Infertility* (New York: E.P. Dutton, 1979).

8. B.E. Menning, *Infertility: A Guide for the Childless Couple* (Englewood Cliffs, New Jersey: Prentice-Hall, Inc., 1977).

9. R.B. Hampson and J.B. Tavormina, "Feedback for the Experts: A Study of Foster Mothers," *Social Work*, Vol. 25 (1980), pp. 108–12.

10. L.C. Burgess, *The Art of Adoption* (Washington, D.C.: Acropolis Books, 1976).

11. N.E. Finkelstein, "Children in Limbo," *Social Work*, Vol. 25, (1980), pp. 100–05.

12. K.H. Laverty, "Psychological Well-Being in Parents and Non-Parents Beyond the Age of Child Rearing: A Comparative and Descriptive Study," *Doctoral Dissertation* (California School of Professional Psychology, 1979).

CHAPTER 4.   MAKING BABIES WITH A LITTLE HELP

1. M. Curie-Cohen, et al., "Current Practice of Artificial Insemination by Donor in the United States," *New England Journal of Medicine*, Vol. 300 (1979), pp. 585–90.

2. E. Chen, "Sperm Bank Donors All Nobel Winners," *Los Angeles Times*, February 29, 1980.

3. D. Smith, "Artificial Birth and Its Effects," *Los Angeles Times*, December 27, 1978.

4. G. Gallup, "Most Favor Funding of 'Test Tube' Births," *San Diego Union*, December 14, 1978.

5. B. Varro, "Scientific Advances in Fertility," *Los Angeles Times*, August 28, 1979.

6. "Test Tube Babies," *Living*, Vol. 10 (1979), p. 4.

7. M. Pines, "How Old Is Too Old to Have a Baby?" *McCalls*, Vol. 107 (1980), pp. 91+.
8. R. Berkow and J.H. Talbott, *The Merck Manual of Diagnosis and Therapy*, 13th ed. (Rahway, New Jersey: Merck Sharp and Dohme Research Laboratories, 1977).
9. "Genetic Counseling Given New Impetus," *Los Angeles Times*, July 13, 1979.
10. "Cutting the Risk of Childbirth After 35: The Reassurance Amniocentesis Can Provide," *Consumer Reports*, Vol. 44 (1979), pp. 302–06.

CHAPTER 5. THE ADOPTION AGENCY GAME

1. Hilde Bruch, *Eating Disorders: Obesity, Anorexia Nervosa, and the Person Within* (New York: Basic Books, Inc., 1973).
2. "They Said We Were Too Fat To Adopt A Baby," *Good Housekeeping*, Vol. 189 (1979), pp. 98+.
3. "The End of the Legal Road for Timmy—And a Beginning in New Mexico," *Behavior Today*, July 3, 1978.

CHAPTER 6. YOUR OWN GAME

1. C.A. Eldred, et al., "Some Aspects of Adoption in Selected Samples of Adult Adoptees," *American Journal of Orthopsychiatry*, Vol. 46 (1976), pp. 279–90.
2. W. Meezan, et al., *Adoptions Without Agencies: A Study of Independent Adoptions* (New York: Child Welfare League of America, Inc., 1978).
3. J. Goldstein, et al., *Beyond the Best Interests of the Child* (New York: The Free Press, 1973).
4. *Statistical Abstract of the United States, 1978*, U.S. Department of Commerce, Bureau of the Census (Washington, D.C.: U.S. Government Printing Office, 1978).
5. L. McTaggart, *The Baby Brokers: The Marketing of White Babies in America* (New York: Dial Press, 1980).
6. R.S. Lasnik, *A Parent's Guide to Adoption* (New York: Sterling Publishing Co., Inc., 1979).

CHAPTER 8. FARAWAY BABIES

1. J. Nelson-Erichsen and H.R. Erichsen, *How to Adopt Internationally: Africa, Asia, Europe and Latin America*, (Minnesota: St. Mary's College, 1980).
2. American Public Welfare Association. *Intercountry Adoption Guidelines.* (Washington, D.C.: U.S. Government Printing Office, 1980).
3. American Public Welfare Association. *National Directory of Intercountry Adoption Service Resources.* (Washington, D.C.: U.S. Government Printing Office, 1980).

4. D.C. Anderson, *Children of Special Value: Interracial Adoption in America* (New York: St. Martin's Press, 1971).
5. J.P. Blank, *19 Steps Up the Mountain: The Story of the DeBolt Family* (Philadelphia: J.B. Lippincott Company, 1976).
6. J. de Hartog, *The Children: A Personal Record for the Use of Adoptive Parents* (New York: Antheneum, 1969).
7. M. Margolies and R. Gruber, *They Came to Stay* (New York: Coward, McCann and Geoghegan, Inc., 1976).
8. J. Rigert, *All Together: An Unusual American Family* (New York: Harper and Row, Publishers, 1973).
9. R. Caudill, *Somebody Go and Bang a Drum* (New York: E.P. Dutton & Company, 1974).
10. L.J. Grow and D. Shapiro, *Transracial Adoption Today: Views of Adoptive Parents and Social Workers* (New York: Child Welfare League of America, Inc. 1976).
11. J.A. Ladner, *Mixed Families: Adopting Across Racial Boundaries* (New York: Anchor Press, 1977).

CHAPTER 9.   THE SPECIAL KIDS

1. J. McNamara, *The Adoption Adviser* (New York: Hawthorne Books, Inc., 1965).
2. A.R. Silverman and W. Feigelman, "Some Factors Affecting the Adoption of Minority Children," *Social Casework*, Vol. 58 (1977), pp. 554–61.
3. P.J. Kravik, *Adopting Children with Special Needs* (Riverside, California: North American Council on Adoptable Children, 1976).
4. J.P. Blank, *19 Steps Up the Mountain: The Story of the DeBolt Family* (Philadelphia: J.B. Lippincott Company, 1976).
5. D. Keyes, *Flowers for Algernon* (New York: Harcourt Brace Jovanovich, 1966).
6. P.J. Kravik, "Adopting a Retarded Child: One Family's Experience," *Children Today*, Vol. 4 (1975), pp. 17–21.
7. J.A. Ladner, *Mixed Families: Adopting Across Racial Boundaries* (New York: Anchor Press, 1977).
8. P.D. Steinhauer and Q. Rae-Grant, *Psychological Problems of the Child and His Family* (Canada: Macmillan, 1977).
9. F. Green, "The High-Risk Adoption and the Highroad to Heartache," *San Diego Union*, February 4, 1980.
10. S. Kety, et al., "Mental Illness in the Biological and Adoptive Families of Adopted Individuals Who Have Become Schizophrenic," *Behavior Genetics*, Vol. 6 (1976), pp. 219–25.
11. C.L. Jewett, *Adopting the Older Child* (Harvard, Massachusetts: Harvard Common Press, 1978).
12. C. Berman, *We Take This Child: A Candid Look at Modern Adoption* (New York: Doubleday & Company, Inc., 1974).
13. A. D. Sorosky, et al., *The Adoption Triangle: The Effects of the Sealed Record on Adoptees, Birth Parents, and Adoptive Parents* (New York: Anchor Press, 1978).

14. A. Carney, *No More Here and There: Adopting the Older Child* (Chapel Hill, North Carolina: University of North Carolina Press, 1976).
15. A. Kadushin, *Adopting Older Children* (New York: Columbia University Press, 1970).
16. J. Rigert, *All Together: An Unusual American Family* (New York: Harper & Row, Publishers, 1973).
17. F.R. Rondell and A.M. Murray, *New Dimensions in Adoption* (New York: Crown Publishers Inc., 1974).
18. P. Beatty, *That's One Ornery Orphan* (New York: William Morrow and Company, 1980).
19. G. Connors, *Don't Disturb Daddy!* (Boston: Brandon Press, 1965).
20. E. Enright, *Then There Were Five* (New York: Holt, Rinehart and Winston, 1944).
21. M. Miles, *Aaron's Door* (Boston: Atlantic Monthly Press Book, 1977).
22. F.S. Murphy, *Ready-Made Family* (New York: Scholastic Book Service, 1972).
23. P. Windsor, *Mad Martin* (New York: Harper & Row, Publishers, 1978).
24. M.M. Gill, "Adoption of Older Children: The Problems Faced," *Social Casework*, Vol. 59 (1978), pp. 272–78.
25. J.A. Ladner, *Mixed Families: Adopting Across Racial Boundaries* (New York: Anchor Press, 1977).
26. A. Howard, et al., "Transracial Adoption: The Black Community Perspective," *Social Work*, Vol. 22 (1977), pp. 184–89.
27. R.J. Simon, "Black Attitudes Toward Transracial Adoption," *Phylon*, Vol. 39 (1978), pp. 135–42.
28. V. Salkmann, *There Is a Child for You: A Family's Encounter with Modern Adoption* (New York: Simon and Schuster, 1972).
29. R.J. Simon and H. Altstein, *Transracial Adoption* (New York: John Wiley & Sons, 1977).
30. C.H. Zastrow, *Outcome of Black Children—White Parents Transracial Adoptions* (San Francisco: R.&R. Research Associates, 1977).
31. C. Bunin and S. Bunin, *Is That Your Sister?* (New York: Pantheon Books, 1976).
32. S.B. Stein, *The Adopted One: An Open Family Book for Parents and Children Together* (New York: Walker and Company, 1979).
33. J. Neufeld, *Edgar Allan* (New York: New American Library, 1968).

CHAPTER 10. THE SPECIAL MOMS AND DADS

1. E. Branham, "One Parent Adoptions," *Children*, Vol. 17 (1970), pp. 103–07.
2. S.A. Dougherty, "Single Adoptive Mothers and Their Children" *Social Work*, Vol. 23 (1978), pp. 311–14.
3. W. Feigelman and A.R. Silverman, "Single Parent Adoptions," *Social Casework*, Vol. 58 (1977), pp. 418–25.
4. C. Berman, *We Take This Child: A Candid Look at Modern Adoption* (New York: Doubleday & Company, Inc., 1974).

5. R.A. Lasnik, *A Parent's Guide to Adoption* (New York: Sterling Publishing Co., Inc., 1979).

6. S.B. Stein, *About Handicaps: An Open Family Book for Parents and Children Together* (New York: Walker and Company, 1974).

7. M. Vieni, "Why Should Physically Handicapped People Want to Adopt?", *Adopting Children with Special Needs* (Riverside, California: North American Council on Adoptable Children, 1976), pp. 43–44.

8. M. Ward, "Large Adoptive Families: A Special Resource," Social Casework, Vol. 59 (1978) pp. 411–18.

9. R.B. Hampson and J.B. Tavormina, "Feedback for the Experts: A Study of Foster Mothers," *Social Work*, Vol. 25 (1980), pp. 108–12.

10. L.C. Burgess, *The Art of Adoption* (Washington, D.C.: Acropolis Books, 1976).

11. J. Goldstein, et al., *Beyond the Best Interests of the Child* (New York: Free Press, 1973).

12. N.E. Finkelstein, "Children in Limbo," *Social Work*, Vol. 25 (1980), pp. 100–05.

13. J.S. Pers, *Government as Parent: Administering Foster Care in California* (University of California, Berkeley: Institute of Governmental Studies, 1976).

14. "Kids of Lesbians Different from Straights." *Lesbian Tide*, Vol. 9, No. 6 (1980), p. 21.

15. "Kids Get Homes with Gays." *Lesbian Tide*, Vol. 9, No. 4 (1980), p. 12.

16. "Numerically, The Handicapped are Far From 'Exceptional,'" *Behavior Today*, March 10, 1980.

CHAPTER 11. DEEP DARK SECRETS

1. R. Dukette, "Perspective for Agency Response to the Adoption Record Controversy," *Child Welfare*, Vol. 54 (1975), pp. 545–55.

2. K.W. Watson, "Who is the Primary Client?" *Public Welfare*, Vol. 37 (1979), pp. 11–14.

3. J.D. Harrington, "Legislative Reform Moves Slowly," *Public Welfare*, Vol. 37 (1979), pp. 49–57.

4. J.W. Small, "Discrimination Against the Adoptee," *Public Welfare*, Vol. 37 (1979), pp. 38–43.

5. A. Haley, *Roots* (New York: Doubleday & Company, Inc., 1974).

6. A.D. Sorosky, et al., *The Adoption Triangle: The Effects of the Sealed Record on Adoptees, Birth Parents, and Adoptive Parents*. (New York: Anchor Press, 1978.)

7. R. Zeilinger, "The Need vs. the Right to Know," *Public Welfare*, Vol. 37 (1979), pp. 44–47.

8. A. Foster, "Who Has the 'Right' to Know?" *Public Welfare*, Vol. 37 (1979), pp. 34–37.

9. F. Fisher, *The Search for Anna Fisher* (New York: Arthur Fields Books, Inc., 1973).

10. J.M. Paton, *The Adopted Break Silence* (Philadelphia: Life History Study Center, 1955).

11. H. Ehrlich, *A Time to Search: The Moving and Dramatic Stories of Adoptees in Search of Their Natural Parents* (New York: Paddington Press, Ltd., 1977).
12. M. Howard, "I Take After Somebody; I Have Real Relatives; I Possess a Real Name," *Psychology Today*, Vol. 9 (1975), pp. 33+.
13. B.J. Lifton, *Lost and Found: The Adoption Experience* (New York: Dial Press, 1979).
14. L. Flynn, "A Parent's Perspective," *Public Welfare*, Vol. 37 (1979), pp. 28–33.
15. L. Lowry, *Find a Stranger, Say Good-bye* (New York: Pocket Books, 1978).
16. L. Dusky, *Birthmark* (New York: M. Evans and Company, Inc., 1979).
17. L.C. Burgess, *The Art of Adoption* (Washington, D.C.: Acropolis Books, 1976).

CHAPTER 12.   LETTING IN SOME LIGHT

1. H.D. Kirk, *Shared Fate: A Theory of Adoption and Mental Health* (New York: Free Press, 1964).
2. A.D. Sorosky, et al., *The Adoption Triangle: The Effects of the Sealed Record on Adoptees, Birth Parents, and Adoptive Parents* (New York: Anchor Press, 1978).
3. R. Conniff, "Adapting to Open Adoptions," *Next*, Vol. 1 (1980), p. 88.
4. L.C. Burgess, *The Art of Adoption* (Washington, D.C.: Acropolis Books, 1976).

BIBLIOGRAPHY

Asterisks indicate books for children related to adoption.

Abernathy, V. "Illegitimate Conception Among Teenagers." *American Journal of Public Health*, Vol. 64 (1974), pp. 662–65.

Adams, B. *Like It Is: Facts and Feelings About Handicaps from Kids Who Know.* New York: Walker and Company, 1979.

Adcock, G.B. *Intercountry Adoptions: Where Do They Go From Here.* Washington, D.C.: Bouldin-Haigh-Irwin, 1979.

"Adoptees Unite." *Newsweek*, April 28, 1975, p. 86.

"Almost 3 in 10 Pregnancies Found to End in Abortion." *Los Angeles Times*, January 6, 1980.

American Public Welfare Association. *Intercountry Adoption Guidelines.* Washington, D.C.: U.S. Government Printing Office, 1980.

_____ . *National Directory of Intercountry Adoption Service Resources.* Washington, D.C.: U.S. Government Printing Office, 1980.

*Ames, M. *Without Hats, Who Can Tell the Good Guys?* New York: E.P. Dutton & Co., Inc., 1976.

Anderson, D.C. *Children of Special Value: Interracial Adoption in America.* New York: St. Martin's Press, 1971.

Anderson, H.C. (retold by L.B. Cauley) *The Ugly Duckling*. New York: Harcourt Brace Jovanovich, 1979.

Andrews, R.G. "A Clinical Appraisal of Searching." *Public Welfare*, Vol. 37 (1979), pp. 15–21.

*Angell, J. *Tina Gogo*. New York: Laurel-Leaf, 1977.

Anonymous, "Because I Loved You, Jennifer." *American Journal of Nursing*, Vol. 74 (1974), p. 471.

Anselm, R. "A Natural Mother's Wish: 'I Would Like to Hold My Son.'" *Los Angeles Times*, June 8, 1980.

Babikian, H., and A. Holdman. "A Study in Teenage Pregnancy." *American Journal of Psychiatry*. Vol. 128 (1971), pp. 755–60.

Baran, A., A. Sorosky and R. Pannor. "The Dilemma of our Adoptees." *Psychology Today*, Vol. 9 (1975), pp. 38+.

Barglow, P., M. Bernstein, D. Exum, M. Wright and H. Visotsky. "Some Psychiatric Aspects of Illegitimate Pregnancy in Early Adolescence." *American Journal of Orthopsychiatry*, Vol. 38 (1968), pp. 672–87.

Barkas, J. L. *The Help Book*. New York: Charles Scribner's Sons, 1979.

Baudry, F., and A. Winer. "A Woman's Choice: Pregnancy or Abortion." *Mademoiselle*, April 1974, pp. 34+.

*Bauer, M.D. *Foster Child*. New York: Laurel-Leaf, 1977.

*Beatty, P. *That's One Ornery Orphan*. New York: William Morrow and Company, 1980.

Beck, M.B. "Abortion: The Mental Health Consequences of Unwantedness." *Seminar in Psychiatry*, Vol. 2 (1970), pp. 263–74.

Benet, M.K. *The Politics of Adoption*. New York: Free Press, 1976.

Benning, B.E. "The Infertile Couple: A Plea for Advocacy." *Child Welfare*, Vol. 54 (1975), pp. 454–60.

Berkow, R., and J.H. Talbott. *The Merck Manual of Diagnosis and Therapy*, 13th ed. Rahway, New Jersey: Merck Sharp & Dohme Research Laboratories, 1977.

Berkow, S.G. *Childlessness: A Study of Fertility, Its Causes and Treatment*. New York: Lee Furman, 1937.

Berman, C. *We Take This Child: A Candid Look at Modern Adoption*. New York: Doubleday & Company, Inc., 1974.

Bernstein, G.S. "Conventional Methods of Contraception: Condom, Diaphragm, and Vaginal Foam." *Clinical Obstetrics and Gynecology*, Vol. 17 (1974), pp. 21–33.

Bernstein, N.R., and C.B. Tinkham. "Group Therapy Following Abortion." *Journal of Nervous and Mental Disorders*, Vol. 152 (1971), pp. 303–14.

Bernstein, R. *Helping Unmarried Mothers*. New York: Association Press, 1971.

Biele, A.M. "Unwanted Pregnancy: Symptom of Depressive Practice." *American Journal of Psychiatry*. Vol. 128 (1971), pp. 748–54.

Bigelow, R.E. "One Father's Dissent." *Los Angeles Times*, June 8, 1980.

Biller, H.B., and D.L. Meredith. "The Invisible American Father." *Sexual Behavior*, Vol. 2 (1972), pp. 16–22.

Bing, E., and L. Colman. *Having a Baby After 30*. New York: Bantam Books, 1980.

Bird, C. *The Two-Paycheck Marriage: How Women at Work are Changing Life in America*. New York: Rawson, Wade Publishers, Inc., 1979.

Black, S., and M. Sykes. "Promiscuity and Oral Contraception: The Relationship Examined." *Social Science and Medicine*, Vol. 5 (1971), pp. 637–43.

Blaine, G.B. "Sex and the Adolescent." *New York State Journal of Medicine*, Vol. 67 (1967), pp. 1967–75.

Blais, M. *They Say You Can't Have a Baby: The Dilemma of Infertility*. New York: W.W. Norton & Company, 1979.

Blake, J. "The Teenage Birth Control Dilemma and Public Opinion." *Science*, Vol. 180 (1973), pp. 708–812.

Blank, J.P. *19 Steps Up the Mountain: The Story of the DeBolt Family*. Philadelphia: J.B. Lippincott Company, 1976.

*Blue, R. *Me and Einstein*. New York: Human Sciences Press, 1979.

Bluford, R., and R.E. Petres. *Unwanted Pregnancy: The Medical and Ethical Implications*. New York: Harper & Row, 1973.

Blumberg, B.D., M.S. Colbus and K.H. Hanson. "The Psychological Sequelae of Abortion Performed for a Genetic Indication." *American Journal of Obstetrics and Gynecology*, Vol. 122 (1975), pp. 799–808.

Boston Women's Health Course Collective. *Our Bodies, Our Selves*. Boston: New England Free Press, 1971.

Bowerman, C.E., D.P. Irish and H. Pope. *Unwed Motherhood: Personal and Social Consequences*. Chapel Hill, North Carolina: Institute for Research in Social Science, 1963–66.

Bracken, M. "Lessons Learned from a Baby Care Club for Unmarried Mothers." *Children*, Vol. 18 (1971), pp. 133–37.

Bracken, M.B., M. Hachamovitch and G. Grossman. "Correlates of Repeat Abortions." *Obstetrics and Gynecology*, Vol. 40 (1972), pp. 816–25.

Bracken, M.B., L.V. Klerman and M. Bracken. "Coping with Pregnancy Resolution Among Never-married Women." *American Journal of Orthopsychiatry*, Vol. 48 (1978), pp. 320–34.

_____ . "Abortion, Adoption, or Motherhood: An Empirical Study of Decision-making During Pregnancy." *American Journal of Obstetrics and Gynecology*, Vol. 130 (1978), pp. 251–62.

Bracken, M.B., and V.K. Stanislav. "Delay in Seeking Induced Abortion: A Review and Theoretical Analysis." *American Journal of Obstetrics and Gynecology*, Vol. 121 (1975), pp. 1008–19.

Braden, J.A. "Adoption in a Changing World." *Social Casework*, Vol. 51 (1970), pp. 486–90.

Bragonier, J.R., R.G. Smith, C.V. Ford, N.M. Simon and J.R. Cavanaugh. "Why do Unmarried Women Fail to Use Contraception?" *Medical Aspects of Human Sexuality*, Vol. 7 (1973), pp. 154–68.

Branham, E. "One Parent Adoptions." *Children*, Vol. 17 (1970), pp. 103–07.

Brew, M.F., and R. Seidenberg. "Psychotic Reactions Associated with Pregnancy and Childbirth." *Journal of Nervous and Mental Disorders,* Vol. 111 (1950), pp. 408-23.

"Brighter Days for 'Unadoptable' Children." *U.S. News and World Report,* Vol. 85 (1978), p. 80.

*Brightman, A. *Like Me.* Boston: Little, Brown and Company, 1976.

Broadhurst, D.D., and E.J. Schwartz. "The Right to Know." *Public Welfare,* Vol. 37 (1979), pp. 5-8.

Brody, S. and S. Axelrad. *Mothers, Fathers, and Children: Exploration in the Formation of Character in the First Seven Years.* New York: International Universities Press, Inc., 1978.

Bruch, H. *Eating Disorders: Obesity, Anorexia Nervosa, and the Person Within.* New York: Basic Books, Inc., 1973.

Bryan-Logan, B.N., and B.L. Dancy. "Unwed Pregnant Adolescents: Their Mother's Dilemma." *Nursing Clinics of North America,* Vol. 9 (1974), pp. 57-68.

*Buck, P. *Welcome Child.* New York: Random House, 1964.

Buck, P. S. *Children for Adoption.* New York: Random House, 1964.

Bumpass, L., and C. Westoff. "The 'Perfect Contraceptive' Population." *Science,* Vol. 169 (1970), pp. 1177-82.

*Bunin, C., and S. Bunin. *Is That Your Sister?* New York: Pantheon Books, 1976.

Burgen, M. "Should Whites Adopt Black Children?" *Ebony,* December 1977, pp. 63+.

Burgess, L.C. *The Art of Adoption.* Washington, D.C.: Acropolis Books, 1976.

*Byars, B. *The Summer of the Swans.* New York: Avon Camelot, 1970.

Cadoret, R., L. Cunningham, R. Loftus and J. Edwards. "Studies of Adoptees from Psychiatrically Disturbed Biological Parents: Medical Symptoms and Illnesses in Childhood and Adolescence." *American Journal of Psychiatry,* Vol. 133 (1976), pp. 1316-18.

Cain, A.C., M.E. Erickson, I. Fast and R.A. Vaughan. "Children's Disturbed Reactions to their Mother's Miscarriage." *Psychosomatic Medicine,* Vol. 26 (1964), pp. 58-66.

*Caines, J. *Abby.* New York: Harper & Row, 1973.

Callahan, D. *Abortion: Law, Choice and Morality.* New York: Macmillan Company, 1970.

Campanella, R., and J.R. Wolff. "Emotional Reaction to Sterilization." *Obstetrics and Gynecology,* Vol. 45 (1975), pp. 331-34.

*Campbell, H. *Home to Hawaii.* New York: W.W. Norton & Company, Inc., 1967.

Campbell, L. H. "The Birthparent's Right to Know." *Public Welfare,* (1979), pp. 22-27.

Caplan, H. "Contraception for Teenagers." *Medical Aspects of Human Sexuality,* Vol. 6 (1972), pp. 192-214.

*Carlson, N.S. *A Brother for the Orphelines.* New York: Yearling, 1959.

——————. *The Happy Orphelines.* New York: Dell Publishing Co., Inc., 1957.

Carney, A. *No More Here and There: Adopting the Older Child.* Chapel Hill, North Carolina: University of North Carolina Press, 1976.

*Caudill, R. *Somebody Go and Bang a Drum.* New York: E. P. Dutton and Company, 1974.

Cawley, P.B. "Natural Parents Seeking Changes in Adoption Laws." *Daily Californian*, November 1, 1978.

Cheetham, J. *Unwanted Pregnancy and Counseling.* London: Routledge & Kegan Paul, 1977.

Chemerinsky, E. "Defining the 'Best Interests': Constitutional Protection in Involuntary Adoptions." *Journal of Family Law*, Vol. 18 (1979-1980), pp. 79-113.

Chen, E. "Sperm Bank Donors All Nobel Winners." *Los Angeles Times*, February 29, 1980.

"Children Now Running Behind Automobiles as a 'Consumer Preference.'" *Behavior Today*, June 4, 1979.

Chilman, C.S. "Teenage Pregnancy: A Research Review." *Social Work*, Vol. 24 (1979), pp. 492-98.

*Chinnock, F. *Kim: A Gift from Vietnam.* New York: World Publishers, 1969.

Claeys, W., and P. De Boeck. "The Influence of Some Parental Characteristics on Children's Primary Abilities and Field Independence: A Study of Adopted Children." *Child Development* (1976), pp. 842-45.

Clothier, F. "Psychological Implications of Unmarried Parenthood." *American Journal of Orthopsychiatry*, Vol. 13 (1943), pp. 531-49.

Cohen, D. "Adoption." *Psychology Today*, November 1977, pp. 128+.

Cohen, M.W., and S.B. Friedman. "Nonsexual Motivation of Adolescent Sexual Behavior." *Medical Aspects of Human Sexuality*, Vol. 9 (1975), pp. 9+.

Colen, B.D. "Use of Pill in Sharp Decline." *Los Angeles Times*, November 18, 1979.

Comfort, A., and J. Comfort. *The Facts of Love: Living, Loving, Growing Up.* New York: Crown Publishers, Inc., 1979.

Conniff, R. "Adapting to Open Adoptions." *Next*, Vol. 1 (1980), p. 88.

*Connors, G. *Don't Disturb Daddy!* Boston: Brandon Press, 1965.

Crisp, W.E. "Ecology of Contraception." *Obstetrics and Gynecology*, Vol. 39 (1972), pp. 931-32.

Cunningham, L., R.J. Cadoret, R. Loftus and J.E. Edwards. "Studies of Adoptees from Psychiatrically Disturbed Biological Parents: Psychiatric Conditions in Childhood and Adolescence." *British Journal of Psychiatry*, Vol. 126 (1975), pp. 534-49.

Curie-Cohen, M., L. Luttrell and S. Shapiro. "Current Practice of Artificial Insemination by Donor in the United States." *New England Journal of Medicine*, Vol. 300 (1979), pp. 585-90.

"Cutting the Risk of Childbirth after 35: The Reassurance Amniocentesis Can Provide." *Consumer Reports*, Vol. 44 (1979), pp. 302-06.

Davids, L. "Foster Fatherhood: The Untapped Resource." *Family Coordinator*, Vol. 20 (1971), pp. 49-54.

Davis, M.E. "Involuntary Sterilization: A History of Social Control." *Journal of Black Health Perspectives*, Vol. 1, pp. 43–51.

Decker, A., and S. Loebl. *Why Can't We Have A Baby?* New York: Warner Books, 1978.

deElejalde, F. "Inadequate Mothering." *Bulletin of the Menninger Clinic*, Vol. 35 (1971), pp. 182–98.

deHartog, J. *The Children: A Personal Record for the Use of Adoptive Parents*. New York: Atheneum, 1969.

Dell, P.F., and A.S. Appelbaum. "Trigenerational Enmeshment: Unresolved Ties of Single-Parents to Family of Origin." *American Journal of Nursing*, Vol. 47 (1977), pp. 52–59.

Denes, M. *In Necessity and Sorrow: Life and Death in an Abortion Hospital*. New York: Basic Books, Inc., Publishers, 1976.

Deutsch, H. *The Psychology of Women: A Psychoanalytic Interpretation*, 17th ed. New York: Grune & Stratton, 1944. 2 vols.

Dewar, D. *Orphans of the Living: A Study of Bastardry*. London: Hutchinson, 1968.

Diddle, A.W. "Rights Affecting Human Reproduction." *Obstetrics and Gynecology*, Vol. 41 (1973), pp. 789–94.

Djerassi, C. "Birth Control After 1984." *Science*, Vol. 169 (1970), pp. 941–51.

*Doane, P. *Understanding Kim*. Philadelphia: Lippincott, 1962.

Doss, H. *The Family Nobody Wanted*. Boston: Little, Brown and Company, 1954.

—————— . *The Really Real Family*. Boston: Little, Brown and Company, 1959.

Dougherty, S.A. "Single Adoptive Mothers and Their Children." *Social Work*, Vol. 23 (1978), pp. 311–14.

Douglas, W. *The One Parent Family*. Nashville, Tennessee: Graded Press, 1971.

Drehsler, A. "Waitress Wages Long Battle for Child." *San Diego Union*, October 12, 1978.

Dukette, R. "Perspectives for Agency Response to the Adoption Record Controversy." *Child Welfare*, Vol. 54 (1975), pp. 545–55.

Dukette, R., and N. Stevenson. "The Legal Rights of Unmarried Fathers: The Impact of Recent Court Decisions." *Social Service Review*, Vol. 47 (1973), pp. 1–15.

Dusky, L. *Birthmark*. New York: M. Evans and Company, Inc., 1979.

Dywasuk, C.T. *Adoption—Is It for You?* New York: Harper & Row Publishers, 1973.

Easson, W.M. "Special Sexual Problems of the Adopted Adolescent." *Medical Aspects of Human Sexuality*, Vol. 7 (1973), pp. 96–105.

Ehrlich, H. *A Time to Search: The Moving and Dramatic Stories of Adoptees in Search of Their Natural Parents*. New York: Paddington Press, Ltd., 1977.

*Eisenberg, E. *The Pretty House That Found Happiness*. Austin, Texas: Steck-Vaugn Co., 1964.

Ekblad, M. "Induced Abortion on Psychiatric Grounds." *Acta Psychiatrica Neurologic Scandanavia*, Supplement 99, (1955), pp. 1–238.

Eldred, C.A., D. Rosenthal, P.H. Wender, S.S. Kety, F. Schulsinger, J. Welner and B. Jacobsen. "Some Aspects of Adoption in Selected Samples of Adult Adoptees." *American Journal of Orthopsychiatry*, Vol. 46 (1976), pp. 279–90.

Elonen, A.S., and E.M. Schwartz. "A Longitudinal Study of Emotional, Social, and Academic Functioning of Adopted Children." *Child Welfare*, Vol. 48 (1969), pp. 72–78.

Engs, R.C. "The Characteristics of Volunteers in Crisis Intervention Centers." *Public Health Reports*, Vol. 89 (1974), pp. 459–64.

*Enright, E. *Then There Were Five*. New York: Holt, Rinehart and Winston, 1944.

Erikson, E.H. *Identity: Youth and Crisis*. New York: W.W. Norton, 1968.

Fanshel, D. *Far from the Reservation: The Transracial Adoption of American Indian Children*. Metuchen, New Jersey: Scarecrow Press, Inc., 1972.

Fanshel, D., and E.B. Shinn. *Children in Foster Care*. New York: Columbia University Press, 1978.

*Fassler, J. *One Little Girl*. New York: Human Science Press, 1969.

——————. *The Boy with a Problem*. New York: Behavioral Publications, 1971.

——————. *Don't Worry Dear*. New York: Behavioral Publications, 1971.

Ferris, P. *The Nameless*, 2nd ed. London: Penguin Books, 1967.

Feigelman, W., and A.R. Silverman. "Single Parent Adoptions." *Social Casework*, Vol. 58 (1977), pp. 418–25.

Fein, E., L.J. Davies and G. Knight. "Placement Stability in Foster Care." *Social Work*, 24. 1979. pp. 156–57.

Feinstein, S.C., and P.L. Giovacchini, eds. *Adolescent Psychiatry*, Volume V. New York: Jason Aronson, Inc., 1977.

Fielding, W.L., M.R. Sachtleben, L.M. Friedman and E.A. Friedman. "Comparison of Women Seeking Early and Late Abortion." *American Journal of Obstetrics and Gynecology*, Vol. 131 (1978), pp. 304–10.

Fine, R.H., and E.P. Shatkin. "Pregnancy and Therapeutic Abortions: A Critical Issue in Adolescence." *American Journal of Orthopsychiatry*, Vol. 41 (1971), pp. 303–04.

Finkelstein, N.E. "Children in Limbo." *Social Work*. Vol. 25 (1980), pp. 100–05.

Fisch, R.O., M. Bilek, A. Deinard and D. Chang. "Growth, Behavioral, and Psychologic Measurements of Adopted Children: The Influences of Genetic and Socioeconomic Factors in a Prospective Study." *Journal of Pediatrics*, Vol. 89, (1976) pp. 494–500.

Fisher, F. *The Search for Anna Fisher*. New York: Arthur Fields Books, Inc., 1973.

Flores, E. "New Surgical Sterilization Methods Told." *San Diego Union*, October 28, 1978.

Flynn, L. "A Parent's Perspective." *Public Welfare*, Vol. 37 (1979), pp. 28–33.

Ford, C.V., R.M. Atkinson and J.R. Bragonier. "Therapeutic Abortion: Who Needs a Psychiatrist?" *Obstetrics and Gynecology*, Vol. 38 (1971), pp. 206–13.

Foster, A. "Who Has the 'Right' to Know?" *Public Welfare*, Vol. 37 (1979), pp. 34–37.

"Foster Parents Win Fight to Adopt 2-Year-Old." *Los Angeles Times*, December 23, 1978.

Frankfort, E. *Vaginal Politics*. New York: Quadrangle Books, Inc., 1972.

Gadpaille, W.J. *The Cycles of Sex*. New York: Charles Scribner's Sons, 1975.

_____ . "Adolescent Sexuality and the Struggle over Authority." *Journal of School Health*, Vol. 40 (1970), pp. 379-83.

Gallagher, U.M. "What's Happening in Adoption?" *Children Today*, Vol. 4 (1975), pp. 11+.

Gallup, G. "Most Favor Funding of 'Test Tube' Births." *San Diego Union*, December 14, 1978.

Garn, S.M., S.M. Bailey and P.E. Cole. "Similarities between Parents and their Adopted Children." *American Journal of Physical Anthropology*, Vol. 45 (1976), pp. 539-43.

"Genetic Counseling Given New Impetus." *Los Angeles Times*, July 13, 1979.

Gessell, A., H.M. Halverson, H. Thompson, F.L. Ilg, B.M. Castner, L.B. Ames and C.S. Amatruda. *The First Five Years of Life: A Guide to the Study of the Preschool Child*. New York: Harper & Brothers Publishers, 1940.

Gill, M.M. "Adoption of Older Children: The Problems Faced." *Social Casework*, Vol. 59 (1978), pp. 272-78.

Gillette, P.J. *Vasectomy: The Male Sterilization Operation*. New York: Paperback Library, 1972.

Goldstein, J., A. Freud and A.J. Solnit. *Beyond the Best Interests of the Child*. New York: The Free Press, 1973.

Gordon, R.H., and C.A. Kilpatrick. "A Program of Group Counseling for Men Who Accompany Women Seeking Legal Abortions." *Community Mental Health Journal*, Vol. 13 (1977), pp. 291-95.

Gould, R.E. "The Wrong Reasons to Have Children." *New York Times*, May 3, 1970, pp. 83-87.

Grayson, J. "Shouldn't Adoptees Know About Their Heritage?" *Seventeen*, March 1975. p. 72.

Green, F. "The High-Risk Adoption and the Highroad to Heartache." *San Diego Union*, February 4, 1980.

Grotevant, H., S. Scarr and R. Winberg. "Are Career Interests Inheritable? *Psychology Today*, March 1978, pp. 88+.

Grotevant, H.D. "Similarity in Adoptive and Biological Families." *Journal of Personality and Social Psychology*, Vol. 35 (1977), pp. 667-76.

Group for the Advancement of Psychiatry. *The Joys and Sorrows of Parenthood*. New York: Charles Scribner's Sons, 1973.

Grow, L.J., and D. Shapiro. *Transracial Adoption Today: Views of Adoptive Parents and Social Workers*. New York: Child Welfare League of America, Inc., 1976.

Haley, A. *Roots*. New York: Doubleday & Company, Inc., 1974.

Hampson, R.B., and J.B. Tavormina. "Feedback from the Experts: A Study of Foster Mothers." *Social Work*, Vol. 25 (1980), pp. 108-12.

Hansen, K., and G. Omenn. "Genetic Counseling: The Search for the Adopted Child." *Journal of Legal Medicine*, Vol. 4, No. 10 (1976), pp. 8AA+.

Haring, B. "Adoption Trends, 1971-1974." *Child Welfare*, Vol. 54 (1975), pp. 524-25.

Harrington, J.D. "Legislative Reform Moves Slowly." *Public Welfare*, Vol. 37 (1979), pp. 49–57.

Harrison, S.I., and J.F. McDermott. *Childhood Psychopathology: An Anthology of Basic Readings*. New York: International Universities Press, Inc., 1972.

Hass, A. *Teenage Sexuality: A Survey of Teenage Sexual Behavior*. New York: Macmillan Publishing Co., Inc., 1979.

*Haywood, C. *Here's A Penny*. New York: Harcourt Brace Jovanovich, 1944.

Helfer, R.E., and C.H. Kempe, eds. *The Battered Child*. Chicago: University of Chicago Press, 1974.

Hendin, D., and J. Marks. *The Genetic Connection*. New York: New American Library, 1978.

Hoffman, L.W. "The Employment of Women, Education and Fertility." *Merrill-Palmer Quarterly*, Vol. 20 (1974), pp. 99–119.

Hook, K. "Refused Abortion: A Follow-up Study of 249 Women Whose Applications Were Refused by the National Board of Health in Sweden." *Acta Psychiatrica Scandanavia, Supplement*, 168. Vol. 39. 1963. pp. 1–156.

Horowitz, J. "Recycling Grandparents as Parents." *Los Angeles Times*, May 4, 1980.

Howard, A., D.D. Royse and J.A. Skerl. "Transracial Adoption: The Black Community Perspective." *Social Work*, Vol. 22 (1977), pp.   184–89.

Howard, J.T., and D. Schultz. *We Want to Have a Baby: The Couple's Complete Guide to Overcoming Infertility*. New York: E.P. Dutton, 1979.

Howard, M. "I Take After Somebody; I Have Real Relatives; I Possess a Real Name." *Psychology Today*, Vol. 9 (1975), pp. 33+.

Hulse, J. *Jody*. New York: McGraw-Hill Book Company, 1976.

Humphrey, M. "Childless Marriage as a Basis for Adoption." *Mental Health*, Vol. 25 (1966), pp. 17–18.

Hunter, N., and N. Polikoff. "Lesbian Mothers Fight Back." *Quest*, Vol. 5 (1979), pp. 55–58.

Jackson, L. "Unsuccessful Adoptions: A Study of 40 Cases Who Attended a Child Guidance Clinic." *British Journal of Medical Psychology*. Vol. 41 (1968), pp. 389–98.

Jewett, C.L. *Adopting the Older Child*. Harvard, Massachusetts: Harvard Common Press, 1978.

*Johnson, D. *Su An*. Chicago: Follett Publishing Company, 1968.

Johnson, J.M. *Thoughts on Adoption*. Greensboro, North Carolina: Children's Home Society of North Carolina, Inc., 1978.

Jones, I.S. "Private Agency in Detroit Eliminates Adoption Obstacles." *Ebony*, June 1976, pp. 53+.

Juhasz, A.M. "To Have or Not to Have—Children? That is the Question." *Journal of School Health*. Vol. 43 (1973), pp. 632–35.

Kadushin, A. *Adopting Older Children*. New York: Columbia University Press, 1970.

Kammerer, P.G. *The Unmarried Mother*. Montclair, New Jersey: Patterson Smith, 1969.

Kane, F.J., P.A. Lachenbruch, L. Lokey, R. Auman, L. Pocuis and M. Lipton. "Adolescent Pregnancy: A Study of Aborters and Non-Aborters." *American Journal of Orthopsychiatry*, Vol. 43 (1973), pp. 769–803.

_____, et al. "Motivational Factors Affecting Contraceptive Use." *American Journal of Obstetrics and Gynecology*, Vol. 110 (1971), pp. 1050–54.

Katchadourian, H.A., and D.T. Lunde. *Fundamentals of Human Sexuality*. New York: Holt, Rinehart and Winston, Inc., 1972.

Katz, L. "Adoption Counseling as a Preventative Mental Health Specialty." *Child Welfare*, Vol. 59 (1980), pp. 161–67.

Kelly, G.F. *Learning About Sex: The Contemporary Guide for Young Adults*, 2nd ed. rev. New York: Barron's Educational Series, Inc., 1977.

Kelly, M. "Birthright—Alternative to Abortion." *American Journal of Nursing*, Vol. 75 (1975), pp. 76–77.

Kenyon, K. "The Littlest Immigrants." *Star News*, November 8, 1979.

Kety, S., D. Rosenthal, P. Wender, F. Schulsingen and B. Jacobsen. "Mental Illness in the Biological and Adoptive Families of Adopted Individuals Who Have Become Schizophrenic." *Behavior Genetics*, Vol. 6 (1976), pp. 219–25.

Keyes, D. *Flowers for Algernon*. New York: Harcourt Brace Jovanovich, 1966.

Kiester, E. "Should We Unlock the Adoption Files?" *Today's Health*, August 1974, pp. 54–60.

Kim, D.S. "Issues in Transracial and Transcultural Adoption." *Social Casework*, Vol. 59 (1978), pp. 477–86.

Kirk, H.D. *Shared Fate: A Theory of Adoption and Mental Health*. New York: Free Press, 1964.

Kittson, R.H. *Orphan Voyage*. New York: Vantage Press, 1968.

Klein, C. *The Single Parent Experience*. New York: Walker and Company, 1973.

Klibanoff, S., and E. Klibanoff. *Let's Talk About Adoption*. Boston: Little, Brown and Company, 1973.

Kline, D., and Overstreet, H.M.F. *Foster Care of Children: Nurture and Treatment*. New York: Columbia University Press, 1972.

Konopka, G. *Young Girls: A Portrait of Adolescence*. Englewood Cliffs, New Jersey: Prentice-Hall, Inc., 1976.

Krames, L.A. *Contraception? Facts on Birth Control*. Los Angeles: Price/Stern/Sloan Publishers, Inc., 1979.

*Kraus, R. *Another Mouse to Feed*. New York: Windmill Wanderer Books, 1980.

Kravik, P.J. "Adopting a Retarded Child: One Family's Experience." *Children Today*, Vol. 4 (1975), pp. 17–21.

_____, ed. *Adopting Children with Special Needs*. Riverside, California: North American Council on Adoptable Children, 1976.

Ladner, J.A. *Mixed Families: Adopting Across Racial Boundaries*. New York: Anchor Press, 1977.

_____. "Mixed Families: White Parents and Black Children." *Society*. Vol. 14 (1977), pp. 70–78.

*Lapsley, S. *I Am Adopted*. New York: Bradbury Press, 1974.

*Lasker, J. *He's My Brother*. Chicago: Whitman, 1974.

Lasnik, R.S. *A Parent's Guide to Adoption*. New York: Sterling Publishing Co., Inc., 1979.

Laverty, K.H. "Psychological Well-Being in Parents and Non-Parents Beyond the Age of Child Rearing: A Comparative and Descriptive Study." Doctoral Dissertation, California School of Professional Psychology, 1979.

Lawton, J.J., and S.Z. Gross. "Review of Psychiatric Literature on Adopted Children." *Archives of General Psychiatry*, Vol. 11 (1964), pp. 635-44.

Leishman, K. "Teenage Mothers are Keeping Their Babies—With the Help of Their Own Mothers." *MS.*, Vol. 8 (1980), pp. 61+.

Liddick, B. "The Agony of Infertility—One Woman's Story." *Los Angeles Times*, September 18, 1977.

Lifton, B.J. *Lost and Found: The Adoption Experience*. New York: Dial Press, 1979.

—————— . *Twice Born: Memoirs of an Adopted Daughter*. New York: McGraw-Hill Book Company, 1975.

Lindley, M. "Adoptive Parents Argue for Keeping Records Closed." *Los Angeles Times*, June 8, 1980.

*Livingston, C. *Why Was I Adopted?* New Jersey: Lyle Stuart Inc., 1978.

*Lowry, L. *Find a Stranger, Say Good-bye*. New York: Pocket Books, 1978.

Lynn, D.B. *The Father: His Role in Child Development*. Monterey, California: Brooks/Cole Publishing Company, 1974.

Maddux, R. *The Orchard Children*. New York: Harper & Row, Publishers, 1977.

Margolies, M. "Adopting a Child If You're Single." *Mademoiselle*. December 1972, pp. 136+.

Margolies, M., and R. Gruber. *They Came to Stay*. New York: Coward, McCann and Geoghegan, Inc., 1976.

Marindin, H. *Handbook for Prospective Single Parents*. Washington, D.C.: Committee for Single Adoptive Parents, n.d.

Marks, J. "Children of Crisis: True tales of High-risk Adoptions." *New York*, Vol. 12 (1979), pp. 31+.

Martin, C.D. "Psychological Problems of Abortion for the Unwed Teenage Girl." *Genetic Psychology Monographs*, Vol. 88 (1973), pp. 23–110.

Matejcek, Z., Z. Dytrych and V. Schuller. "Children from Unwanted Pregnancies." *Acta Psychiatrica Scandanavia*, Vol. 57 (1978), pp. 67–90.

Maxtone, Graham K. *Pregnant by Mistake: The Stories of Seventeen Women*. New York: Liveright, 1973.

McEwan, M.T. "Readoption with a Minimum of Pain." *Social Casework*, Vol. 54 (1973), pp. 350–53.

McFadden, M. *Bachelor Fatherhood: How to Raise and Enjoy Your Children as a Single Parent*. New York: Walker and Company, 1974.

McNamara, J. *The Adoption Adviser*. New York: Hawthorne Books Inc., 1975.

McTaggart, L. "Babies for Sale: The Booming Adoption Racket." *Saturday Review*, November 10, 1979, pp. 15+.

_____ . *The Baby Brokers: The Marketing of White Babies in America.* New York: Dial Press, 1980.

Mead, M. "In the Best Interests of the Child." *Redbook*, October 1978, pp. 100+.

_____ . "What's Right and Wrong About Adoption Today." *Redbook*, September 1978. pp. 39+.

Meezan, W., S. Katz and E.M. Russo. *Adoption Without Agencies: A Study of Independent Adoptions.* New York: Child Welfare League of America, Inc., 1978.

Menning, B.E. *Infertility: A Guide for the Childless Couple.* Englewood Cliffs, New Jersey: Prentice-Hall, Inc., 1977.

*Meredith, J.C. *And Now We Are a Family.* Boston: Beacon Press, 1971.

*Miles, M. *Aaron's Door.* Boston: Atlantic Monthly Press Book, 1977.

"Motherhood Rated on Happiness Scale." *Los Angeles Times*, May 9, 1980.

*Murphy, F.S. *Ready-Made Family.* New York: Scholastic Book Service, 1972.

Nash, A.L. "Reflections on Interstate Adoptions." *Children Today*, Vol. 3 (1974), pp. 7–11.

Nelson-Erichsen, J., and H.R. Erichsen. *How to Adopt Internationally: Africa, Asia, Europe and Latin America.* Graduate Research Project in Human Development, Saint Mary's College, Minnesota, 1980.

*Neufeld, J. *Edgar Allan.* New York: New American Library, 1968.

"New Contraceptives for Both Sexes Seen." *Los Angeles Times*, October 24, 1978.

Norvell, M., and R.F. Guy. "A Comparison of Self-concept in Adopted and Non-adopted Adolescents." *Adolescence*, Vol. 12 (1977), pp. 443–48.

Notman, M.T., and C.C. Nadelson. *The Woman Patient: Sexual and Reproductive Aspects of Women's Health Care,* Volume I. New York: Plenum Press, 1978.

"Number of Children in Divorces Triples." *Los Angeles Times*, July 2, 1979.

"Numerically the Handicapped are Far from 'Exceptional.'" *Behavior Today*, March 10, 1980.

*Palmer, F. *And Four to Grow On.* New York: Rinehart, 1960.

Palmer, S.E. "Predicting Outcome in Long-term Foster Care." *Journal of Social Service Research*, Vol. 3 (1979), pp. 201–14.

Pannor, R., F. Masserik and B. Evans. *The Unmarried Father: New Approaches for Unmarried Young Parents.* New York: Springer Publishing Co., Inc., 1971.

Pannor, R., and E.A. Nerlove. "Fostering Understanding Between Adolescents and Adoptive Parents Through Group Experience." *Child Welfare*, Vol. 56 (1977), pp. 537–45.

Paton, J.M. *The Adopted Break Silence.* Philadelphia: Life History Study Center, 1955.

Pers, J.S. *Government as Parent: Administering Foster Care in California.* University of California, Berkeley: Institute of Governmental Studies, 1976.

Pierce, R.I. *Single and Pregnant.* Boston: Beacon Press, 1970.

Pines, M. "How Old is Too Old to Have a Baby?" *McCall's*, Vol. 107 (1980), pp. 91+.

Platts, H.K. "Mothers Seeking to Relinquish Children for Adoption." *Children*, Vol. 17 (1970), pp. 27–30.

"Problems Seen in Artificial Insemination." *Daily Californian*, March 15, 1979.

Rains, P.M. *Becoming an Unwed Mother*. Chicago: Aldine Atherton, Inc., 1971.

Rao, L.M. "A Comparative Study of Childlessness and Never-pregnant Status." *Journal of Marriage and the Family*, Vol. 36 (1974), pp. 149-57.

Rauh, J.L., R.L. Burket and R.R. Brookman. "Contraception for the Teenager." *Medical Clinics of North America*, Vol. 59 (1975), pp. 1407-18.

Raymond, L. *Adoption and After*. New York: Harper & Row, Publishers, 1955.

*Read, E. *Brothers by Choice*. New York: Farrar, Straus and Giroux, 1974.

Remsberg, C., and B. Remsberg. "The Baby Everyone Wanted." *Redbook*, January 1973, pp. 73+.

Richards, M.P.M., ed. *The Integration of a Child into a Social World*. London. Cambridge University Press, 1974.

Rigert, J. *All Together: An Unusual American Family*. New York: Harper & Row, Publishers, 1973.

*Rodowsky, C.F. *P.S. Write Soon*. New York: Laurel-Leaf, 1978.

Rondell, F., and R. Michaels. *The Adoptive Family: Book I, You and Your Child*. New York: Crown Publishers, Inc., 1951.

_____ . *The Family That Grew*. New York: Crown Publishers, Inc., 1951.

Rondell, F., and A.M. Murray. *New Dimensions in Adoption*. New York: Crown Publishers, Inc., 1974.

Rosenthal, D., P.H. Wender, S.S. Kety, F. Schulsinger, J. Welnew and R.O. Rieder. "Parent-child Relationships and Psychopathological Disorder in the Child." *Archives of General Psychiatry*. Vol. 32 (1975), pp. 466-76.

Rothenberg, E.W., M. Goldey and R.M. Sands. "The Vicissitudes of the Adoption Process." *American Journal of Psychiatry*, Vol. 128 (1971), pp. 590-95.

Rovinsky, J.J. "Abortion Recidivism: A Problem in Preventive Medicine." *Obstetrics and Gynecology*, Vol. 39 (1972), pp. 649-59.

Ryberg, H.M. "Are You My Real Mother?" *Parents*. February 1974, pp. 56+.

Salkmann, V. *There is a Child for You: A Family's Encounter with Modern Adoption*. New York: Simon and Schuster, 1972.

Sandberg, E.C., and R.I. Jacobs. "Psychology of Misuse and Rejection of Contraception." *Medical Aspects of Human Sexuality*, Vol. 6 (1972), pp. 34-72.

Sanderson, J. "Bringing Up the Subject of Baby." *Los Angeles Times*, May 4, 1980.

Scarr, S., and R. Weinberg. "I.Q. Test Performance of Black Children Adopted by White Families." *American Psychologist*, Vol. 31 (1976), pp. 726-39.

Schultz, A.L., and A.G. Motulsky. "Medical Genetics and Adoption." *Child Welfare*, Vol. 50 (1971), pp. 4-17.

Sherman, E.A., R. Neuman and A.W. Shyne. *Children Adrift in Foster Care: A Study of Alternative Approaches*. New York: Child Welfare League of America, Inc., 1974.

"Should Grandparents Adopt? A Saigon Orphan Says Yes—with a Philadelphia Accent." *People Magazine*. Vol. 9 (1978), pp. 80×.

Siegel, B. "Why One Mother Gave Up Her Children." *Los Angeles Times*, February 27, 1978.

*Silman, R. *Somebody Else's Child*. New York: Dell Publishing Co., Inc., 1976.

Silverman, A.R., and W. Feigelman. "Some Factors Affecting the Adoption of Minority Children." *Social Casework,* Vol. 58 (1977), pp. 554–61.

Simon, R.J. "Black Attitudes Toward Transracial Adoption." *Phylon,* Vol. 39 (1978), pp. 135–42.

_____, and H. Altstein. *Transracial Adoption.* New York: John Wiley and Sons, 1977.

Simross, L. "The DeBolts and Their 19 Children: 'Loving Tough.'" *Los Angeles Times,* December 10, 1978.

Small, J.W. "Discrimination Against the Adoptee." *Public Welfare,* Vol. 37 (1979), pp. 38–43.

Smith, D. "Artificial Birth and Its Effects." *Los Angeles Times,* December 27, 1978.

Smyth, E. "The Paper Maze to Lost Identity." *San Diego Union,* December 3, 1978.

Snider, A.J. "Motherhood Rated on Happiness Scale." *Los Angeles Times,* May 9, 1980.

*Sobol, H.L. *My Brother Steven is Retarded.* New York: Macmillan, 1977.

Sokoloff, B. "Should the Adopted Adolescent Have Access to his Birth Records and to His Birth-parents?" *Clinical Pediatrics,* Vol. 16 (1977), pp. 975–77.

Sorensen, R.C. *Adolescent Sexuality in Contemporary America: Personal Values and Sexual Behavior Ages Thirteen to Nineteen.* New York: World Publishing, 1973.

Sorosky, A.D., A. Baran and R. Pannor. *The Adoption Triangle: The Effects of the Sealed Record on Adoptees, Birth Parents, and Adoptive Parents.* New York: Anchor Press, 1978.

Stein, S.B. *About Handicaps: An Open Family Book for Parents and Children Together.* New York: Walker and Company, 1974.

_____. *The Adopted One: An Open Family Book for Parents and Children Together.* New York: Walker and Company, 1979.

Steinhauer, P.D., and Q. Rae-Grant. *Psychological Problems of the Child and His Family.* Canada: Macmillan, 1977.

Stone, H.D., and J.M. Hunseker. *Education for Foster Family Care: Models and Methods for Foster Parents and Social Workers.* New York: Child Welfare League of America, Inc., 1975.

Sugar, M., ed. *Female Adolescent Development.* New York: Brunner/Mazel, Publishers, 1979.

*Taber, B.G. *Adopting Baby Brother.* New York: 1974.

"Test Tube Babies." *Living,* Vol. 10 (1979), p. 4.

"The End of the Legal Road for Timmy—And a Beginning in New Mexico." *Behavior Today,* July 3, 1978.

"They Said We Were Too Fat to Adopt a Baby." *Good Housekeeping,* Vol. 189 (1979), pp. 98+.

Tizard, B. "Adopting Older Children from Institutions." *Child Abuse and Neglect.* Vol. 3 (1979), pp. 535–38.

Statistical Abstract of the United States, 1978. U.S. Department of Commerce, Bureaus of the Census. Washington, D.C.: U.S. Government Printing Office, 1978.

Van Deep, P.A. and H. Schmidt-Elmendorff. "Involuntary Childlessness." *Journal of Biosocial Science,* Vol. 7 (1975), pp. 37–48.

Varro, B. "Don't Expect Perfection in Birth Control." *Los Angeles Times*, March 24, 1980.

——————. "Help for the Heartbreak of Infertility." *Los Angeles Times*, August 23, 1979.

——————. "Scientific Advances in Fertility." *Los Angeles Times*, August 28, 1979.

——————. "The Pill: Controversy Rages On." *Los Angeles Times*, March 21, 1980.

Veenhoven, R. "Is There an Innate Need for Children." *European Journal of Social Psychology*, Vol. 74 (1974), pp. 495–501.

Veevers, J.E. "Childlessness and Age at First Marriage." *Social Biology*, Vol. 183 (1972), pp. 292–95.

——————. "The Moral Careers of Voluntarily Childless Wives: Notes on the Defense of a Variant World View." *Family Coordinator*. Vol. 29 (1975), pp. 473–87.

——————. "The Social Meanings of Parenthood." *Psychiatry*, Vol. 36 (1973), pp. 291–310.

Ward, M. "Large Adoptive Families: A Special Resource." *Social Casework*, Vol. 59 (1978), pp. 411–18.

——————. "The Special Needs of the Adopted Child." *Parents Magazine*, December 1972, pp. 942+.

*Warren, M. *Walk in My Moccasins*. Philadelphia: Westminster Press, 1966.

*Wasson, V.P. *The Chosen Baby*. New York: J.B. Lippincott Company, 1939.

Watson, K.W. "Who is the Primary Client?" *Public Welfare*, Vol. 37 (1979), pp. 11–14.

*Waybill, M. *Chinese Eyes*. Marshall, Arizona: Harold Press, 1974.

Weidell, R.C. "Unsealing Sealed Birth Certificates in Minnesota." *Child Welfare*, Vol. 59 (1980), pp. 113–19.

Whelan, E. *Boy or Girl?* New York: Pocket Books, 1977.

Whelan, E.M. *A Baby . . . Maybe? A Guide to Making the Most Fateful Decision of your Life.* New York: Bobbs-Merrill Company, Inc., 1975.

"White Family, Black Child." *Christian Century*, May 6, 1973, pp. 526–27.

"Why a Sudden Drop in Baby Adoptions." *U.S. News and World Report*, July 30, 1973, p. 62.

Wieder, H. "The Family Romance Fantasies of Adopted Children." *Psychoanalytic Quarterly*, Vol. 46 (1977), pp. 185–200.

*Windsor, P. *Mad Martin*. New York: Harper & Row, Publishers, 1978.

Wishard, L., and W.R. Wishard. *Adoption: The Grafted Tree*. San Francisco, California: Cragmont Publications, 1979.

Zastrow, C.H. *Outcome of Black Children-White Parents Transracial Adoptions*. San Francisco: R.&R. Research Associates, 1977.

Zeilinger, R. "The Need vs. the Right to Know." *Public Welfare*, Vol. 37 (1979), pp. 44–47.

Zigler, E., and K. Anderson. "The Last Victims of Vietnam." *Psychology Today*, Vol. 12 (1978), pp. 24+.

INDEX

A

Abortion
  after amniocentesis, 69-73
  declining birthrate and, 17
  as method of contraception, 22-23
  question of when "life" begins and, 58
Adolescents, concerns about being
  adopted, 240
Adoptees in Search, 222
Adoptees' Liberation Movement
  Association (ALMA), 222
Adoption
  changes in, 216-17
  lack of advocacy groups for, 31
  lack of children available for, 77
  of older children, 184-87
  of racially mixed children, 189-91
  of sibling groups, 187-89
Adoption agencies
  advantages of, 100-101
  approaches to, by parents seeking to
    adopt, 81-82
  attitude of social workers toward
    birthparents, 243-45
  counseling for clients, 246, 264-65
  criteria for selecting adoptive parents,
    77-93
  as guardian of child until finalization of
    adoption, 79-80
  as information centers on adoption, 267
  open adoption and, 254-55
  openness in adoption process and,
    265-66
  power of, 98-100
  ratio of adoptive parents to available
    infants, 77
  recommendations for changes in, 260-67
  sealed birth records and, 230-32
  waiting list, 76
Adoption laws and surrogate mothers, 67
Adoption process through agencies, 12,
  77-82
Adoption records, 217
Adoption Resource of North America
  (ARENA), 174
Adoptive Research Council, 254
Adoptive parents
  attitude toward opening of sealed birth
    records, 225-27
  counseling for, by agencies, 264-65
  proposed licensing of, 267-68
  payment of birthmother's expenses in
    private adoption, 110-12
  qualifications of, 12-13, 77-93
  recommendations for approaching the
    adoption process, 271-76
Advertising for an adoptable baby, 150-52
Age and adoption agencies' criteria for
  parents, 83, 200-202
AID. See Artificial insemination by donor.
AID Research, 63
Aid to Adoption of Special Kids (AASK),
  174
Alternatives to agency adoption, 103 ff.
American Fertility Society, 46, 48
Amniocentesis, 68-72
  abortion and, 69-72
  cystic fibrosis and, 69
  detection of child's sex, 70
  Down's syndrome and, 69
  factors to consider in deciding its use,
    71-72
  Klinefelter's syndrome and, 69
  for mothers at high risk for genetic
    disorders, 68
  for older mothers, 68
  physician's potential legal liability and,
    71
  Rh-factor incompatability and, 69
  risks of using, 71-72
  and possibility of correcting defects *in
    utero*, 70
  sickle-cell anemia and, 69-70
  spina bifida and, 69
  Tay-Sachs disease and, 69
  Turner's syndrome and, 69
  use of with ultrasound, 71
Anonymity in adoption, 110
Artificial insemination
  anonymity of donors, problems with,
    62-63
  defined, 59
  donor's response to fathering multiple
    children, 63
  using father's sperm, 59-60
  risk of legal problems for donors, 62-63
  secrecy surrounding, 63
  for single women, 60-61
Artificial insemination by donor (AID)
  characteristics of donors, 61
  screening for, 61

B

Baby search
  by individuals wishing to adopt, 129 ff.
  information sheet, 138-39
  persons to contact, 40-49

Baby selling. *See* Black market adoptions.
Basal thermometer, 25
Becker, Dolores, 71
"Best interest of child" policy, 99, 216, 262
Big Brother/Big Sister organizations, 52, 197
Birth certificate, amended, 116. *See also*
  Sealed birth record.
Birth Control Institute, 153
Birth control pill
  age of woman and, 21
  decrease in numbers of users, 21
  effectiveness as contraceptive, 21
  health risks and, 20-21
Birth records. *See* Sealed birth records.
Birthmother
  contact with adoptive parents, 109-10,
    249-57
  drugs and, 135
  financial aid for, 110-12, 263-64
  relinquishment papers and, 114-15
  specific requests about adoptive home,
    79, 87, 263-64
Birthparents
  agency pressure to relinquish child
    and, 14
  attitude toward opening of sealed birth
    records, 227-30
  counseling for, by adoption agencies,
    264-65
  search for, by adult adoptees, 221-25
  social workers' attitudes toward, 243-45
Birthright, 143
Black children
  adoption by white parents, 86-87
  adoptive homes for, 97
Black market adoptions, 10, 120-26
  fitness of parents and, 123
  proposed changes in current adoption
    laws, 124
  risks in, 124-26
Bonding of infant and parent, 119, 136, 266
Burgess, Linda, 255

C

Cervical mucus and infertility, 40
Child Welfare League of America, 52
Childless marriages compared to those
  with children, 53
Colleges as a source of adoptable babies,
  147-48
Community outreach programs for
  adoption, 97
Conception outside the mother's body, 57
Concerned United Birthparents, Inc.
  (CUB), 228
Condoms
  drawbacks to use of, 24

effectiveness in preventing pregnancy,
  23-24
Consent-to-adopt papers. *See*
  Relinquishment papers.
Contraception
  declining birth rate and, 17-19
  failures of, 20
  techniques, 20-26
  techniques undergoing testing, 25-26
Counseling for unplanned pregnancy,
  29-32
Court proceedings in private adoption,
  116-17
Crippled Children's Services, 179
Cystic fibrosis, 69

D

David Livingston Missionary Foundation
  Adoption Program, 156
DeBolt family, 174, 177, 203
Declining birth rate and available adoptees,
  18-19
Diabetes and lowered sperm count, 39
Diaphragm
  drawbacks of using, 22
  effectiveness as a contraceptive, 22
  increased use of, 21
Divorce and declining birth rate, 19
Down's syndrome, 69

E

Eastern Medical School, Norfolk,
  Virginia, 65
Educational level as criterion for selection
  of adoptive parents, 84
Edwards, Dr. Robert, 64, 65
Eggs, release of and infertility, 40-41
Embryo implantation, 66-67
Emotional disturbance, causes of, 182-83
Emotionally handicapped children,
  adoption of, 181-84
Employment of mother, adoption agencies'
  view of, 88-89
Expenses incurred by birthmother payable
  by adopters, 110-12
Experimental techniques
  to correct infertility, 59-66, 70
  to measure intelligence of unborn child,
    70-71

F

Fallopian tubes, 41
Families for Children, 156
Family adoptions, 120
Family histories, 79, 96
Father. *See* Natural father; Birthparents.
Female infertility
  causes of, 40-42
  treatment of, 41-42

Feminine hygiene products as
   spermicides, 40
Fertility and adoption agencies' policies, 78
Fertilization, probability of, 41
Financial assistance
   for birthmother, 110-12, 263-64
   for families adopting special-needs
     children, 96, 178-79
Financial status required of adopters, 82-83
Finalization of adoption
   consent of older child required, 113
   legal process, 80
   six-month wait for, 79-80
   state agencies' role in private adoptions,
     113, 116
Flexibility of attitude as criterion for
   selection of adopters, 90
Foam contraceptive, 25
Foreign Adoption Center Inc., The, 156,
   164
Foster care
   adoptive placement and, 266-67
   characteristics of children placed,
     51-52, 206
   proposed time limits for, 269
Foster parenting, compared to adoption,
   50-52
Foster parents
   financial aid for handicapped child, 178
   interaction with adoption agencies,
     206-209, 247-48
   right to contest adoption, 113-14
   screening of, 51
   types of, 206
Free clinics, 97, 142-44
Friends for All Children, 156

G

Gonorrhea and scar tissue preventing
   conception, 39
"Good cause," legal meaning of, 217
Graham, Robert, 62

H

Hard-to-place children. *See* Emotionally
   handicapped children; Mentally
   handicapped children; Older children;
   Physically handicapped children;
   Racially mixed children; Sibling
   groups.
Health as a criterion for selection of
   adopters, 85-86
High school pregnant minors program, 145
High schools as a source of adoptable
   babies, 145-47
Holt, Henry, 154
Holt Adoption Program, 154, 156, 160-62
Home visit by adoption agency worker,
   78-80

Homosexuals as adopters, 209-10
Honesty in adoption, 237-49

I

Immune reaction to sperm, and
   infertility, 40
Infection
   as cause of infertility in females, 41
   of prostate gland and lowered sperm
     count, 38
Infertility
   adoption agencies' attitude toward, 85
   and alcohol, tobacco, and drugs, 37
   causes of in the male, 38-40
   causes of in the female, 40-42
   coital position and, 36-37
   male body temperature and, 37
   medical advances and, 36
   psychological stress and, 35-36, 42-45
   sexuality and, 42-43
   sources of information about, 46-48
   state of general health and, 36-37
   too-frequent sexual intercourse and, 36
Infertility Association of San Diego, 142
Infertility groups and information about
   adoptable babies, 142
International adoption, 153-71
   adoption agencies and, 155-56
   characteristics agencies seek in adopters,
     159-60
   procedures for, 157-59
Intrauterine device (IUD)
   drawbacks of, 22
   effectiveness of, 22
IUD. *See* Intrauterine device.

L

Large families as adopters
   adoption agencies' criteria and, 203-205
   characteristics of children to be placed
     and, 204
Laws regarding adoption, need for changes
   in, 260, 267-71
Lawyers
   role in private adoptions, 107-108, 112,
     117-18
   role in private international adoption, 163
   as source of information about adoptable
     babies, 40-41
Legal aspects of private adoption,
   107-108, 112
Legal process for finalization of
   adoption, 80
Letters of recommendation, required by
   adoption agencies, 78
Los Niños International Aid and Adoption
   Referral Center, 156

M

Male contraception, 24
Male infertility
    diagnosis of, 40
    treatment of, 39
Marital relationship as a criterion for
    selection of adopters, 87-88
Medical advances in aid of reproduction,
    58-59
Medical consent forms in private
    adoptions, 112
Medical problems of potential adopters,
    202-203
Menstrual cycle and fertility, 37
Mentally handicapped children, adoption
    of, 179-81
Microsurgery to correct infertility, 65
Model State Subsidized Adoption Act, 178
Mother, surrogate. *See* Surrogate mother.
Mumps and lowered sperm count, 38

N

National Alliance for Optional Parenthood,
    53
National Association of Black Social
    Workers, 189
National Foster Parent Association (NFPA),
    207
National Foundation — March of Dimes, 72
National Genetic Foundation, Inc., 72
Nationality and adoption placement, 86-87
Natural father, rights regarding consent to
    adopt, 114-15. *See also* Birthparents.
New York State Court of Appeals, 71
North American Council on Adoptable
    Children, 175

O

Older children, adoption of, 184-87
Older parents as adopters, 200-202
Open adoption, 249-57
    adoption agencies and, 254-55
    involving maximum contact, 252-54
    involving minimal contact, 249-51
    involving moderate contact, 251-52
    risks in, 256
Open Door Society, 141, 191
Openness in adoption and adoption
    agencies, 265-66
Organization of Foster Families for Equality
    and Reform (OFFER), 207
Organization for a United Response
    (OURS), 164
Orphan Voyage, 222
Overweight as a handicap in seeking to
    adopt, 85
Ovulation, 25

P

Parenting skills and adoption agencies'
    criteria, 92-93
Parents of large families as adopters,
    203-205
Parents with medical problems as adopters,
    202-203
Patton, Jean, 222
Peirce-Warwick Adoption Service, 254
Personality factors sought in adoptive
    parents by agencies, 90-91
Physically handicapped adopters, 85-86,
    198-200
Physically handicapped children
    adoption of, 176-79, 198-99
    subsidization of medical costs for, 96,
    178-79
Physicians as source of information about
    adoptable babies, 140
Planned Parenthood, 143, 144
Pregnancy counseling agencies, 98
    kickbacks from hospitals performing
    abortions, 32
    proposed licensing of, 269-70
Pregnancy for pay. *See* Surrogate mothers.
Private adoption agencies with
    international contacts, 156-62
Private adoptions
    advantages of, 118-19
    versus agency adoptions, 105-106
    expenses paid by adopters, 110-11
    legal status of, 104, 134
    medical consent forms required, 112
    procedure for, 106-17
    risks of, 117-18
    and single parents, 197-98
    success of, 104-105
Private international adoptions, 162-71
    case study, 167-71
    making contacts in foreign lands, 164-65
    risks of, 166-67
    state regulations governing, 163
Pro-abortion counseling groups, 30-31
Probationary period before finalization of
    adoption, 113
Psychological parent, 115, 208

R

Race and adoption placement, 86-87
Racially mixed children, adoption of,
    189-91
Radiation and male sterility, 39
Recruiting babies for adoption, 260
Recruiting minority homes for racially
    mixed children, 189-90
Rejection of applicants by adoption
    agencies, 13, 93-95

Religion and medical care, 87
Religious requirements for adopters, 87
Relinquishment papers, 113-16, 118
Repository for Germinal Choice, 61-62
RESOLVE, Inc., 142
Retarded children. *See* Mentally
 handicapped children.
Reunions between adult adoptees and
 birthparents, 96
Revised Uniform Adoption Act, 108
Rh-factor incompatability, 69
Rhythm method of contraception, 24-25
Right to Life groups, 65
Rubin's Test, 41

S

Scar tissue as cause of male infertility, 39
Sealed birth record, 14, 214, 217, 221 ff.
 adoptees' demands for viewing and,
  216-17, 221-25
 state laws and, 214-15
Sealed birth record, opening of,
 adoption agencies' policies, 230-32
 adoptive parents' attitudes, 225-27
 birthparents' rights, 228-29
 emotional issues surrounding, 218-19
 prospects for legal changes, 232-34, 271
Secrecy in adoption, 13, 14, 213-14, 237 ff.
Sibling groups, adoption of, 187-89
Sickle-cell anemia, 69
Single parents' advocacy groups, 31
Single parents as adopters, 194-98
 adoption agency requirements, 194-96
 private adoption, 197-98
 special-needs children, 196
Smoking
 attitude of adoption agencies, 85
 infertility and, 37
 use of birth control pill and, 21
Social workers in adoption agencies
 interviews with adoptive parents, 77-79
 power of, 98-100
Special-needs children. *See* Emotionally
 handicapped children; Mentally
 handicapped children; Older children;
 Physically handicapped children;
 Racially mixed children; Sibling
 groups.
Sperm count, low,
 diabetes and, 39
 infectious diseases and, 38
 thyroid dysfunction and, 39
 too-frequent ejaculation and, 38
Spina bifida, 69
Stanley v. Illinois, 108, 114

State agency, role of in private adoption,
 113
State courts and natural father's role in
 consent to adopt, 114-15
Stepparent adoptions, 120
Steptoe, Dr. Patrick, 64, 65
Sterilization, 18-19, 23
Substitute parenting of relatives' children,
 52-53
Surrogate mothers, 10, 66-68

T

Tay-Sachs disease, 60, 69
Television in seeking homes for
 special-needs children, 96-97
Test-tube birth, 10, 57, 64-65
Thalassemia, 69
Thyroid dysfunction and lowered sperm
 count, 39
Tubal ligation and declining birth rate,
 18-19
Turner's syndrome, 69

U

Ultrasound used with amniocentesis, 71
Unplanned pregnancy
 adolescents and, 27
 availability of babies for adoption and,
  19-20, 26-28
 contraceptive failures and, 19-20
 counseling and, 29-32
 father's legal rights in abortion, 30
 as a result of unconscious desire to be
  pregnant, 26-27
U.S. Bureau of Consular Affairs, 165
U.S. Department of Immigration, 155-56

V

Vaginal pH and infertility, 40
Vaginal sponges, 25
Vasectomy and declining birth rate, 18-19
Vietnam conflict and orphans available for
 adoption, 153, 154, 189
Visa required for foreign child adopted, 159

W

Women's Clinic, 143
Working women and declining birth
 rate, 18
World War II
 European orphans available for
  adoption, 153
 genetic planning by Nazis, 58
 women in labor force, 18

Z

Zero population growth, 17